ALSO BY KENNEDY FRASER

Scenes from the Fashionable World
The Fashionable Mind

KENNEDY FRASER

Ornament and Silence

Kennedy Fraser grew up in England and has lived in New York City for many years. A longtime writer for *The New Yorker*, she is also a contributing writer to *The New York Times* and *Vogue*. She has been a Guggenheim Fellow and the recipient of a Whiting Writer's Award, and is the author of two previous books published by Knopf, *The Fashionable Mind* and *Scenes from the Fashionable World*.

Ornament and Silence

KENNEDY FRASER

*O*rnament
and
*S*ilence

*Essays on Women's Lives
from Edith Wharton
to Germaine Greer*

Vintage Books

A DIVISION OF RANDOM HOUSE, INC.

NEW YORK

Most of the essays in this collection were originally published in the following:
The New Yorker: "Fritillaries and Hairy Violets" (1987), "Ornament and Silence"
(1989), "Demented Pilgrimage (1990), and "Stones of His House" (1991).
Vogue: "A Normal Man" (1992); "Meat" and "Warmed Through and Through"
(1993); "Love, Longing, and Letters" (1994); "My Sister, Myself,"
"The Poet of Everyday Life," and "Valentina" (1995).

The Library of Congress has cataloged the Knopf edition as follows:
Fraser, Kennedy
Ornament and silence: essays on women's lives / by Kennedy Fraser.—1st ed.
p.   cm.
ISBN 0-394-58539-9
1. Women authors. 2. Women artists. 3. Authors' spouses. 4. Artists' spouses.
I. Title.
PN471.F69   1996
809'.89287—dc20   96-11479   .
CIP
Vintage ISBN: 0-375-70112-5

Author photograph © Sam Jones

Printed in the United States of America

Random House Web site: www.randomhouse.com

For Ibs, with love

———

"[The history of most women is] hidden either by silence, or by flourishes and ornaments that amount to silence."

—*Virginia Woolf*

Contents

Acknowledgments

I WISH to thank the editors who supported me while I was writing these essays: Bob Gottlieb and Charles McGrath at *The New Yorker*; Anna Wintour, Shelley Wanger, and Susan Morrison at *Vogue*; and Ann Close at Alfred A. Knopf. I have been sustained by Andrew Wylie and Sarah Chalfant, of the Wylie Agency; I thank them for that. I feel honored to have been the recipient of a Whiting Writer's Award.

Foreword

ONE OF the many privileges of being a professional writer is that in rereading what you have written, you can take stock of how far you've come and see the stepping-stones along the way. I couldn't, for instance, have written my farewell to the world of the old *New Yorker* magazine—the center of my life for many years, and the subject of this book's final essay—without first grappling with the life stories of women who stood on their own feet quite satisfactorily. In the period covered by these essays, it feels as though I've travelled quite a distance.

Any progress I have made is probably more visible to me than it is to the reader—who may see, more easily than I, how far I need to go. But I harbor the modest hope that my retelling of these stories of creative women—in love affairs, friendships, marriages, and families; in relation to each other and to talented men—will prove a fraction as helpful to some reader as it has proved to me. To those women of the past who left a record of their lives, as well as to those of my subjects who are still living, I owe a tremendous debt of gratitude. I am especially thankful for my encounter with the Russian writer Nina Berberova, one of the most remarkable literary women of her generation. I am sorry that she died, as she did, after giving me of her time but without seeing her "profile" appear in *The New Yorker.* But if this trick of fate had to happen to anyone, she was philosophically better equipped to handle it than most: throughout her long life she had eerie intuitions about mortality and time. Her story remains as full of what she liked to call "juices" as when she was alive. I have elected to leave my piece just as I wrote it— as if, indeed, she were. (I have also left the world of the extraordinary Miriam Rothschild just as I found it in May 1987.) For Nina, bold and honest writers could seem more vital, even after death, than living people who dwelled in the past and let themselves be silenced or ground down.

I don't believe I could have written about women in the way I have without all the biography and criticism by and about women that has made itself felt in the past twenty years or so. Many a new book, article, or memoir guided by feminist principles shone a spotlight on aspects of experience that had previously been neglected or repressed. I remember that when "Ornament and Silence," the title essay of this book, first appeared, one male novelist of my acquaintance—a great man, famous for the subtle perceptiveness of his prose— admitted to being shaken by the piece and by the strong response it had evoked in his wife. He said it was as if, for the very first time, he was tuning in to a private language in which women had been communicating among themselves all along.

Two events of significance for me occurred as I was embarking on the period covered by this book. The first was apparently very small and very personal: A man of my own age, with whom I was talking at a party, withdrew his attention from me to look hungrily over my shoulder at a pretty young woman many years my junior. As a younger woman I had relied on the attention of older men and depended on their approval. I saw very clearly, in that instant when the man's gaze shifted, that one kind of power had passed from me. The time had come to develop other resources. The second event, which took place in stages, was larger and very much more public: the sale of *The New Yorker*, where I had worked for more than half my life; the abrupt end of the long tenure of its second editor, the extraordinary William Shawn; and, eventually, the painful dispersal of the tightly knit, decent, and fiercely independent little community of writers and artists among whom I had had the luck to come of age. I can see that, among other things, these essays have been my attempt to come to terms with these personal and public losses, and to move beyond them. I wasn't going to be able to fall back on being an attractive young thing anymore; I could no longer hide behind being a daughter of the paternal old *New Yorker*. For the next stage of my life, I would need to summon up new courage and explore new forms of speech.

KENNEDY FRASER
New York, 1996

Ornament and Silence

ORNAMENT AND SILENCE

*T*HERE WAS a time when my life seemed so painful to me that reading about the lives of other women writers was one of the few things that could help. I was unhappy, and ashamed of it; I was baffled by my life. For several years in my early thirties, I would sit in my armchair reading books about these other lives. Sometimes when I came to the end, I would sit down and read the book through from the beginning again. I remember an incredible intensity about all this, and also a kind of furtiveness—as if I were afraid that someone might look through the window and find me out. Even now, I feel I should pretend that I was reading only these women's fiction or their poetry—their lives as they chose to present them, alchemized as art. But that would be a lie. It was the private messages I really liked—the journals and letters, and autobiographies and biographies whenever they seemed to be telling the truth. I felt very lonely then, self-absorbed, shut off. I needed all this murmured chorus, this continuum of true-life stories, to pull

3

me through. They were like mothers and sisters to me, these literary women, many of them already dead; more than my own family, they seemed to stretch out a hand. I had come to New York when I was young, as so many come, in order to invent myself. And, like many modern people—modern women, especially—I had catapulted out of my context; in important ways, the life of my mother, in her English village, was not much help. I remember reading in those dark years a review by John Updike in which he smoothly compared the lives of Jean Rhys and Colette. The first was in the end a failure, the second a triumph, he said. I took it personally, felt a stab in the heart. And poor Jane Bowles, said someone else, in the *Times*—you'd have to admit that hers was a desperate life. The successes gave me hope, of course, yet it was the desperate bits I liked best. I was looking for directions, gathering clues. I was especially grateful for the secret, shameful things about these women—the pain: the abortions and misalliances, the pills they took, the amount they drank. And what had made them live as lesbians, or fall in love with homosexual men, or with men with wives?

Often the secrets were buried in footnotes or almost elided in the text. Such was the case with Virginia Woolf's memoir "A Sketch of the Past," which happened to be published (in the volume *Moments of Being*) some thirty-five years after her death, around my armchair time. Like someone climbing into an old governess cart, I had embarked on the first pages and set off to joggle and drowse down the rhythmic byways of her so very English prose. Here were the dear old familiar things again—the nursery, the drawing room, the girlhood in the tall Victorian dollhouse that was the Stephen family home in Hyde Park Gate. Here the luminous, bee-buzzing, flower-scented Eden of summers at St. Ives. She was so seductive, so charming, such a stylist always. Then, suddenly, the cart was stopped, the lullaby cut off. Something—what was it?—had happened to her in the hall. Her half brother Gerald Duckworth, already a young man then, had set her on a ledge when she was six and sexually molested her. It was a

shock seeing all this written down. "I can remember the feel
of his hand. . . . I remember how I hoped that he would stop,"
she wrote. The story was like a dream; it came and went,
enfolded by the text. She was a woman in her late fifties,
within a year of committing suicide, when she took up
her pen and wrote the memory down. "By putting it into
words . . . I make it whole; this wholeness means that it has
lost its power to hurt me," she said. "I have no motive for
lying about it." Here was her introduction to powerlessness,
to shame, to the trance. Afterward, she was always ashamed
of her body and of seeing her face in a mirror. She called it
her "looking-glass shame." As far as I know, I was not
molested as a little girl, but as a woman I knew about powerlessness, and I knew about the trance. Honest personal writing is a great service rendered the living by the dead. She, too,
read hungrily about the lives of others, for the consolation of
knowing that whatever she had experienced and felt they had
experienced and felt as well. But so much about people was
still a mystery; so much in their memoirs was unspoken or
suppressed. "Something has been left out from fear. Something has been altered, from vanity," she once wrote. She
could read, at the beginning of the twentieth century, far
fewer life stories of women than we can read at its end. (The
question of women's stories is thoughtfully addressed by
Carolyn Heilbrun in her book *Writing a Woman's Life*.) Virginia Woolf was a feminist, and she knew and lamented that
much of women's side of history has been lost in anonymity
and self-deprecation—"hidden either by silence, or by flourishes and ornaments that amount to silence."

THE BOOK about Virginia Woolf by the American scholar
Louise DeSalvo makes a real contribution to the literature of
women's lives truthfully described by women. *Virginia Woolf:
The Impact of Childhood Sexual Abuse on Her Life and Work* is
an original and courageous work. It carries to a deeper level
the dialogue that I (like so many others) have long continued

with the life of a prodigiously creative, life-loving woman who was at the same time so powerless against self-hatred that after a lifetime of trying she finally killed herself. DeSalvo's subtitle, with its emphasis on the crucial fact that Virginia was a survivor of incest, may not do full justice to the rich texture of the book, which also embraces the lives of other women in her family and has broad and valuable lessons for women now. Both in form and in emphasis, the book feels vigorous and new: not linear but looping organically through time and around the aspects of the young Virginia's experience in her family to build a compelling and, in the end, forward-rushing kind of truth. Insights, events, personalities appear in one of the essays, vanish for a while, then resurface in a later essay to be viewed from a different angle and in ever-clearer light. DeSalvo is a professor, and she has clearly read deeply in published and unpublished texts about her subject, which she approaches sometimes with indignation and always with a woman's heart.

Virginia Woolf's previous biographers have dealt with her childhood sexual experience according to their limitations: tactfully, awkwardly, snidely, or with angry denial. DeSalvo honors the extensive testimony of Virginia Woolf herself, in letters and memoirs and juvenilia, and the obvious clues in her mature fiction, including early, unpublished drafts. *Virginia Woolf* looks squarely at the link between its subject's incestuous encounters with Gerald Duckworth and the even more destructive ones with his older brother, George (both were sons of Virginia's mother, Julia Stephen, by her first marriage), and Virginia's sadness, madness, fear of sex with men, and death. Her relations with George seemed to have begun when she was thirteen, after her mother's sudden death. She had the first of her nervous breakdowns then. DeSalvo (and at least some Woolfians before her) would claim that, far from being the onset of the inexplicable "madness," this shutting down was a natural response in a young girl being sexually abused by an older relative who might have been expected to protect her in a time of grief. Many of

her symptoms, such as wildly changing moods and a racing
pulse, may have been brought on by drugs that were pre-
scribed to treat her—drugs whose effects were ill understood
in 1900.

George's sexual attentions persisted until another bereave-
ment—the death of her father, when she was twenty-two—
and another, more devastating breakdown. She heard voices
telling her to starve her hateful body, and jumped out of a
window; fortunately, it was too low for her to hurt herself.
Her older sister, Vanessa, who had also been sexually involved
with George, was at last driven to break their girlhood's long
silence by telling an outsider—Dr. Savage, Virginia's physi-
cian—and Dr. Savage confronted him. When, a few years
later, Virginia wrote the first of her memoirs of childhood,
"Reminiscences," she referred to the time after her mother's
death as one of "oriental gloom," when "a finger was laid on
our lips." She wrote of the family's "sultry and opaque life
which was not felt, and had nothing real in it, and yet swam
about us, and choked us and blinded us." There was more
than mourning going on. As her nephew and biographer,
Quentin Bell, put it, in his tolerant, silver-age way, there was
"George making himself disagreeable . . . Eros came with a
commotion of leathern wings, a figure of mawkish, incestuous sexuality." He recorded his aunt's conviction that
"George had spoilt her life before it had fairly begun."

In maturity, Virginia made a point of telling about
George. In her late thirties, she wrote the memoir "22 Hyde
Park Gate," an amazingly candid account of George as the
"lover" of "those poor Stephen girls," and read it aloud to the
members of the Memoir Club. These were mostly old friends
from the inner circle of Bloomsbury, but nonetheless it was a
public gathering. Speaking frankly to a group of men and
women was a far greater emotional risk than writing a letter
to some indignant, tenderhearted female or confiding in her
by the embers of the teatime fire. Victims of incest often stay
silent at the time because they are afraid that by speaking
they will break the family apart, and later because they feel

that the universe might split open; it seems safer to pretend that nothing happened or that they themselves are loathsome or mad.

With her reading to the Memoir Club, she was taking a heroic step; she was "coming out." Even so, she would do her little self-deprecatory dance. "Maynard, Desmond, Clive, and Leonard all live stirring and active lives . . . all constantly affect the course of history one way or another," she said. "Who am I?" She could always turn things so wittily, charm you with that famous hooting laugh. *Her* memoirs, she told Maynard & Co., were only about herself, about an intimate, feminine world, were "always private and at their best only about . . . seductions by half-brothers." Yet her whole work shows how passionately she valued the substance of the "private" world, exploring the most secret, fluid feelings of women and children in a culture that, like today's, more highly valued the solid, public actions of men. In her time, there was little public information about the great taboo of incest, but she did think of joining something called the British Sex Society, in order to find out how common incest was. She had no access to today's collective wisdom and "support groups." She was alone in her commitment to airing her pain, and could not know that many of the symptoms of her lifelong illnesses were shared by many, many others who had been sexually abused as children. Her style was never more prancing or her wit more dazzling than when she described the merry-go-round of manipulation, seduction, rivalry, and rage that involved her, her sister, and George. Yet, however endearingly these disclosures are packaged, she is in deadly earnest about the damage; she knew that those "seductions by half-brothers" mattered very much.

"The happiest time of a happy childhood" was how Bell referred to Virginia's summers before her mother's death. In promoting the myth of an unclouded beginning, with an angelic mother and a father—Sir Leslie Stephen—who was an adorably eccentric genius, many of her biographers have been content to follow the more comfortable markers laid down by Virginia Woolf herself. The innocent, spritelike girl-child—Alice in cherub wings of pinafore—in the sheltered paradise of the upper-middle-class nursery was a powerful stereotype, dear to the Victorians, and it remains so to us, their successors. DeSalvo paints a bleaker picture, of children ignored by their parents, taught—by any means and at any cost—to control what they feel, and left to the care of servants who were no more than children themselves. Virginia Woolf described in her fiction her characters' pain in childhood and linked it to their emotional lives as adults in a way that was ahead of its time. "It's a fallacy to think that children are happy. . . . I've never suffered so much as I did when I was a child," says Richard Dalloway, M.P., in *The Voyage Out.*

In her final period, she was working on her posthumous novel, *Between the Acts*, a story of children in a pageant who confront adults with their cruelty and failure. At the same time, she was writing about Gerald molesting her, and describing depression in her childhood well before her mother's death—including an experience of "hopeless sadness" and "dumb horror" that left her feeling unprotected and numb, cut off even from her beloved Nessa, who was sponging herself at the other end of the bath. Yet she still fled back into denial, lost her nerve. "How beautiful they were those old people," she wrote after reading her father's letters to her mother. "With . . . the little hum and song of the nursery." For many years, when she wrote directly of her parents the portrait was idealized; she borrowed her memory of her mother from her father's sentimentalized memoir of his late wife. Yet in the main her later memoirs and her fiction give views of parents that seem more real. The father in *To the Lighthouse* is, like Sir Leslie, given to fits of violent, flowerpot-throwing temper. Stephen seems to have been an emotionally unstable man, demanding even by the standards of Victorian patriarchs. "I am a man without a skin," he would wail. He expected women to march to his emotional drum. "When I am sad, you should be sad. When I am angry, you should weep," he is said to have told Vanessa, who (unlike Virginia) openly admitted to being angry with him. Woolf was lenient with her particular patriarch, perhaps, but she was harsh on patriarchs in general. She thought that the model of the patriarchal family, with men given license to bully and rant while women and children submitted and served, was unwholesome. She went further: such a model in private life, when it was mirrored in the public life of nations, led to Fascism. "The tyrannies and servilities of the one are the tyrannies and servilities of the other," she wrote.

In her final memoir Virginia Woolf described the Stephen-Duckworth family as a lonely "caravan, absolutely private, silent, unknown." Brothers came and went in a larger world—away to boarding schools, to university, into professions. Of the girls and women cloistered in the dim, tall house DeSalvo draws a poignant group portrait. There was, for Virginia as a child, the frightening example of young Laura, the daughter of Sir Leslie's first marriage: first violently punished for "badness" and slowness in reading, then segregated from the rest (like Mrs. Rochester) in a distant part of the house, and, finally, banished to an asylum. Then there was the beautiful Stella Duckworth, George and Gerald's sister, who had been given the family nickname of The Old Cow. She worshipped her mother with a never-satisfied yearning, while Julia pushed her away, first with long, grim mourning for the dead Duckworth, then with absorption in her new husband, her sons, the four children of her second marriage, and her elaborate, debilitating ministry to the Deserving Poor. She treated young Stella like a personal slave. She was the charming, self-sacrificing "angel in the house" of Virginia Woolf's essay "Professions for Women," who must be killed off if a young woman is to realize herself. Julia knew she treated Stella harshly, but she also drove herself unmercifully hard. "She sank, like an exhausted swimmer, deeper and deeper in the water" was Virginia's way of describing her mother's overwork before her death, at the age of forty-nine. Julia burdened her firstborn daughter with duties beyond a child's capacities because "Stella seemed to her more a part of herself" than a person in her own right. Julia had, moreover, waited slavishly on *her* mother, Maria Jackson, and continued to do so when summoned by her. (Maria Jackson had at some point decided to take refuge from life in a fairly mysterious invalidism, in the style of Alice James, and often stayed in bed, medicating herself with morphia and chloral.) When her mother died, young Stella was expected, in the custom of the time, to take over supervision of the household, with its nine family members and seven servants, and to become mother to the younger children. In addition, she spent hours in tearful embraces with the widower and in visits to the Deserving Poor. After Stella's marriage, which was shortly followed by her death, it was young Vanessa who was moved up to the front line of domesticity, just as, some years later, fresh waves of young men were hurled into the battles of the First World War.

THERE WAS always Vanessa, Virginia's "co-conspirator," "The Saint." Vanessa had been there from the beginning, knew all that she knew. "How did we ever get out of it? It seems to me almost too ghastly and unnatural now ever to have existed," Vanessa wrote after reading her sister's "Reminiscences," which Virginia presented in the form of a story of Vanessa's life. Vanessa wasn't going to forget or to leave her stranded, Virginia made sure of that: she clung with a grip that Vanessa's daughter, Angelica Garnett, later called a "stranglehold." Vanessa was the painter, the silent one, the one who always coped. Virginia was the writer, the clown, the one who broke down. For, in spite of the sister, there were always times when Virginia seemed to lose herself, to be desolate and alone. And, in spite of husband, work, friends, and fame, the feelings were there all her life. "I feel at the moment a helpless babe on the shore of life, turning over pebbles," she said when she was a woman in middle age. "So the ocean tosses its pebbles, and I turn them over, naked, a child, and no one helps me." Writing helped. From childhood on, it was a way to create a self, "set up some stake against oblivion." It was her escape rope out of the princesses' tower and into a larger world, into the "great conspiracy of civilized people." If you're bent on saving your life by speaking out, naturally you get it wrong sometimes, you go too far. She gossiped; she gave away people's secrets; she tried to talk to old Lady Strachey about homosexuality—which was obviously absurd. "You have the wildest ideas about such things," her older sister wrote reprovingly. She made a point of informing Clive Bell, the new husband Vanessa was so dotty about, that Vanessa had been madly in love with Jack Hills, Stella's widower, right after their half sister died. (It was illegal in England at that time to marry your dead wife's sister, but the couple could have gone to live abroad.) The sisters exchanged a mountain of letters, writing sometimes twice each day; they talked and talked. But there was much that was never spoken, a fund of silence at the core. Virginia wrote often in her fiction of the agony of unexpressed feeling between people who love each other: the chasm, she called it, the abyss. Divisions between people were the source of all evil, she said. But the sisters played "the Victorian game of manners" so beautifully—the game that could be so "helpful in making something seemly and human out of raw odds and ends," she said.

For women, especially, the odds and ends of Bloomsbury could be extremely raw. After a year of ecstatically happy marriage to Clive, Vanessa gave birth. Straightway, he turned his back on mother and child and began some sort of affair with Virginia. ("He came from a society which hunted birds, animals, and in his case, girls," his son, Quentin, said.) There is no evidence of Vanessa's taking the pair to task. Incest breeds incest. From their experience with their half brothers and their brother-in-law, the sisters had learned that no one is off limits; that men could change partners at will; that jealousy and rivalry are tolerable because they serve the greater good of keeping the group bound up together, the magic circle intact; and that only the familiar, however painful, is safe. Vanessa's self-respect was already low; even more than most women, she found it hard to say, "No more! Enough!" Before long, Vanessa fell in love with a former lover of her brother Adrian—the handsome young painter Duncan Grant. Soon after the birth of Angelica (who was the couple's daughter but until she was disillusioned, at the age of seventeen, believed that Clive was her father), Duncan lost interest in being Vanessa's lover. For the rest of her life, until her death, at the age of eighty-one, Vanessa continued to run an elaborate household for him and a succession of his male lovers and to paint side by side with him in the studio at Charleston.

"There must have been a strong element of masochism in her love for him," said Angelica, who tried to come to terms with her life and her mother's in her own valiant, elegant memoir, *Deceived with Kindness: A Bloomsbury Childhood*, which came out in 1984. Like her mother, her aunt, and her grandmother, Angelica was both beautiful and frequently depressed. All the women in the family were beauties except Great-Aunt Julia Margaret Cameron, who became a well-known photographer and took photographs of the rest. So many of the women's portraits have a pall of sadness— the suggestion of a self locked off, and a distant, down-cast eye. Angelica hung a group of them in the passageway at Charleston, and could see that depression and self-denigration were a legacy handed down. Feelings and habits of mind "like motes of dust spiralling downwards settle on the most recent generation," she said. Her mother was one "in a chain of women who, whether willingly or not, had learnt certain traits, certain attitudes from one another through the years."

In her own, unconventional way, Vanessa reproduced the old family life of Hyde Park Gate. She was still the angel in the house. She justified her self-sacrifice and Duncan's self-ishness by declaring him a genius. She cocooned Angelica, neglecting her education—trained her for the magic circle but not for life in a larger world. "The walls round us were high and the conditions inside the castle odd," Angelica wrote of her childhood years at Charleston. She had been another sprite, another make-believe princess, living in a shimmer of Post-Impressionist color and avant-garde sex. She was in her late teens, reeling from the news of her father's identity and from the death of her older brother in Spain, when Duncan's former lover David (Bunny) Garnett made his move. He was almost thirty years her senior and had a wife who was dying. The seduction of Angelica told the old, old stories of incestuousness and the aphrodisiac effects of premature death. He was still emotionally tied to Duncan and to Vanessa, whom he had also at one time tried to seduce; after some chilliness when he and Angelica were first married, the four of them remained very close.

"I seemed unwittingly to have plunged into a stagnant pool where nothing ever changed," Angelica wrote, looking back, and using the watery imagery so frequent in her family's myth. (It is no coincidence that in the end Virginia chose to drown herself.) Like her aunt at the time of her last memoir, Angelica was a woman in her late fifties when she wrote; she found herself quite alone, and she was writing for her life. She had been hospitalized for depression and treated with "jade green pills." Unlike Virginia, she had seen her mother grow old, and more and more sad. She had witnessed the price Vanessa paid for the choiceless choices, for the life of the trance—for a lifetime of pretending that nothing untoward was happening or that things didn't hurt. For years and years, Vanessa went on humbly yearning for Duncan to take her as a lover again. Virginia, who called herself "a sexual coward," liked to reinvent her sister as the great Earth Mother, the sensual adventuress, but in fact both women were celibate for most of their lives. Vanessa longed for Duncan to accept her as a woman and, even more, for him to validate her as an artist. Her continual self-denigration became embarrassing to her daughter and their intimates, and so did the way her paintings began to look more and more like his. (Virginia was also tormented by self-doubt, and after finishing a book was greatly at risk of breakdown or suicide.) In spite of a life that included laughing children, brilliant visitors, sexual drama, and the making of art, Vanessa, too, felt disconnected and alone. In 1918, the year of her daughter's birth, she had painted what Angelica believed to be a self-portrait, of a young woman standing naked and solitary beside a tub of water. It seemed to Angelica to be Vanessa's attempt at sending a message to the "great conspiracy"—a parting of the curtain and a clear insight into the truth of her life. But the canvas was put away, hidden in the attic, out of sight. So at the end of Vanessa's life she and her daughter sat facing each other in silence across the family abyss. "When I visited Charleston I would sit with her by the studio stove, unable to utter a word," Angelica wrote. "Neither of us knew what was wrong: we were submerged by inertia and depression. . . . The key to emotion was lost." But by telling strangers about this secret sadness Angelica has found the key. Here is real courage: this revelation of her truth, this determination of a middle-aged, underwater woman to break the surface of the myth and come up for air.

DeSalvo's book has something of the same momentum, carries the same kind of hope. I suspect that the world of Bloomsbury scholars is itself a kind of magic circle, carrying an unspoken threat of punishment to any initiate who betrays it or launches out. I was touched by DeSalvo's thanks to her husband, at the beginning of her book, for urging her not to obfuscate; he supported her, then, while she took her own risks, violated the taboos. She has done a considerable service. My admiration for Virginia Woolf has increased, and I am more than ever saddened by the example of her death. And I am affected by the other lives DeSalvo shows with such sensitivity: the silent ones, powerless to help, sitting with their sponges at the far end of the tub. Less gifted, less overtly self-destructive women than their brilliant relative, they yet found the old female ways of keeping themselves from living life. Shutting down behind self-pity and secret shame; sacrificing themselves to childish mothers and selfish men; vaguely yearning, self-medicating; painting someone else's pictures; obediently tracing the magic circle, afraid, entranced. There are so many different ways to drown.

1989

GOING ON

*T*IME IS flowing fast for me now," said the Russian
writer Nina Berberova, who is ninety-one. "I must
not lose time. That is my secret. Now that I am an
old woman, I give my secrets away." She was inviting me to
spend the day at home with her in Philadelphia; her voice on
the phone was deep and strong, with a heavy Franco-Russian
accent. When I first met her, she was eighty-nine; she was
still dyeing her hair a robust red-brown. After she turned
ninety, she let her hair go snow white, and she looked quite
transformed. From the very first encounter, I was amazed by
everything about her: her freedom, her mystery, her curiously galvanizing presence, which is also felt (by the susceptible reader) in her prose.

"Where does it come from, the divine electrical energy in
you?" she once asked Maxim Gorky, when she was a girl in
her twenties, living under the great man's roof. I can just
imagine the look she gave him.

"Where does it come from in you?" Gorky said.

I'll always be grateful that I met Nina. After my first visit, I came back from Philadelphia to New York like someone bewitched. The train was rattling and rattling along, and I stared blindly out. You've met a great woman, I thought.

She dresses quite dashingly, in the good-quality clothes she has been able to afford since she became internationally famous, in her late eighties. Before international fame overtook her, she was living in exile, first in France (for twenty-five years) and later in America (since 1950), and writing all the time. But most French and American readers knew nothing at all about Nina Berberova. She and her gifts were screened off from the West by the Russian-language ghetto of the émigrés (who had their own newspapers, journals, and publishing houses) and then by the somewhat hermetic community of professional Slavicists. Before she left her native St. Petersburg, in 1922—travelling by boxcar with her lover, the famous poet Vladislav Khodasevich, and his precious eight-volume set of Pushkin—all that Nina had published was a single poem. The thread of her whole long life would be spun outside Russia, and, with that long life, the twin thread of a prodigious body of work: poetry, novels, novellas, short short stories, reportage, plays, theatre and literary criticism, four biographies, and a lengthy autobiography.

Her fourth biography—a semi-fictionalized meditation on the life of the Baroness Moura Budberg, who was Gorky's companion in the years when Nina and Khodasevich were also part of his household—is subtitled *The Iron Woman.* Written when Nina was in her late seventies and first published when she was eighty, the book may well be her masterpiece. She was in her early twenties when she lived under the same roof as Moura, who was nine years older than her. She admired Moura's physical vitality, her lack of sentimentality, her determination to forge for herself a new, post-Revolutionary female destiny. At the time, Moura was already a full-blown femme fatale surrounded by clouds of mystery and with a carefully managed public image. Long after their lives had diverged and Nina had rejected the amoral political means Moura was willing to use for personal survival, the older woman and her legend drew her in. "I knew in 1938, as in 1958 and in 1978, that I would write a book about Moura," Nina wrote in its introduction. Even now, the relationship between the biographer and her subject (who died in 1974) seems eerily alive and far from simple.

The volume on Moura forms a companion piece—a literary-emotional glossary, a dark but invaluable mirror—to Nina's powerful meditation on her own life and times, *The Italics Are Mine*, written a decade earlier. ("I wrote my own life first!" she says.) This autobiography must be classed not only as a historic, if unabashedly subjective, record of the vanished world of the Emigration—the community of people, great and small, uprooted by the Russian Revolution—but also as a luminous inside account of a twentieth-century woman courageously journeying (a pilgrim, a female hero) in search of herself. In writing her works, Nina kept the faith with her mother tongue. I once asked her whether she had ever been tempted to try her hand at French or English—whether she had always written in Russian. Although slight and a little frail these days, Nina can still draw herself up with the best of them. "In Russian?" she said indignantly, rolling her Russian "r" in my direction like a boulder from a sling. "Of *course* I wrote in Russian!"

THE TIME: 1985. Enter Hubert.

Gallant, mustached, pipe-smoking, mature enough to have aided in the Resistance as a youth—Hubert Nyssen, founder and editor-in-chief of Actes Sud, who became Nina's French publisher. A Philip Larkin to her Jean Rhys, a Kenneth Tynan to her Louise Brooks. In time, with trust, Nina's *cher Hubert*. A French translation of *The Accompanist*, a novella she wrote in 1934, is what brought Nina to Nyssen's attention. It is the tale of Sonechka, a plain young woman living with her never-married mother and half starving (like so many Russians) in the period of famine and blockade right after the 1917 Revolution. She finds work playing the piano for a beautiful soprano some ten years older than she is, and moves with her employer's household to Paris. She observes the dramas of the artiste's romantic life and develops a passionate attachment to her patron, who finally moves to America (singing, as it happens, in Philadelphia) and leaves Sonechka behind. The style, as in all Nina's bèst fiction, is extraordinarily controlled and virtuosic—a fine, tautly vibrating net flung over historic world events and tectonic plates of individual feeling.

On Hubert Nyssen the Berberovan effect was total. Then he learned that the author was still alive, and that she was living (as she was then) in Princeton, New Jersey.

"Your timing is perfect," she told him composedly on the transatlantic phone in February of 1986. "I have to be in Paris for my first husband's centennial."

"Did you write anything else?" he asked her when they met in May in a café on the Place Saint-Sulpice.

She was not in any hurry. "Let's make a start with this and see how it goes," she said.

"It was very strange, that first meeting," Nyssen told me not long ago. "Not demonstrative at all. Not much was said. But it was as if each of us entered the other through our eyes." He paused. "*Oui*. I felt her enter me. I entered her. It began."

He learned of *The Italics Are Mine*, which had appeared in the late sixties in an English translation, published in America by Harcourt, Brace, and, three years later, in Munich, in the original Russian. At that youth-quaking, greening-of-America moment, the timing for a fat book by an unknown foreign woman in late middle age was less than perfect. Torpedoed by a hostile review in the *Times*, *The Italics Are Mine* sold a little more than a thousand copies and then sank without trace. To introduce Nina's work to the readers of France, the country she had lived in so long ago and so intensely, Nyssen astutely elected to begin with the novellas, of which she had written a dozen or so in addition to *The Accompanist*. Most of them first appeared in the émigré press in the 1930s, and they are rather classically constructed. The narrator is often a woman, and the plot often involves erotic passion: a dispiriting view of it, sometimes, as (to quote one novella) love affairs that start as Gypsy love songs and end as "the smell of unchanged sheets." A collection of the novellas was published in Russian in the 1940s by the Paris branch of the Russian Y.M.C.A.—an improbable sponsor but one in possession of a Cyrillic printing press. Some busybody riffled through the book, however, and declared it pornographic. Distribution was stopped, and piles of the books lay moldering in the basement for several decades. Now Nyssen commissioned first-rate translations, published the "little novels" one by one in exquisite miniature books ("One can't take works of such impact and stack them up like saucers," he said, explaining why they didn't come in collections), and shepherded them onto the French best-seller lists, where they congregated in companionable bunches, sometimes for months. In this country, Knopf brought out a collection of six of the novellas in 1991, in the elegant translations of Marian Schwartz, under the title *The Tattered Cloak*. (*The Iron Woman* has not yet appeared in English translation.) American critics hailed the book; one placed their author in importance alongside Chekhov and Turgenev.

I'm not sure what ninety-one is supposed to look like, but it's clear that for most of her adult life Nina has looked younger than her age. This youthfulness may have combined with her physical stamina to help her lead her courageous life. Or perhaps her inner strength produced a body to fit it— a flexible and vital vehicle to carry her through the saga that her character and twentieth-century history impelled her to lead. Inner and outer are one for her. Her vitality must have made many things happen in her life, and so must her expressive eyes. These have kept their deep-brown color and clear whites into extreme old age. The recurrent experience of poverty and uprootedness schooled her in not setting store by much except friendship, spirit, mind. Her eyes, and the powerful intellect that plays in them like sun and shade, may be her most valuable possessions. A gaze like Nina Berberova's makes people want to gaze right back at her or it scares them to bits. Vladimir Nabokov, born two years earlier than she, on Morskaya, the same St. Petersburg street, recorded in a letter in Paris in 1932 the sparkle of Nina's already famous eyes. She came over to where he was sitting in one of the Montparnasse cafés frequented by the émigré intelligentsia. By then, she had lived for a decade with Khodasevich, whom Nabokov once called "the greatest Russian poet of our time." Nina's brown eyes flashed. "I've left him!" she said.

RUSSIA, France, America. "My long life is divided into three parts, like Caesar's Gaul," Nina wrote in an introduction to the French edition of *The Italics Are Mine*. The assertive comparison is only mildly ironic; Nina has a warrior's will. For people like me, growing up in the West in the period of relative stability after the Second World War, the trials endured by people like Nina are almost unimaginable. She grew to maturity in what she called, in her biography of Moura Budberg, "pitiless and cruel" times. She wrote, "That generation born between 1890 and 1900 was almost completely wiped out by war, revolution, emigration, the gulag, and the terror of the 1930s." Many of Nina's friends, escaping Stalin, were killed by Hitler as Freemasons or Jews, or else they committed suicide. Readers of her fiction are often struck by its quality of "pitilessness." As if she were an animal lifting her head from grazing to stare at predators and prey from a species quite separate from her, she depicts her émigré characters acting upon each other and struggling to survive. Unflinching, she gazes at her waiters, milliners, taxi drivers, charwomen, night-club doormen—former members of the czarist ruling class, often—living in cheap hotels and dingy restaurants, in the swamp of difference between There and Here. "I am not the crying sort," she often says. Sentimentality in any form appalls her. Yet I'm not sure I agree with those who accuse her, as a fiction writer, of having no compassion. Love only begins, after all, at the point where you see other people clearly and accept them unreservedly for what they are.

Nina Nikolaevna Berberova was born almost with the century—on the old Imperial-calendar equivalent of August 8, 1901. Her father, Nikolai Ivanovich Berberov, a high-ranking civil servant in the czarist Ministry of Finance, came from a family of Europeanized Armenian merchants and professional men. Nina adored her father. She loved to sit with him in his study—he in the armchair, wearing his tasselled smoking cap, she on the rug at his feet—talking things over and "speaking with their eyes." He had charm and was something of a boulevardier, and he was for his young daughter "the incarnation of the masculine principle." She knew that he loved women and also that he was pained if she brought home school friends who were plain. The family of Nina's mother, Natalia Ivanovna Berberova, was titled, possessed the proverbial vast estates (at Tver, in the Volga region), and was thoroughly Russian. Her maternal great-grandfather was such an Old Russian type that he was said to be the model for Goncharov's Oblomov.

When Nina was a girl, her feelings for her mother were very mixed. She both loved and hated her, she wrote in her sixties, when her mother was long dead. (In extreme old age, Nina speaks of her mother without anger and with great tenderness. "I don't suppose it was easy to raise me," she says.) Nina was her parents' only child. She was precocious and gifted; because of this, perhaps, her mother saw her as a threat. And then, like many a mother's daughter in that class, place, and time, Nina represented the new era that would violently and irrevocably smash the old. Natalia led a life that her daughter (who has been extremely industrious all her adult life and remains so) describes as idle and pleasure-seeking. Natalia, Nina wrote, did not seem completely *genuine*. She used one voice to address a servant, another for a child, and a third for the gentlemen at some soirée where she wore the silk gowns that bared her lovely bosom and throat. Natalia told the young Nina that she was not pretty—wrote this in her daughter's album. If Natalia tried to encircle her with her arm, Nina would furiously shrug it off. She never wanted protection—she wanted more of *life*. Not for her were powerlessness, frivolousness, or domesticity—what she calls, with the mimicry of gagging that sometimes punctuates her talk, "the nest."

"When did you become a liberated woman, Nina?" I asked her one afternoon in her apartment.

"At eight, it started. At nine. At seven, maybe. I looked around and saw that women with children were silly and boring. That women with a profession were not boring. I decided to have a profession."

She wrote a long list and settled on "poet." What she has called the "rigorous sense of her vocation" sank into her then and has never left. (Only decades later, when she was struggling to put food on the table, did she conclude that she was better at prose than at verse.) Little Nina taught herself to write with her left hand, just in case she lost her right.

"Sometimes children do not want only boxes of chocolates," she told me that afternoon. "Happy? Unhappy? I wasn't interested in that at all. I had such *curiosity*. At seven, at eight, I thought, I will grow up and meet interesting people. I will read interesting books. I will *write*." She was rapping on her chest with the knuckles of her two hands, for emphasis. Her wrists are fragile now, and the bones of the hands stand out under thin skin freckled by the years. The fingers are long, with unusual nails: big, oval, and domed like the eggs of small birds. Unlike her feet, which are tiny, Nina's head—too big to fit into most hats—and hands are, in proportion to the rest of her, rather large. She has good teeth and a dazzling smile.

"I thought, How wonderful my life will be!" she said, opening her hands and flinging them out to frame a radiant face in a gesture of gratitude. "Difficult, complicated things. An enigma to solve. I thought that would give me the greatest pleasure in life. And it did! There is something wonderful in the desire to experience life even if it's ugly, even if you have to suffer. It may be that you have to be poor, to be lonely, to lose someone you cherish. Maybe, maybe. But at least I have had plenty of *thinking* about my life. This helped me in life enormously—that I am not rushing where there are bonbons and presents." She made her retching sound. "Aaargh. Only sweet things—what a life!"

Before October 1917, there had been a fine apartment in Petersburg; English and French governesses; family tours abroad. (Nina and her family had to scramble their way out of Paris because the First World War arrived at its gates.) There were family summers on the estates of "Oblomov's" son. But Nina's parents held politically progressive views ("Protest was my environment," she would write), and, unlike the White Russian émigrés whom she would depict in much of her fiction, the Berberovs welcomed the downfall of the Romanovs. Nina's hatred of Nicholas II, the last czar, is unwavering. She holds him responsible for balking at democracy and failing to steer his country safely into the twentieth century. She sees no reason to forgive the fellow just because he's dead. Her chums in the girls' liberal secondary school she attended (whether or not they were pretty enough for her father's taste) were already caught up—as poets, members of the Socialist Revolutionary Party, future members of the Cheka—in the extraordinary artistic and political ferment of pre-Revolutionary St. Petersburg. Many of them would come to early, violent ends. Theirs was the last class to squeak under the wire and complete its studies in the old world; they graduated in 1917.

People ten or fifteen years older than Nina—Khodasevich, for example, or Nikolai Makeyev, who became her second

husband much later on—had university degrees and promising careers under way when the historic cataclysm came.
Timing was all.

For Nina, the old world could not end fast enough. But no
one could have prepared her or anyone else for the blood-
shed, horror, and starvation that ushered in the new. Her
parents "more or less survived" the Revolution, Nina says.
Her father even found work with the Bolshevik government,
and the family moved with it to the new capital of Moscow in
1918. No more fine apartment, servants, or bare-shouldered
silk gowns; as "former" people, the Berberovs were lucky to
escape with their lives. Nina's family went hungry, like
everyone else, and lived in a single room with dingy rags of
laundry hanging over the ill-fed stove. (If there is an excep-
tion to Nina's lack of interest in material things, it is her
appreciation for clean sheets and towels.) Young Nina wandered dazed and alone in Moscow streets filled with gunfire
and dead horses, and learned to elbow for a crust of straw-
filled black bread in a communal cafeteria. There seem to
have been some passionate and sometimes brutish encounters
with boys and men in those years. "If I were to decide to
write a book about the lost years of my life," she writes in her
autobiography, "it would begin with these four Moscow
months."

In 1921, after three years in Rostov-on-Don, Nina and her
parents returned to a Petersburg that had completely
changed. The alphabet and even the length of days were
being radically adjusted by the Revolutionary powers. She
was destined to remain there only briefly—just long enough
to publish the poem and make the contacts that would
provide her boost into the world of professional literature.
Some years earlier, she had gone with her mother to hear
Alexander Blok and the great Anna Akhmatova—then at
the height of her fame and beauty—read their poetry. Afterward, Nina had shaken the hands of the literary luminaries.
Now she attended Blok's funeral—an occasion that had
seemed to mark the end of a culture, and not just a life. She

took some poetry classes and hung about at the House of Arts—an institution, sponsored by Gorky, that acted as, among other things, a kind of glorified soup kitchen to keep writers and intellectuals from starving. The leading light at the House of Arts was the poet Gumilev, Akhmatova's first husband. He was a tall, rather ugly man with a squint, which did not prevent him from staring at Nina (she writes) and sizing up the would-be poet's bosom and legs. "I created Akhmatova, I created Mandelstam . . . I can, if I want, create you," he said. The flirtation came to an abrupt end when he was taken by the Bolsheviks, accused of counter-revolutionism, and summarily shot.

It was in the House of Arts that Nina met Khodasevich. One evening, she listened in awe as he recited a poem about his wet nurse. He was already being hailed as a poet of genius. Gorky, who was in almost all ways the polar opposite of Nabokov, shared his opinion of Khodasevich as "the greatest Russian poet of our time." Khodasevich was thirty-five when he met the twenty-year-old Nina; he had already been married and divorced twice. His health had never been robust, and in the famine years of 1918 and 1919 he had nearly died. His stomach and lungs were weak, and he suffered from recurrent boils. But he still seemed young when the couple met and fell in love. "He did not yet know the taste of ashes in his mouth," she wrote forty years on. "He still had, like all of us, a homeland, a city, profession, a name." He would sit at the window of his room at the House of Arts, looking down the Nevsky Prospekt and working on poems for his book *The Heavy Lyre*. And he was often to be found at Gorky's place.

Even as families like Nina's were retracting to a single room, Gorky was expanding his already large apartment—knocking through walls to accommodate his ever more extended family, which included people who came for tea and stayed for years, as well as a former wife, a present wife, and eventually Moura.

In the Thermidorian Moscow of 1918, Moura had also

been struggling to keep her footing. If Nina was losing parts of her life story, Moura was well embarked on a lifework of mythologizing or deliberately deep-sixing parts of hers. "In order to survive, she had to be wary, deft, bold, and surrounded by legends from the start," Nina would write. Her girlhood and young womanhood seem to have been more conventionally hidebound and upper class than that of her future biographer. She liked to claim that she had a degree from Cambridge University but Nina, in the first of many unmaskings, exposed that sham; there were no degrees for women from Cambridge at that time. But there had certainly been cotillions and velvet trains and curtsies in courts at home and abroad. There was a first marriage, to a Count Benckendorff, a diplomat who owned estates in Estonia, and two children by him. (She once told Nina she had them "simply because everyone has children," and lived mostly apart from them in later years. They were brought up by a governess, first in Estonia and later in England.) In 1917, she learned from someone she met on a St. Petersburg street that her husband had been hacked to pieces by a mob of peasants on his estates. She sold her velvet court train to buy a bag of flour and used her wits in order to stay alive. She picked her way through the "cracked and crumbling" world in an increasingly shabby velvet coat and feathered hat—all she retained from her life before. And she fell passionately in love with Robert Bruce Lockhart, a young British diplomat who was using all *his* wits in a doomed and virtually single-handed attempt to keep the new Russian government at war with England's enemy, Germany. In the Red Terror following the attempt on Lenin's life in 1918, Moura found herself along with her lover in the fearsome, blood-soaked Lubianka prison, accused of plotting counterrevolution.

Moura had an iron constitution and a nerve of steel, any loss of which was as rare in her as tears in Nina. Lockhart wrote admiringly in his journal of her thoroughly aristocratic and unbourgeois approach to love. She made no secret of the pleasure she took in sex or of her willingness to use it. "This truth shocked and irritated women, disturbed and excited men," Nina wrote of Moura, whom Gorky first admiringly dubbed the iron woman. Yakov Peters, the ruthless and powerful vice-president of the Cheka, interrogated Moura and showed her some intimate photographs of her and Lockhart together. Moura did something unprecedented for her: she fainted. Then she did the only thing she could think of to save her life and her lover's as well: she went to bed with Peters. He was a man of his word, and had both Lockhart and Moura set free. To the end of their long lives, Lockhart (who died in 1970, at eighty-three) and Moura (who died in 1974, at eighty-two) maintained the public fiction that *he* had got *her* released, through "diplomatic channels." The following year, after Lockhart had gone home, she was thrown into jail again, for a barter involving her mink muff. But by then she had a powerful protector in Gorky, Lenin's old friend and "the stormy petrel of the Revolution." She was forging her own survival. She was being reborn as a kind of woman as yet unknown—a woman with new emotions. There were "new fears for new generations: fear of prison; fear of hunger and cold; fear of having no passport . . . fear of having her secrets unveiled," Nina later wrote. "But the joys were of a new order, too: joy of freedom in private life, without constraint of moral code or the opinions of neighbours; joy of escaping death and surviving; joy of not having been destroyed by those she loved."

Moura made herself indispensable to Gorky—translating his many literary works and his worldwide correspondence into French or English and running his household (where there were servants, still) with admirable efficiency. Gorky was spellbound by Moura. So was his friend H. G. Wells, who came over to Petrograd in 1920 to give his imprimatur to the Revolution and to stay in Gorky's apartment on a kind of semiofficial visit. Both men were in their fifties and at the height of their renown and commercial success. They were sure of their power to remake the world according to their own ideas of progress. No writer of today could ever rival the international influence of such men; they were more like heads of state or of television networks. Wells was also, of course, a proponent of free love, and the proximity of Moura's bedroom to that of his host did not inhibit the Englishman from turning up at the foot of her bed one night in his pajamas. When he got home, he assiduously informed Rebecca West of what might (with a woman other than Moura) have been a sexual conquest. Far from being conquered, though, Moura was probably using the encounter with Wells as an insurance policy—a vital link in the chain of her escape from danger and degradation.

There's a famous photograph of Gorky, Wells, and Moura taken in Petrograd in 1920. The men are turned toward each other in what looks like admiring and animated conversation. ("You're a great and excellent man, Wells!" Gorky once wrote in a letter. "You've written a magnificent book!") They are twin Titans, in their vested suits and Edwardian mustaches—Gorky's drooping and stained yellow by tobacco smoke—discussing their schemes for enlightening the masses. Moura looks away from them and directly into the camera lens in a thoroughly modern way. She is smiling a feline smile, as though she had already drunk the blood of the two oblivious pontificators and would at any moment lick her lips with a pink tongue and make a start on the photographer.

" D O N O T take from me five minutes of my time, or I will *kill* you," Nina said to me one day not long ago. We were sitting companionably side by side on a bench in the plaza of her apartment complex in Philadelphia. She has found in this most recent home of hers an environment that seems to suit her. It's an American place, completely modern: a plaza—a clean, bland space—surrounded by tall residential towers. Nina likes America very much, its freedoms ("What is on

paper is what is the law") as well as its youthfulness and open-
ness. (Americans, she told me once, are "happy day and
night.") Like many artists who came of age in the first decades
of the twentieth century, she enthusiastically embraces the
whole notion of modernity. The towers were designed by
a famous architect in what turned out to be the last great
modernist moment, the 1960s. They are arrogant, idealistic
structures—as touching and as much a period piece as the
cobble-streeted neighborhood of Benjamin Franklin, on
whose peaceable roofs the floor-to-ceiling window of Nina's
high rise look down.

Perhaps I had flinched when she spoke about wasting
her time.

"I don't mean this, sitting here with *you*, now," she said,
giving my sleeve a little pat. Her talk is by turns indignant, seductive, crisp, conspiratorial, historical, intimate,
secretive, and astoundingly frank. She once described Gorky
as having the natural charm of an original and intelligent
person who has had a difficult life, and that charm is in
her, too: a lightness after bridges crossed. Often, when I'm
with her I have a tingling sensation of the present moment,
even—or especially—when she reaches into her remarkable
memory for tales of long-gone times. She has always rejected
the idea of eternity, and even the idea of living, like Wells
and Gorky, for future generations, in favor of living in the
here and now. "The most ferocious immanence," she calls it,
using a phrase from Herzen.

On the way to our bench, we had skirted a fountain. The
walk was still a new one to her, and she was compiling
mental notes about the fountain. The hours of its operation
mattered to her. She wished to know precisely when the
water gushed and when it lay still. She watches the world and
herself in the world (mind, body, feelings) with great intensity. "I always wanted to know myself before I die," she
writes.

"I worship time! I cherish it!" she told me now. "As a
child, I felt it, the weight of time." Once the writerly die was

cast, she resented all distraction from literature. She would have gladly scrubbed the floor at Blok's house, but she balked at piano practice and at paying social calls with her mother. "At eight or nine, I understood that there is an *end*. I understood there is no God. That only weak and feeble people look to God." She hates the idea of religion with as much passion as she hates the memory of the Czar. Yevgeny Yevtushenko, coming to pay homage to her once, made the mistake of bringing an icon as a gift. It was all she could do not to throw it at him; she had him take it away.

We were sitting on the bench and speaking about love. "The *amours* thing," she said. She used to refer to Khodasevich and Makeyev as her first and second "husbands." In the course of becoming famous and giving hundreds of interviews, she has come to call them her "companions." "There are things I didn't understand when I loved at twenty, at forty," she said, speaking low. A heavyset nursemaid passed in front of us, slowly pushing a baby in its stroller. "Sometimes I think I have a little bit the two sexes in me," Nina went on. "People didn't understand these things before. They thought there was only one way to be."

The baby leaned forward in his seat, gazing fiercely at Nina. He flung an imperious and dimpled fist in her direction. She stared back intently. She has always been fascinated by living memory and the chain of being: one generation touching fingers with the generations on either side, like paper dolls. The deaths of Chekhov and Tolstoy took place when Khodasevich was a young man, and he felt them as personal tragedies. Nina's friend and fellow-writer Mark Aldanov had known—as a youth, in Paris—the old Empress Eugénie, who had known in her youth the men of the French Revolution. "Perhaps in fifty years someone will remember having met me," Nina wrote in *The Italics Are Mine*, never dreaming of how long she would live, how many new admirers she would meet. The stroller rolled on and away from us toward the fountain, with the child turning around and staring back from under the raised hood. He might have been a passenger in a horse-drawn cab in St. Petersburg, where, in 1910 (she never forgot it), Nina saw Halley's comet rising over the Neva. I felt like pinning a note to the baby's chest: "I met the gaze of Nina Berberova."

"I think about these old stories. I think there is so much I will never understand," she said now, with something that was very like a sigh. "And, to tell you the truth, I don't care anymore."

There was a silence.

"Look at that tree," she said, lifting her face. The tree was freshly green, with trembling, feathered leaves. "How beautiful it is!"

"Do you know the name of that tree, Nina?" I asked.

"Its name? Oh, no," she said, in the Russian voice that Americans thought was French when she moved here. "I know only a little bit of botany. I see only that in spring the magnolia is the first tree. That it lasts a few days and is gone."

"When I hear the birds sing in America, I do not know their names," I said. "I used to know the names of the birds back home in England."

"What? What's that you say?"

"Birds. I was saying I don't know the names of American birds."

"Oh. Birds."

"Were you ever interested in birds, Nina?"

"*Birds!* I was more interested in *wolves!*"

IN ST. PETERSBURG, Nina and Khodasevich made a pact: that they would "stay together and survive." The repression of the old bourgeois culture was well under way, and his name was on a list of proscribed voices, their owners scheduled for banishment or worse. In 1922, the year of the mass exodus of the intelligentsia, Nina took her lover by the hand and told her mother she was leaving Russia with him. Nina was to see her mother only once more—in the late twenties, when they met at the house of a cousin who lived in Ireland. It was a gathering of women, and there was much discussion of domestic servants; lots of children were running around. "It was awful, absolutely not I," Nina told me, with a shudder. As for her father, she never saw him in person after her departure. But in the thirties he was trying to make ends meet by working as an extra for the Soviet movie industry, so at a screening sponsored by a Communist cell in a Paris back street she sat in a smoky room and watched her father on film. He was cast in the role of an enemy of the people—a man of the *ancien régime* in a starched collar and tie—who gets his comeuppance from a righteously indignant proletariat. As he was marched off under escort through the howling mob, presumably to his movie death, Nikolai Ivanovich turned back to look into the camera, giving his daughter a farewell gaze.

Her parents died in the winter of 1942, during the terrible siege of the city that had by then become Leningrad. Nina knew only that they had been lost. She assumed that they were just two more of the hundreds of thousands who died of hunger and cold, and whose bodies, frozen and stacked like logs, went unburied for months. Then she heard some details from a second cousin she spoke to in Moscow in 1989: it seems that her father died of a heart attack as he sat on a train ready to run the German blockade. She learned nothing about how her mother died. "Perhaps she threw herself in the Neva." The conversation with the cousin took place during a return visit that Nina was able to make to Russia—the cog of her individual life and the wheel of Russian history having turned—after an absence of sixty-seven years. On this trip, she was tireless, she was stoic, she took great pains to smile and smile. Secretly, she was horrified by much of what she found. "Everyone hates his neighbor, everyone lies," she says. "There are no more Russian people." Hubert Nyssen, admiring and protective, went along. He kept a journal and later published it as a book. The Gallic Boswell was on hand to observe how, as she set foot on Russian soil, a single tear rolled from her eye and she immediately crushed it with her thumb.

She visited her native city and Moscow, trailed at every turn by crews from French television, on which she had become a great favorite. (She made two appearances on the intellectual talk show "Apostrophes.") In Russia, she read from her works and conducted lengthy question-and-answer sessions with feverish audiences, sometimes several thousand strong. For the heirs of five generations of Soviet history, she was an awesome survivor—a lucid memory bank of so much of their authentic national story. Not many people live to her age anywhere, and in Russia, where life expectancy is far lower than in the West, she was a miracle. "Touch her, she's real," she heard someone say in a stage whisper. The purity of her pre-Revolutionary accent and syntax amazed them. And the poet Andrei Voznesensky, who contributed an admiring ode to one of the public sessions, told me how fearlessly and vigorously ("not at all like an old woman") Nina had stood up to hostile heckling from the anti-Semitic, right-wing nationalist movement Pamyat.

o p p o s i t e the austere and narrow bed in Nina's modern, glass-walled bedroom hangs a row of four male poets. Blok; Andrey Bely; Valery Bryusov, and, naturally, Khodasevich. The portraits are there (instead of icons, instead of Apostles) to watch over her while she sleeps. They are the first thing she must see on waking. Her autobiography gives the impression that much of her life was spent in the company of men. "Of course. Because the profession was mostly men," she said when I brought up the subject.

Above the desk in Nina's living room hangs a formal group portrait made in a photographer's studio in Berlin in 1923. (Apart from lengthy stays with Gorky in the early twenties as he moved his household from one out-of-season European resort to another, Nina and Khodasevich followed the classic émigré trail of Berlin-Prague-Paris.) The portrait shows young Nina with seven Russian literary men, including Bely and Khodasevich. For all the Revolutionary upheaval they have just left, the hand-to-mouth, boarding-house nature of their present, and the precariousness of their future, the men have dressed in suits, starched collars, and neckties and have mustered a tolerable impersonation of complacency, like the governors of a Victorian bank. Nina is sitting in the front row—in a pale, soft blouse among the sober suits, and with a fox fur draped over her crossed knees. She's a strikingly feminine and sexual presence. "Half of them were in love with me," she murmured when she saw me looking at the picture. Afterward, I wondered if I'd imagined this remark. It seemed uncharacteristically boastful.

It's a peculiar thing: the young Nina among the suits reminds me of the elderly Nina in her own apartment. In both cases, there's something almost talismanic about her femininity. Apart from the fluffy pink towels in Nina's bath-room and apart from Nina herself—in her pretty blouses, with costume-jewelry necklaces; petite-size pants and dainty shoes; carefully applied lipstick in a fashionable shade—there is nothing about the Philadelphia apartment that would reveal the sex of its owner in her absence. The living-room furniture is distinctly unpretentious: a table covered in a brown-and-white checked oilcloth; a couple of carved chairs with brown velours seats; a sofa covered in a faded, slightly threadbare linen in a yellow-and-white print that was in style in the sixties. The impression (at odds not only with Nina's appearance but with the luxurious view of the old roofs, and beyond them, the Delaware River) is of faculty housing on a campus where Nabokov's Pnin might have been grateful to find work, or of a room in one of the residential hotels on New York's West End Avenue, where Nina lived when she started out in America. There is not a single shawl, scatter cushion, ornament, or darling little lampshade in sight. The sole framed photograph is the one above the desk, of Nina and her fur piece with the pleiad of Russian Berlin—and that is less a personal souvenir than something recorded with the public and posterity in mind. A stranger seeing the shabby but orderly shelves of old Russian books, the coffee table with the literary reviews, and a dish of stubby, sharpened pencils (like a dish of well-loved pipes) might take this for the home of a frugal, elderly, and scholarly man.

One of the bookshelves is filled with brand-new books in bright-colored jackets: the still-proliferating editions of works by Nina Berberova. The fiction, the book about Moura, the book about herself (the latter translated into many different languages). The biographies of Borodin (1938), Tchaikovsky (1936), and Blok (1947). Here is her book about the Kravchenko libel trial of 1949 (when pro-Communist French intellectuals and an English bishop testified that there was no such thing as the gulags), and the book about twentieth-century Freemasonry, written and published when she was in her seventies. Secrets, taboos, censorships, lies, "gas lightings" both public and private have been meat and drink to her as a writer. "Secrets have their juices," she writes. In Paris, she worked for fifteen years as a reporter on the émigré daily *The Latest News.* In that capacity and as a biographer, she has been a formidable detective—tireless and patient. "Intimate papers fell into my hands now and then by pure chance," she once wrote. "The list of documents read by me seems . . . quite incredible." The bookcase containing Nina's works is a yeasty, organic business. Books keep arriving from distant publishers and flowing out again in the hands of her many visitors. "My books are all in order, everything is arranged," she told me once. "I am ready to die." But then she plunged back into the bookshelf and rummaged happily about, like a busy baker.

Several of the editions of the autobiography use on their jacket a photograph taken of Nina in her mid-twenties. Her dark hair is softly arranged around a heart-shaped face and disappears into a chignon at the nape of a long, slender neck. The eyes are large and luminous and seem to be ringed with kohl; the mouth is wide and full.

"You were beautiful," I said, weighing one of the books and looking at its jacket portrait.

"No! Never was! Attractive, yes. It was the photographer who made me look like that—the lights."

No doubt there are some documents, some third-party accounts (apart from Nabokov's) of what Nina really looked like in her youth. But the witnesses who knew her then are all dead now. Secrets die with people, says this writer who has revealed and concealed so many secrets. Memories are gone. "The house burns down . . . the undergrowth grows up," she writes. I rely on Nina's own testimony for this account of her; she takes the stand in her own behalf. Now she was glancing dismissively at the smoldering beauty in the photograph. There's no way I can see that this girl with the doelike air and sideways-sliding glance could have written the rich, bold book she ornaments. Nina could see herself most clearly, she wrote in that book, as a child and after she was fifty. The dialogue with herself was faintest when she was between twenty and thirty and looked her loveliest.

"It is so *black*, this picture," she said now. The kohl, it seems, was the photographer's idea; he added it to the negative. The hair seemed too black to Nina, and the mouth as well.

"Were you wearing lipstick that day?"

"Lipstick? What strange questions you ask."

When I asked about the lipstick, I couldn't help thinking about Nina's romantic friendship with a young woman she calls only Virginia. They bought a single lipstick once and shared it by breaking it in two. This was during the civil war, in Rostov-on-Don. The story is in Nina's autobiography. The Red Army was passing under the window as the two young women lay reading in each other's arms. Virginia smelled of Coty's l'Origan and was already sick with T.B., which would kill her in a few short years. (At the end, Nina would visit her friend in her French sanatorium, changing her nightgown and emptying her sputum cup.)

" 'Love is a breeze rustling in the roses,' " Virginia said (quoting Hamsun) back then in Rostov-on-Don.

Not at all, Nina said to Virginia. "Love is *one* artichoke leaf eaten by *two* people."

The italics are Nina's. There was something remarkable about this friendship, Nina wrote, recalling it as a woman in her sixties. She and Virginia were equals. "Neither was superior to the other, neither dominated."

"H O W many men of genius I have known," Nina once wrote. As Khodasevich's girlfriend, she moved directly into a close-knit community of famous literary men, many of them as old as her father. "I knew the last great men in Russia," she added. They would be a university for her. By the time she'd enrolled in undergraduate courses in Rostov, the jig was up; the professors were too hungry and too terrified to teach. Nabokov, with his two years' head start, also had a leg up in other ways. He was a man; his family was well established outside Russia in 1917; there was enough money to send him to Cambridge to read for a genuine degree in English. Nina's education had to come through her own reading and through being around brilliant men. In Berlin in 1922, Nina would dress up in Khodasevich's trousers, hat, and cane, and walk the streets half the night with him and the writer Pavel Muratov, soaking up ideas like a sponge. As part of Gorky's peripatetic entourage for three years—in Herringsdorf, on the Baltic coast; in Saar, in the German forest; in Marienbad; in Sorrento—she absorbed his talk. His writing never interested her, and in her opinion he was limited by a streak of Victorian prudery, but she loved hearing him tell his famous fireside tales, even if (as soon happened) she had heard him tell them many times before.

At a banquet after the Berlin group portrait, Bely picked a drunken fight with Khodasevich, and never saw him again. Before that, Bely had been a frequent visitor. He would rant and rave and ooze self-pity, but he was writing brilliantly through it all, and for Nina "his genius was so powerful that each encounter illuminated life." Along the great-men route to education, she makes clear, there were crosses to be borne. The novelist Ivan Bunin (who later became the first Russian to win the Nobel Prize in literature) treated her with "tender irony" when she was in her doelike days, but also tested her (as he liked to test all women, especially women writers) by telling her dirty jokes. As for Aleksandr Kuprin, the author of a book called *The Pit* ("a semidocumentary study of Russian brothels," according to the appendix of *The Italics Are Mine*), he caught Nina alone one night in the drawing room of Prince Baryatinsky's house in Paris and asked her to let him eat a cherry off her chin. He reminded her vaguely of her grandfather at Tver. Obediently, she held the stalk between her teeth. Kuprin ate the cherry and spat out the pit; he said that life was nearly over for him. It's as if she's in a movie, in slow motion and with the sound off, as she tells it. "I was terribly sorry for him but said nothing," she writes.

There are some remarkable photographs from the twenties. She leans kittenishly on the shoulder of Khodasevich; she holds a cat (with an awkward, hungry sensuality) in her arms; she stands behind a deck chair occupied by Bunin and, geisha-like, shields his eyes with her parasol. Once, Nina showed me a group of photographs taken in the garden of Gorky's house in Sorrento in 1924. She brought them out, it seems to me in retrospect, like a magician bringing out his doves, and fluttered them rapidly out of sight again. There exist, though I haven't seen them, photographs of Nina and Moura sitting with Gorky on a stone bench. One version, owned by Nina, shows only Gorky and Nina, with Moura carefully scissored out. Another version, seen by Nina in the Gorky museum of Moscow, has only Gorky and Moura on the bench, with Nina carefully snipped off. But I did see a photograph in which Khodasevich hovers like Prospero in some shrubbery near an enchanting young Nina with what looks like a tan. In the photographs, Gorky looks handsome and heroic—full of that superabundant vitality which Nina admired above all in him, and which was present in spite of, or perhaps because of, his own T.B. Moura had long since discarded the threadbare velvet and the feathered hat. In her new incarnation, and to the end of her life, she would go hatless, with soberly tailored clothes, hand-made shoes, and a man's wristwatch. Here she is, standing with Gorky in Sorrento, looking even more abundantly full of life than he does. She has a well-cut coat slung like a British officer's round her shoulders; a silk-clad bosom; a fur piece at her throat.

"But, Nina," I said, amazed. "Moura was *beautiful!*"

"No! Handsome, yes. Her face was intelligent, expressive. But beautiful, never." The doves were fluttering again. "And she had such big feet. Like a man."

In Sorrento, with a view of Vesuvius beyond the window, and the crackle of an olive-wood fire on the hearth, Nina would listen while Moura, Gorky, and Khodasevich talked. Moura had kept her balance on the tightrope of the previous years, had refashioned herself and survived. From a never-consummated marriage to another Estonian noble—this time a ne'er-do-well young baron called Budberg, in 1921, she gained new papers, giving her a new title and name; then she conjured up enough money to pay for her bridegroom's one-way passage to South America. She was also writing to Lockhart, and Nina has read some of the letters.

"She certainly loved Lockhart very much," Nina said to me, with a note of tenderness in her voice, and she added, with something like satisfaction, that the Englishman had fallen out of love not long after his release from prison. "I think when she slept with Peters this calmed Lockhart down a bit."

"You think Lockhart knew what she'd done?"

"Of course he knew."

Although Nina had her hair bobbed—like every modern girl—when she reached Paris, Moura never did cut hers. She wore it in a chignon with loosely escaping wisps. But in Gorky's house at Marienbad both women had long hair. It was when Nina was washing her hair and Moura was helping her to rinse it with water from a jug that Moura told her the story of Peters and the compromising photographs. Moura almost never spoke about her feelings or betrayed them; she was known for stoicism and serenity. When Gorky's arch-enemy, Zinoviev, had her room searched in Petersburg, she noted with satisfaction that her hands didn't shake. When Mussolini sent his men to search her room in Sorrento, she went straight to see him, confronting him and making him laugh. There were so many things back then that Nina didn't understand. "She was one of the most exceptional women of her time," Nina would write. "She was more interesting to me than all the rest, including Gorky." Moura would leave for lengthy trips. She was full of mystery, which Nina liked. "But there could be no intimacy between us, because we weren't equal."

BY THE LATE TWENTIES, when Nina and Khodase-vich had set up very modest housekeeping in Paris (with a broom, a couple of pots, a tea cozy with an embroidered rooster), she was beginning to publish her writing in *Contemporary Annals*, the most highly regarded émigré quarterly, as well as in *The Latest News*. Khodasevich discussed her work with her and told her she would be a good writer someday. But they were far too poor to wait for that day to arrive; she published anyway. She also did piecework embroidery, typing, and movie-extra jobs, and painted Christmas cards to make ends meet. Like all émigrés, the couple were officially stateless, and France did not grant them the legal right to salaried work. A portrait of her from this period shows newly bobbed hair, a pugnaciously forward-leaning neck, with a dramatic pussycat bow at the side, and eyes that look at the viewer directly. This is no pliant flower in the garden of the great men.

"I was more like that," Nina said, waving at this picture. "Here I recognize myself. Much more *activity* in the face."

I asked what she thought when she saw the portrait of that young woman.

"What do I think? I think she was right. *Damn* right!"

In those days, she was laying claim to a seat of her own at the Paris café tables where the émigré writers met and talked—becoming a member of what Khodasevich called "the club of people who can still tell the difference between an iambic and a spondee." One night, Nina writes, "around midnight we began to talk of Tolstoy—Bunin, Khodasevich, Aldanov, Nabokov, and I." Historically, Russian literature has been inclined to take itself quite seriously as a kind of sacred trust. This fiery, life-or-death idea of writing and reading sprang naturally from the risk—under the czars, as later, under Stalin—that a writer might pay for an honest sentence or line of poetry with prison, exile, or death. In the twenties and thirties, Nina's milieu had a commitment to the literary ideal which is rather rare. No other group of refugees can ever have been quite so top-heavy with poets as the one making its way to Paris after the Bolshevik rise to power. "Stay together and survive," the motto of Khodasevich and Nina, was only the group imperative writ fine. The writers of the emigration loved each other, and sometimes hated each other even more, but, either way, they gave each other visibility. They recited for each other, they formed an audience of listening ears, they read each other's work in manuscript and in type. They held fund-raisers to enable colleagues who used to be rich and famous to get their teeth or their hernias fixed. In cafés where sympathetic Russian waiters let them linger all night over a single coffee; in night clubs with vodka, Gypsy fiddlers, and steaming plates of blinis; in rented rooms with bathtubs in the kitchen and festoons of drying sheets— they talked and talked.

The writers of the emigration were shut out of publishing in their abandoned country and went largely unnoticed by writers and readers in the outside world. Their materially deprived and intellectually luxuriant community was invisible, for instance, to the more casually knit web of English-speaking writers in Paris in the twenties. James Joyce, F. Scott Fitzgerald, Ernest Hemingway, Katherine Mansfield, and Gertrude Stein must sometimes have been at the Dôme or the Coupole with the Russians, but at separate tables and a world apart. The ignorance was mutual. The older émigré writers, those of the so-called First Generation, tended to discount contemporary Western writing; they were resistant to new forms even among the Russians of their own New Generation, including Nabokov. As a group, the writers of the emigration were doomed to become extinct. Russian dancers, visual artists, and musicians in exile fared better. (Nina describes herself—a young woman in a sleeveless blue chemise dress reflected in the mirror of the theatre stairs—proudly attending the first night of her compatriot Igor Stravinsky's *Rite of Spring*.) But the writers were stuck with the language of a country from which, year by year, they were more efficiently squeezed out.

Khodasevich was only one of the many who felt the creative life draining out of them. "Here I can neither write nor live," he would moan to Nina. "And over there I no longer have the right." It was by a quirk of fate that Nina's work floated up through history: that she lived long enough to see her work translated and distributed around the world (like Nabokov) and (unlike him) lived long enough to see it acclaimed and openly sold in Russia itself. I spoke to her once about how easily the pendulum might have skipped, how easily her writing might have been lost. She shrugged. There were so many good writers, she said, who could not get published then. Nabokov fought unsuccessfully for years to get his novels translated into English before he became famous for *Lolita*. "It was not my tragedy alone," she said. Many of the émigrés, whether skilled at writing or not, had unbelievable life stories and felt impelled to set them down. "Every émigré wrote his memoirs," Nina wrote in what is, she avers, not memoirs but autobiography, being first and foremost about herself. "The Empress's lady-in-waiting wrote about

Rasputin choosing ministers, the Social Revolutionary wrote about assassinating them," she said. "Others wrote about their lost estates with lime-tree walks and portraits of their ancestors."

THE ITALICS ARE MINE is a compendious, digressive book more than five hundred pages long. It is like an émigré's travel trunk, fitted with mirrored compartments and secret drawers and stuffed with all sorts of memorabilia and written forms. Among them are:

(a) Lists, including the list of his prior loves Khodasevich wrote in pencil on a piece of cardboard and gave to Nina as they began life together.

(b) Scraps and jottings, including the rough draft of the poem which K. used in Petersburg to stuff the toe of some too big galoshes and which surfaced a year later in Berlin.

(c) Letters, including those intended for one intimate friend and those intended to awaken the conscience of the world.

(d) Philosophical digressions and meditations.

(e) Accounts of Nina's dreams, including the most significant dream of the Well and the Source and the dream of playing chess while talking to Dostoyevsky.

(f) Stories of real people's lives: some many pages in length and reading like novellas; others often quite acerbic, no more than epigrams ("He was a perfectly ordinary man but his life was quite eventful as though it were intended for someone more energetic and intelligent").

(g) Chunks of quotation from the prose and verse of Russian and European authors.

(h) Literary essays and reviews.

(i) Two sections of intimate journal: a painful day-by-day account of the final illness and near-pauper's death of Khodasevich, in 1939, and The Black Notebook, which includes Nina's diary of her life under the German Occupation.

(j) Confessions.

(k) Veils. Palpable omissions. Pockets of air. Silences.

Her whole life has been a process of conserving and of letting go—of saving the tiniest scraps for the archive while refusing to regret the passing of anything at all.

"Sometimes I think that reading and writing are very old-fashioned," I said to her one day. "But important."

"Very important," she said. A pause. "Or maybe literature will be finished," she said, looking almost perky at the idea. "Because of the computer, the fax—all that." She is an enthusiast of the word processor.

"Do you think people are losing the sense of history?" I asked.

"Maybe. *Many* things are lost. But new things will come. The new generation has no tears to shed about the end of something. They have new things to think about."

If Nina writes about books and thoughts as if they were lively and full of juices, she writes about people as if—like plays or books—they were subject to stringent standards of review. After all, each of these others, like Nina herself, was allotted a store of energy at birth which simply runs out with death. There is nothing more, she insists. The light bulb simply clicks off. What, she demands of all these characters who shared the earth with her for a span, did they make of their measured amount of the cosmic charge? What choices did they make? What place was there for love in their lives and how did they survive it? What was their strategy for survival in general? All the émigrés suffered Job-like tests. France, which had denied them civil rights, drafted them to fight; Germany sent them to forced-labor camps, and forbade them the free use of their language. For the inhabitants of the cemetery in the émigré district of Boulogne-Billancourt, even death brought no respite: in an Allied bombing raid one night, their skulls and bones flew about. Nina seemed, at the time she wrote about Moura, to have admired and identified

with her modernity, her vitality, her sexual freedom, and her
ability to survive. But she drew the line at Moura's amoral
survival methods—"like a hawk or a leopard."

For the émigrés, Nina's checklist gets even more specific. Did you survive morally and mentally as well as physically? Did you try to look inside yourself, or did you play the
victim and look for others to blame? The great Russian question: Did you speak out and tell the truth? Were you bold in
your work? Were you modern—pushing yourself away from
the nineteenth century with sufficient vigor? Did you fulfill
your promise, develop the talent you were born with? And
this question, overarching all: Were you cooperating with the
life force, or were you willfully moving in the direction of
suicide?

Khodasevich's genius was far from unrecognized. "He had
such great glory," Nina told me that day on the bench. "He
was not a martyr in any way." Scores of admiring friends and
disciples sought him out in the rented rooms; he would sit up
half the night talking with them or writing. Nina would go
to sleep hugging his pajamas to warm them for him. She was
the fledgling writer; he came into exile already a star. People
called her his finest creation, his "Galatea." "The thought
that I could be his equal never crossed my mind," she writes.
The pages where he appears have a mythic resonance. The
silhouette is strong: in a coat to his ankles and in a strange
pointed hat in a Petersburg square lit by flaming brands; with
his arms outstretched in the window when she left him, like a
man crucified.

"Nothing will ever destroy you," he used to tell her. "You
will simply die." His erstwhile fame worked against him in
the new world. He suffered greater humiliation as he steadily
lost ground. She was young and healthy and had nothing to
lose. Unlike him, she was not afraid of life. Ever since his
youth, he had played with the thought of committing suicide.
He liked her strength but was secretly alarmed by it. He
"built a private hell and tried to pull her in," she wrote. For

the first time, as she listened to his laments, she felt time standing still. She never left the house without wondering whether he would jump out of the window or turn on the gas while she was out. This suicide idea was his ace in the hole. It never left him until (completely disillusioned by literature and by life) he died, of cancer, at the beginning of the war. As a little girl, Nina had gone through a phase of playing with dolls—pretending they were male, bandaging them, and lining them up in hospital beds. She soon gave up that game. Now she began to spend intervals separated from Khodasevich, and observed that time began to flow again when they were apart. Their physical life was unsatisfactory ("I spoke to the doctors and finally I understood," she says now. "He was not a normal man"), but she did not wish to embarrass him by leaving him for someone else. As soon as she detected a hint of romance between him and a woman named Olga Margolina, she felt free to leave; there was another woman to look after him. (Before Khodasevich married Olga, he asked Nina's permission.) "I expect she darned his socks and made soup for three days," said one of the couple's mutual friends upon hearing that Nina had left Khodasevich. Leaving him everything, including the embroidered rooster, she moved into a hotel.

It is a great thing for a Russian woman to be the wife, girlfriend, or widow of an important artist. Well into old age, Nina still defined herself in relation to the dead Khodasevich. Even today, the couple are bound together as long as she is alive and is thinking about him; death ends a life, it is said, but not a relationship. After Khodasevich and Olga were married, they used to come and stay with Nina and Makeyev, who had married within months of the other pair and bought an old farmhouse at Longchêne, outside Paris. After her husband died, Olga (who was Jewish) came alone, and even lived there for a while before she was sent to Auschwitz, where she died in 1942. Nina went to Olga's apartment just before it was confiscated by the authorities and rescued a suitcaseful of Khodasevich's papers and unpublished writings. After the

war, these followed her to America and formed the basis of
the poet's archive at the Hoover Institution, in California. It
is a measure of how she saw herself, and typical of the records
of women's lives compared with records of the lives of men,
that her own papers had no separate archive then but were
mixed up with his. Most of her papers are now in an archive
of their own, in the Beinecke Library, at Yale. Nina oversaw
the posthumous publication of Khodasevich's verse and his
essays, both in Russian and in French. In spite of all these acts
of devotion, there are some lovers of Russian literature who
have not forgiven Nina for abandoning the failing Khodasevich. In an émigré world that has often been split by cruel
feuds and savage rumors, Nina has made more than her
share of enemies.

"Some people blamed you," I said to her once.

"Probably."

"They say 'that terrible woman.' "

"Very Russian," she said, looking wry.

"What is that? Machismo?"

"Machismo, of course. I lived with him for ten years. I
wrote. I kept house. He was very sick. It was not easy." A
long silence. "No, I have no pangs of conscience that I left
him. Absolutely not." An even longer silence. "I saw that I
could go on."

M O U R A H A D also gone on. She was also surviving, making
decisions and existential leaps. "We did not consider our
actions as feminine caprices . . . . but as a part of ourselves for
which we were personally responsible," Nina wrote of herself
and Moura, looking back. As a young woman, she had
watched with admiration as the "manly, firm, and serious"
Moura took energetic action to break with the conventions of
her "erroneous" past and remake herself. "No one was going
to hand her a scholarship, clothes, a nice apartment in an elevator building. . . . She did not have the luxury of sure tomor-
rows, of money in the bank." After Gorky returned to Russia,

Moura lingered in Berlin for a while on enigmatic business and then moved to London, taking with her, at his request, a suitcase full of letters from correspondents who would be in jeopardy if the letters fell into Soviet hands. Before long, Moura became the companion of H. G. Wells. In the thirties ("that frightful time," Nina calls it), while Nina was living in France on a Nansen passport and writing non-stop in order to eat, Moura was effortlessly becoming a British subject and a highly visible member of London café society. She also kept up her frequent and mysterious journeys abroad.

Lockhart, too, was back in Moura's life, not as a lover but as an old friend and as the other half of what looked increasingly like a professional team. After his return from his swashbuckling efforts on behalf of His Majesty's Government in St. Petersburg, Lockhart had become first a kind of commercial spy for the international banking business and then a journalist. He wrote a column for the *Evening Standard* and became a right-hand man to Lord Beaverbrook, the newspaper's owner. Moura fed him up-to-date information about Russia and the politics of Europe, which he would publish in his column. She reproached him for not being more serious about his writing and prodded him to finish his book *Memoirs of a Secret Agent in Russia*. Because he was a gentleman and because the book included a version of his love affair with Moura, he showed her the manuscript in advance. There was no hint of the transaction with Peters, but even so Moura surprised Lockhart by demanding changes worthy of Gorky at his most prissily Victorian. She insisted that Lockhart refer to her throughout by the formal and now obsolete title of "the Countess Benckendorff." She also asked him to change his description of her hair. The book, published in 1932, became a hit in both England and America, and it later became a movie, *British Agent*, and the real-life protagonists sat uncomfortably through a private screening while Leslie Howard and Kay Francis re-created their old romance.

Lockhart was a man of honor, a man of action, a man of

charm. There's always, in *The Iron Woman,* a kind of lightness whenever Lockhart's about, as if a sprightly little theme
tune accompanied him on the harpsichord. He's no Victorian, to be sure; but he's not exactly a twentieth-century man,
either. He's more like a man from eighteenth-century
London, fluffing his wrist linen and heading for the gaming
tables and the club. Sometimes I think (reading about the
man in Nina's book) that she is a little in love with Lockhart;
sometimes that he is Nina in some way. (A man once sought
to compliment her by saying she had a sense of honor like a
man's.)

H. G. Wells wanted Moura to marry him, but she said no.
By Nina's account in *The Iron Woman,* the couple were as
close to being equals as a man and a woman might hope to
get. There was no question of dominance, of submission.
"For these two experienced partners, that would have been
far too simple, pale, and banal, in the tradition of male supe-
riority and female inferiority," Nina wrote. "The love of
Wells and Moura was played on the stage of a completely
empty theatre."

Some of the gloom of Wells' last years stemmed from his
discovery that Moura had probably been planted on him as a
Soviet spy. He lived with this knowledge from 1934 until,
with Moura at his bedside, he died, in 1946. He felt incapable
of giving her up. Even before Lockhart, it seemed, she had
been in thrall to one spymaster or another. The Germans had
sentenced her to death for spying for Russia in 1916. Lockhart's acquaintances assumed she was working as a secret
agent for the British, but she seems to have lied to him and
perhaps she spied on him as well. Gorky knew she had been
planted on him by his political enemies, but got around the
awkwardness by declaring that he had known all about it all
along—that he and Moura had freely discussed it. The Esto-
nians thought she spied on them for the Soviets in the twenties; the émigrés thought she spied on them for the Germans
in the thirties. When Lockhart was back at M.I.-5 during the

Second World War, she reported to him on, among other things, the activities of the Free French. Wells, who had taken her at her word when she said she had not been back to Russia since 1931, because to have gone back would have meant risking prison or death, was stunned to find out that she had been coming and going with impunity all along. Nina hypothesizes that when Gorky was on his deathbed, in 1936, Moura made a bargain with Stalin: she would have access to the closely attended Gorky if she brought the suitcase full of politically compromising letters he had entrusted to her for safekeeping outside Russia. The contents may have been used in evidence in the show trials mounted by Stalin to eliminate fellow-countrymen who were still around and still brave enough to oppose him.

W H E N Nina left Khodasevich, she moved into a cheap little room in an attic. But the view from the window was grand. She hung up her hand-me-down dresses, unpacked her clean towel and pillowcase, set out her papers on the rickety little table, and untied the bundle of books. Then she slept like the dead for three days and nights. (Khodasevich came round once to wake her and take her out to eat.) On the fourth day, she woke, found herself alone, and felt "flooded with happiness." It was a hot summer that year in Paris, and she wandered the city's parks and streets—a female version of the Baudelairean *flâneur*—or lay on the bed of the stuffy little room reading into the night. She turned away from the Russian classics and plunged for the first time into the contemporary writers of the West—devouring Huxley, Lawrence, Woolf, Joyce, Gide, Valéry, Kafka, and Proust. As always, life and literature went together for her. A new emotional moment, like a new idea, called for new form and style. She closed a chapter and turned the page.

In the 1960s, when Nina was writing of her life, there were few accounts by women of moments like this—of turning points where the "whole self" is exercised in an autonomous decision, with "joy independent of the success or lack of it." A quarter of a century ago, there were few really honest accounts in autobiography or biography of women standing in the center of their lives. Even now, there are not enough biographies of talented women writers who were not seeking, one way or another, to destroy themselves. Nina's life story right up to the present—a healthy, lighthearted, and thoughtful old age, solitary but not lonely ("I have no children or grandchildren to stop me doing what I want"), and with her talent financially and critically valued—is an extraordinarily helpful one. Yet, although she has led an emancipated life, she is not in any conventional sense a feminist. It seems to gall her that, this time around, her autobiography was reviewed less by experts on Russia than by women who celebrated her survival as a woman and wished to learn from it. Progressives of her generation did not make a distinction between progress for men and progress for women. She despises the idea of "women writers" or "women readers," apparently associating both with sentimentality, which she calls, along with its twin, cruelty, the greatest twentieth-century sins. In fact, as she often says, the cruel collective miseries of her era served her rather well. The Revolution, the Depression, war all kept closing escape hatches behind her, forcing her to develop herself and go on. But I have been taken aback sometimes to hear her speak of her own sex with a kind of contempt. "Women are always so *jealous*," she told me once, with a grimace.

Next to her hatred of the Czar, the Czar's God, and wasted time, Nina has hated the idea of making babies. She has told me several times that only once in her life did she ever contemplate committing suicide, and that was when she thought she was pregnant. In fact, the musty, Old Russian God and the making of babies seem connected in her mind. In her autobiography she describes the chapel at Tver with the coffins of dead babies lined up on the altar steps: the infants look pink, like suckling pigs at an Easter banquet—as if leaves of lettuce should garnish their mouths.

"I was very hard," she said to me one afternoon in her kitchen, looking up sharply from a scoop of Russian tea leaves she had been measuring carefully into a pot. "One day in Tver, my mother said to me, 'Put on your hat! We are going to visit the daughter of the priest.' We went into the house. It was so poor. So dark. She was there in a sort of bed, and beside her there was . . . a *baby*! One day old. And I looked, and then I went and was sick in the toilet. I knew *then* I had more important things to do than playing the piano or visiting babies."

The village priest had seven daughters. Nina used to play with the two youngest. He was an uneducated man, but he sent his girls to school in winter in a nearby town, intending that they should be teachers. The older girls were ashamed of their small sisters' bare feet squelching through the manure in front of their hovel. The young Nina, for her part, was already ashamed of her own bare feet in sandals, her bare arms and legs in summer dresses. She was ashamed of her body in the bathing suit she was forced to wear even though she stayed away from the water, having inherited from her father a fear of drowning.

NINA SAYS she obeyed two laws when it came to writing down her life: "The first, reveal yourself completely. The second, conceal your life for yourself alone." Around the halfway mark in her life and that of the century, the tone of her autobiography shifts, like the bathwater that is said to spiral counterclockwise after the equator is passed. It's as if concealment became more urgent as she contemplated the writing of her life and the living of it for herself alone. The play of light and shade is felt intensely in the writing she did in her forties and in the writing that describes that time of her life. Makeyev, with whom she lived between 1936 and 1946, is called N. or N.V.M. in the English-language editions; only in an appendix note in the French edition is he identified by his full name and as a writer, a politician, and a painter who studied with Odilon Redon. The couple were happy at first. "With Nikolai," she told me one day when I caught her in a tender mood, "I knew for the first time what it was to have a mate." At the old farmhouse they fixed up at Longchêne, there were humble, shared contentments even through the cross fire of a world at war. (For Nina, there was interrogation by the Gestapo, the loss of Olga, strafing and bombing by the Allies, a near-lynching by French neighbors, and the news from Leningrad.) Between the giant parentheses of first an army of occupation and then an army of liberation rumbling past the garden gate, there were beehives and strawberries at Longchêne and a much loved dog called Rex. There was a husband with charm and many talents, and jokes that made her laugh. There's a snapshot of Nina at that time, standing in her garden in a sun hat and an apron, beside a clothesline where a pair of men's pants hangs upside down. "I loved and love the human body," she wrote in *The Black Notebook*, her journal of that time. "Shoulders and knees, its smoothness and strength, the smell of a human being, his skin, his breathing, and all the noises within him." This passage, present in the English versions, is left over from the sixties and has been excised from the later, French editions—along with surrounding observations on "femininity" and on sometimes faking submission to a man. Unlike the parting with Khodasevich, that with Makeyev was very bitter. "There was a sudden duel between us, a struggle between him and me for a third person who deliberately became the center of this struggle, determined to split us up," she wrote. In the end, she also wrote, N.V.M. was one of those Russians who accomplish nothing of significance in life.

"Nikolai?" she said sharply when I caught her in a different mood. "Nikolai played such a small role in my life that in a few years from now I will even forget his patronymic!"

There was also in these years a woman friend—called M in the book. Nina was caught in a bombing raid with her in Paris, and covered her frightened eyes with her hand. M is not identified in any index, but a footnote to the afterword of the French paperback suggests that she may be Mina Journot, to whom Nina dedicated her biography of Blok in 1947. (Alone among all her books, this was originally published not in Russian but in French.) In Berberova country, the most interesting things often happen in the fine print of a footnote or are hidden between the lines; the same French footnote links this Mina with the author of a bundle of love letters that Nina gave Hubert Nyssen to read one day when he visited her in Princeton in 1987. Naturally, he wrote all this in his journal. He sat up all night reading the letters and trying to puzzle out the story behind Nina and Mina.

"What happened to the letters you wrote to Mina?" Nyssen had asked Nina as she handed him the letters from Mina.

She shrugged.

"Lost, I suppose. Like the woman."

I have never asked Nina about Mina Journot. But I once asked her what she thought about her *cher Hubert* publishing his sometimes revelatory journals.

She shrugged again. "I believe in liberty," she said.

THE END of the war brought public and private liberations for Nina. The horror was over, and, with it, the honey-and-strawberry time with Makeyev. The café tables were empty of German generals but were filling up with pro-Stalinist French intellectuals. The iambic-and-spondee club was disbanded, its members scattered or dead. "Night fell on the Russian Parnassus," Nabokov said. In 1946, Nina journeyed to Sweden, where her biography of Tchaikovsky was being published. ("What a pity it was written by a woman and not by one of us," said an émigré prince who, like the composer, was homosexual.) She was reading Strindberg's very frank autobiography and expressing to her journal her desire to write about

her life in an open, modern way. She returned to Sweden in
1947 and spent the month of June on a remote island with
a friend named Greta Gerell, and Gerell's partner, Fru
Asplund. They were physically powerful and active women
(Asplund, a retired gym teacher, was a fencer and champion
yachtswoman) leading lives that did not depend on men. They
offered Nina a new kind of nurturing.

In the thirties, Nina dreamed that she would someday be
freed of the fear of drowning which was her inheritance from
her father. With the unshakable authority of a sibyl, Asplund
challenged Nina and pointed her firmly in the direction of
her life, saying, "If you do not stop fearing water, which is an
element . . . your harmony will be destroyed. . . . If you deny
water in yourself, you will gradually turn into a pillar of salt."
So Nina learned to swim at last and took to setting off alone
in a rowboat, like Wordsworth in *The Prelude*. Under the
watchful eyes of her hostesses (who pretended not to be
watching, from the shadow of their balcony), she charted a
zigzagging course far out across the water in the endless,
pine-scented midsummer nights.

She took stock. Just as, on the eve of an earlier departure,
Khodasevich had written a list of his former loves, Nina now
wrote a list of her present freedoms:

> From what, exactly?
>
> From intellectual anarchy
> From opinions subject to the caprices of mood
> From dualism (everything has been synthesized)
> From a sense of guilt (now gone)
> From anxiety
> From fear of the opinion of others
> From neurotic restlessness and disorders in the body
> From the pedantry of early years
> From formless overflowing with contradictory emotions
> From the fear of death
> From the temptation to escape
> From pretense

Living alone once more, she camped for a time in a borrowed Paris apartment in the process of renovation—sleeping with no walls or roof sometimes, and with a view of the stars. There was a meeting with Olga's niece, who had married an Englishman and was the only one of her large family to have escaped the Holocaust. "But you survived!" the niece told Nina. "Now you must live as if you alone in all the world had survived." In the late forties, Nina made what she recognized as the greatest and most significant leap of her life—the decision to immigrate to America. Upon leaving Paris and her remaining friends there, she wept uncontrollably on the train. She was forty-nine when she arrived in New York, "narrow and tall like a Gothic temple," which reminded her, in its "unique mixture of functional and symbolic," of her lost St. Petersburg. She had seventy-five dollars to her name, and she parted with thirty-five on landing, in settlement of a debt. With her two suitcases, she once again moved into a hotel room and began a new life.

In order to support herself, Nina took a series of modest jobs—seven in as many years, including private secretary, addressograph operator, and file clerk. In 1958, she was hired to teach a freshman Russian course at Yale. The head of the department discovered some of her books in the library and promoted her to teaching literature. It was around this time that she started to cover the gray in her hair. "It wasn't good for my students. It wasn't good for me," she says. She taught Bely, Blok, and Khodasevich to graduate students first at Yale and then at Princeton, where she moved in 1963. Her students have gone on to teach at Yale and Princeton; one of them became head of the Russian department at Harvard.

"You are proud of them," I once observed.

"Yes. I enjoyed teaching clever men."

Her new life in America burst right out of the novella form, with its unities and constraints. Here was a world without memories or history for her—where Flaubert and Turgenev had never lived, where nobody went around quoting from Akhmatova or Lermontov. "Where am I? How many towns have I passed through . . . Where is the horizon I was promised?" says the protagonist of her most recently published novella, *In Memory of Schliemann*, which is a surrealistic piece set in America and reads like a transportation dream. She is fond of this story for its modernity, seeing it as "an egg laid in the middle of her century." Like the story she wrote just before it, it is written in the voice of a man.

Like everyone else in America in the 1960s, she hit the road, setting off in her car to drive across the continent, exploring her new world without walls, the new state of consciousness that she now called home. After first detaching herself from Paris by revisiting it, to establish that both she and the city had moved on, she spread out her papers on the big American desk and started in on her life story. A writer I know remembers seeing her at Yaddo, the artists' colony, one summer when she must have been working on *The Italics Are Mine*—an unprepossessing little woman who kept herself to herself. "I thought I would 'become someone,' " she wrote at the end of her book, recalling herself when young. "But I haven't 'become anyone,' I've simply 'been.' " There's another, slightly later glimpse of her—in 1979, after the autobiography had appeared and swiftly vanished, and eight years after her retirement from what had been, considering its late start, quite a successful academic career. Someone took a snapshot as she was about to receive an honorary degree from Glassboro, a small liberal-arts college in southern New Jersey. (As if swept up in Berberovan flux, the institution has since changed its name.) She is an elderly, somewhat weary-looking woman wearing sunglasses, a too small mortarboard, and a plain black academic gown. Patiently clutching her handbag, she stands sandwiched between two imposing-looking men in much fancier regalia, who seem to be ignoring her. This might so easily have been the apogee: a female sparrow on the lawn of an obscure provincial campus, looking rumpled and just the tiniest bit defeated.

"WHAT IS this woman to me?" Nina said angrily. Her old hands moved in a gesture of agitation. She was showing me a new Moscow edition of *The Iron Woman*, which she had been checking and rechecking word for word against her original. To her satisfaction, not a word had been altered or omitted. ("I think this is a very good book," she says.) There's an expressive, evil mask of smiling hypocrisy that Nina adopts to speak of traitors. She wears it now to speak of Moura with a rage not present in the book. "She lied and lied and lied. She slept with *everyone*. No, reading again this book, I understand that I have no sympathy with her. She was interesting to me because she had an interesting life. She had interesting *men*. But I did not like *her* at all."

Wells had tried to confront Moura about her life as a spy. How *could* she? Didn't she believe that some things were so dishonorable that it would be better for a person to die than to go on living with the knowledge of having done them? Moura laughed. He was an Englishman. He'd never known what it meant to be alone and completely defenseless—to be living the life of the cave. There was only one law in life: survival. And Nina wrote in *The Black Notebook* that she couldn't understand why anyone would say that honor was more precious than life. "How could anything be more precious than life?" she asks. Sometimes I feel that the pages of *The Iron Woman* are an eerie, dimly lit gallery filled with the dust-sheeted statues of great men and echoing with what I imagine to be the whispered dialogue of Moura and Nina.

"You compromised?"

"Yes."

"Me, too."

"I had sex with him, but I made believe it didn't bother me."

"You did what you did."

"You know, it was Lockhart who said I should hand over Alexei Maximovich's letters."

"You had dealings with that butcher, Stalin. How *could* you? Aaargh!"

Since the Age of Chivalry, a man of honor has been able to kill or go whoring, but he is not supposed to be a liar. An honorable woman may use tricks, ruses, and manipulations—may lie, in short—but she is supposed to be faithful. Moura was living by new rules, and Nina, in writing about her, was in uncharted literary and emotional waters. Sometimes Nina seems to celebrate and endorse Moura's sexuality unfettered by procreation or sentiment. ("Moral questions, fake modesty, and ordinary taboos did not spoil her liaisons. . . . She was free long before women's liberation.") At other times, Nina adopts a masculine view that irresistibly sexy, emotionally detached women are a threat to men and may be used (by them or against them) as lethal weapons in time of war. Nina may be curious to know how Moura survived Wells' depressions; I would be even more curious to know how, after she used her body to save Lockhart's skin, his "calming down a bit" had made her feel.

"I think she was a little bit frightened of me," Nina says. After leaving Gorky's house, Nina scarcely caught sight of Moura again. They met for the last time in Paris in 1937, on the centennial of the death of Pushkin. Nina told Moura she hadn't changed; the other woman looked flattered.

"I can't wait for you to write your memoirs," Nina said.

Moura looked terrified. "I'll never have memoirs. Only memories," she said, giving Nina her hand and moving off.

Moura was fifty-four when Wells died, leaving her the equivalent of $100,000—a substantial sum for postwar London. By then, she knew everyone who was anyone. Over the years, she went on publishing her translations of great Russian men; worked as a consultant to Sir Alexander Korda and the British movie industry; came up with a new version of *The Seagull* for her friend Larry Olivier. Her appetite for food was gargantuan, and she needed vodka more and more. She let her figure go. She took to smoking big cigars and,

Bunin-like, telling dirty jokes. By her seventieth birthday, she had run through all her money, and her friends took up a collection to bail her out. She was caught shoplifting once. In 1970, Moura was seventy-eight, the age Nina would be when she really sat down to write *The Iron Woman*. (It was a book she had been planning to write for forty years, she says; it is also a book she could not have written a day sooner than she wrote it.) That year, *Vogue* sent Kathleen Tynan around to interview the legendary Baroness Budberg, who rarely left her flat. By dim light filtering through heavy curtains, Tynan made out a crowded and dusty nest: ancient velvet-covered armchairs; decanters; framed photographs; little tables jammed with bibelots and objects that looked (Tynan said) like prizes from a fun fair; icons; a tapestry of Nicholas and Alexandra that had been a gift from H. G. Wells. In the interview, Moura rolled out the old, old legends about herself. "When I began to verify," Nina (in a very different room, across an ocean) was gearing up to write, "I found that all her life she had lied."

Vogue also sent a photographer, who recorded Moura sitting on the edge of her narrow bed. She is surrounded by the signs of her life as a woman of letters—books, journals, bundles of correspondence, and notebooks, all piled higgledy-piggledy on a nearby bookshelf and on the floor. (Within a few months of this photographic record of their existence, Moura would pack all her papers into ten cartons and ship them off to Italy, where her son had rented a house. There was a trailer parked beside the house, and Moura spread out her papers, intending to use it as a study—a place to work. "To 'work,'" Nina would write in a footnote—waiting with her contemptuous punctuation like a patient hunter. The trailer and everything in it was destroyed by fire.) In the portrait, Moura wears a plain, dark-colored, shapeless-looking dress. The face is still strong, and even handsome, but there's a grimness to the set of Moura's mouth. And she gazes away from the camera with more despair than stoicism, as if there were something in the corner of her bedroom that she alone could see: some force that has already picked her up and lifted her out of ferocious immanence and dropped her in a falsely sentimental past; a force that isn't finished with her yet. She's powerless; the acrobatics have failed her. Moura Budberg's met her match.

1992

Nina Nikolaevna Berberova
b. St. Petersburg, August 8, 1901
d. Philadelphia, September 26, 1993

WARMED THROUGH AND THROUGH

O N E   W A Y or another, the great Edith Wharton was always writing about sex. She was afraid of it for the longest time. That's why you feel it's a force in all she wrote. She is best known as a novelist of manners and morals in New York a century ago and, most unjustly, as a junior version of her friend Henry James. But the unsealing of her private papers, subsequent biographies, and the surfacing of her love letters, secret journal, and even erotica by her have made us view her with new compassion and increased respect. Her life was quite a journey. She herself said that she only came into "a real personality of her own" at thirty-seven, when she published a collection of short stories—the first of what would prove to be a remarkable output of thirty-nine books. Those books—notably *The House of Mirth*, *The Custom of the Country*, *The Age of Innocence*, and *Ethan Frome*—were also part of an inner process by which their author freed herself to fall madly in love, at forty-five, and ecstatically discover sex.

Although she was an intense observer and delineator of feminine psychology in her characters, Edith Wharton would no doubt have been appalled to know that the secrets of her own heart would be laid bare. She was very much the grand Victorian lady. She inherited a great deal of money and made a great deal more by her pen. She relished and demanded a life of luxury. She loved laughter; riding in her motor behind her chauffeur; brilliant conversation; and small, fluffy dogs. But the eyes gazing out from photographs of her, especially in youth, are very sad. With strangers, her manner could be frosty; with friends, it was warm. In spite of her gargantuan zest for socializing and dining out, she was really very shy. She was "an odd, contradictory creature," she wrote in her unpublished autobiographical sketch called "Life and I."

Edith was born in her father's house on New York's West Twenty-third Street when Lincoln was President, and she died in her small château near Paris after Hitler and Mussolini had come to power. Her mother, Mrs. Lucretia Rhinelander Jones, was prominent in the "old New York" society her daughter would evoke with such wit and photographic sharpness—such a tautness of love and hate—later on. Lucretia was also a fashion plate. She had an advanced case of what Newland Archer, the male protagonist of *The Age of Innocence*, refers to as "the religious reverence of American women for the social advantages of dress." He supposes (this observer/hero who is one of a line of sensitive, self-conscious, and ultimately flaky Whartonian men) that dress is women's "armor" and "defense against the unknown." Edith inherited her mother's faith in the protective powers of stylish clothes. She dressed in French couture to the end of her days. As a girl, she was encouraged to believe herself the ugly one in her family; her feet were big and her smile wasn't right, somehow. But she was tall and lithe, with nice red hair and a slender, shapely figure that she maintained well into middle age. Her husband, Edward ("Teddy") Wharton, liked shooting, fishing, and smoking cigars. He was "terrified" by his wife's intellectual friends and her career, as it bloomed. "Look at that waist!" he said to one of the couple's men friends, pointing proprietorially at his wife as if she were a horse. "No one would ever guess that she had written a line of poetry in her life!"

"I had to fight my way to expression through a thick fog of indifference," Edith Wharton wrote in *A Backward Glance*, the autobiography she chose to publish. The world of old New York did not encourage the kind of risk-taking involved in Wharton's literary work. It was, Newland Archer understood, a "hieroglyphic world" of genteel people who avoided painful, unpleasant, or scandalous topics and who regarded art as "something between a black art and a form of manual labor." Edith's childhood revolved around summers in Newport and winter seasons in the proper world of lower Fifth Avenue and its surrounding blocks, where town houses like her parents'—with Dutch stoops, façades "the color of cold chocolate sauce," and windows shielded by triple layers of shades and drapes—presented a united front. It was a comfortable, conformist, and conservative little world, where everyone was related to everyone else. Its inhabitants were cushioned by money inherited from fathers and grandfathers who were far more pushy than they were themselves. Neither Edith's father, George Frederic Jones, nor her two brothers (who were twelve and fifteen years older than she was) ever worked much. The chocolate brown tribe, or at least Edith's version of it, was constantly resisting and invariably surrendering to "new money" and its attempt to gain a foothold in their midst. The mannerly and clubbish little world of New York blue bloods, a place of "faint implications and pale delicacies," was powerless in the end before the likes of Undine Spragg, the amoral Midwestern social climber in *The Custom of the Country*. Undine is able to crash the magic circle so uninhibitedly because she is ignorant of the unspoken rules.

Lucretia taught her daughter not to talk about money and to think about it as little as possible. But Edith became a hardheaded businessperson, negotiating on her own behalf with publishers in order to support her lavish way of life. Lucretia also taught Edith not to even *think* of sex. Almost everything to do with what James called "the great relation" between men and women was dismissed by Mrs. Jones as being "not nice." Even by the prevailing standards of her time, Edith's girlhood seems to have been puritanically repressive. As a child, she tried to puzzle out where babies came from and got no further than concluding that God made them by looking at the bride and groom through the church roof. In "Life and I," Edith told of a desperate shot at extracting the facts from Lucretia on the eve of the wedding to Teddy.

> Her handsome face at once took on the look of icy disapproval which I most dreaded. "I never heard such a ridiculous question!" she said. . . . But in the extremity of my need I persisted. "I'm afraid, Mamma—I want to know what will happen to me."

The answers never came. Although Teddy was nice enough and very kind to dogs, the marriage was doomed from the start. It wasn't consummated until three weeks after the wedding night and was celibate for the twenty-eight years it lasted after this false start. Generally the couple slept in separate rooms. If Edith was forced to share a room with her husband, she would almost suffocate from asthma attacks.

HER SECOND PUBLISHED BOOK was *The Decoration of Houses*, written in collaboration with architect Ogden Codman, Jr. Its design theories were a slap at homes like Lucretia's: gloomy Victorian nests of repression "crammed with smug and suffocating upholstery." Houses, like fashions, would be an essential buffer for Edith's restless and vulnerable self down the years. "I was always vaguely frightened by ugliness," she once said. In all, she created seven homes for herself, each more refined than the last. She was in her fifties and divorced from Teddy when she fell head over heels in love with a house in the South of France. "I feel as if I were going to get married—to the right man at last!" she said breathlessly to a friend. Married to her handsome houses, she processed between them—with a retinue of servants and in costly dresses—like Elizabeth I.

She even gathered round her a kind of court: a group of adoring friends who shared her interest in books and gossip of a high-toned sort. Henry James would often come to stay. He knew she was a powerhouse, and she scared him just a bit. Angel of Devastation was one of his tongue-in-cheek names for her. He was much older, but most of the others were younger than she—generally either homosexual or (like James himself) vibrating in a fastidious and asexual bachelorhood. At the age of forty-two, when she "turned from a drifting amateur into a professional" by producing *The House of Mirth* to meet the installment deadlines of *Scribner's Magazine*, she did her stint of daily writing, sitting up in bed each morning for several inviolable hours. After giving the day's orders to her devoted servants (a housekeeper and a lady's maid were with her for many decades), she straightened her silk cap and buckled down. In her firm, no-nonsense, rather manly writing she covered sheet after sheet on her lapboard, then let the completed pages slide to the floor. Then she dressed to the nines and went downstairs to join the courtiers for lunch.

"A woman's nature is like a great house full of rooms," she wrote in one of her early stories, which have an atmosphere of desolation unrelieved by the later wit. There were, she wrote, rooms meant for formal visits from strangers and others meant only for the family itself. "But beyond that, far beyond, are other rooms, the handles of whose doors are never turned . . . and in the inmost room, the holy of holies, the soul sits alone and waits for the footstep that never comes." There was a hunger in her as a girl, a sense of loneliness, what she called a "long inner solitude." The great Mrs. Wharton in her maturity was loaded down with furs and houses and motors; with fame, and honors of every kind. She was the first woman to win a Pulitzer (for *The Age of Innocence*) and to be awarded an honorary doctorate from Yale. The French gave her the Légion d'honneur as a reward for her herculean refugee work during the First World War. There was even talk of giving her the Nobel Prize for literature. But Edith was wounded, still. Still mad as hell at her mother. Lucretia had not loved her enough. She'd tried to crush her daughter's spirit when she lived at home and failed to prepare her to leave it. Lucretia's silence about sex, Edith said, "did more than anything to falsify and misdirect my whole life." When she wrote this, she was an old woman and her mother long dead. Lucretia had been thirty-seven when her daughter was born. Her boys were growing up, and she was far too interested in paying calls or unpacking the trunk of dresses from Paris to pay as much attention as little Edith craved.

There was Mr. Jones, of course. Edith loved her father very much. He died when she was twenty. The hidebound life of his tribe and the prosaic materialism of his wife had conspired, Edith thought, to squeeze the poetry right out of him. She speaks of him protectively. He had been lonely, she felt sure (as she, his little girl, had been lonely), and "haunted by something always unexpressed and unattained." Something in Edith didn't fit in the house of her family; didn't quite fit in the house of her tribe. The idea that she was a changeling reverberated with sufficient truth for her to half believe the rumor she heard in middle age that she was the daughter not of her father but of an Englishman who was living with the Joneses as a tutor to her brothers. Between the ages of four and ten, Edith lived outside the chocolate-brown ghetto when her father took the family to live in Paris and in Italy for a while. After this, and even after she'd been back in America for decades, she felt she didn't belong. She was "a wretched exotic produced in a European glass house," she said. At fifty, she returned to France and lived as an expatriate until her death at seventy-five. She never ceased to set her fiction in America, although she saw it again only twice.

It was during the childhood stay in Paris that her father taught her to read. Then he gave her free run of the books in his library in New York. The library was one of the house's dimly lit rooms, with windows muffled in green damask and a massive mantel held up by carved-oak figures of visored knights. Whatever the tutor had meant to Lucretia, he taught her boys the manly things: Greek and Latin and the connections between titanic ideas. Then Edith's brothers were gone, first to Harvard or Cambridge, then out into the world, leaving their sister to the crumbs of education considered appropriate for a young Victorian girl—a well-meaning but ineffectual governess, some manners, music, drawing, and conversational French. Undaunted, Edith augmented all that with what she picked up for herself in the library under the gaze of the visored knights. Her mother and her aunt read stacks of books by lady novelists. But too "indolent," Edith said, to vet the reading for anything "not nice," Lucretia simply forbade her daughter to read novels at all. Instead Edith plunged promiscuously into the books of the great men of the past: Plutarch, Homer, the Elizabethan and Restoration dramatists, Macaulay, Addison, Ruskin, Darwin, Shelley, Keats. The foundation of the wide-ranging erudition of Edith's maturity was laid here by a young girl "squatting on the Turkey rug" and pulling down volume after volume from her father's shelf. When it came to her education, she was, as someone said of her, a self-made man. "A secret ecstasy of communion," she said it was for her, with the knights and the books. Even before she could read, she'd told stories with a book in her hand: a highly ritualized, even compulsive activity she called "making up." It was a devastating passion, she remembered; it gave her exquisite relief. Even her entry into what she called her "secret garden" of creative life sounds remarkably like sex.

The novel *The House of Mirth* and the life of its lovely,

maddeningly immature, and narcissistic heroine, Lily Bart, is indeed a house of many rooms. Outwardly, in her gorgeous clothes, she goes through the motion of parading from one Gilded Age place to another in her quest for a man. At a deeper level, she's a child left hungry and neglected in the handleless room while a showy, noisy banquet for grown-ups goes on far down the hall. Lily is an artifact, a commodity, an Ornamental Woman. She's not looking for a mate—a lover to embrace her and father their child—but an investor, a collector, a real connoisseur. She wants a husband with capital— someone to bankroll her in the luxuries for want of which (she suspects) she'll die. But she's thirty already; it's five minutes to midnight and something uncomfortably like a pumpkin has its meter running at the door. She's getting older and wearying of the cynical game of using and being used by people much richer than herself. But she's trapped. Parasols, pearls, veils, décolleté gowns from Doucet and Worth, verandas on the island, private ballrooms, men's hats and canes on marble hall tables outside closed doors; cash, checks, stocks, deals; the "piece of the action," the "vigorish" and all so very New York. A worldly world, a gilded cage with no exit at all. "The doors stood open," observes Wharton. "But the captives had forgotten how to get out."

Lily comes within a whisker of being normal, of falling in love with Lawrence Selden, another passive, oversensitive Wharton man. She feels a zephyr of freedom one day in springtime as they're sitting under a tree. But then she's back "gasping for air in a little black prison-house of fears." And Selden simply joins the tribe of Lily's former friends who watch impassively as she loses ground. The time in the den at Gus Trenor's house was the point of no return. He's helped her with her bridge debts, and now he wants some sexual favor in return. "Hang it, the man who pays for the dinner is generally allowed to have a seat at table," he says. He's florid and drunk and he tries to make her, this girl who's a friend of his wife's. It's a very authentic sexual-violence scene. Lily flees with her "virtue" intact, but it makes no difference to her reputation and to her sense of shame. "I am bad—a bad girl—all my thoughts are bad," she moans. She is unable to break her silence about what happened even to Gerty Farish, her most unconditionally loyal and loving friend.

It is not society that kills poor Lily, you feel. It is some force, some resident Furies within herself. It is her strange misfortune to be punished by her former world as if she were a "fallen woman" but without having fallen, or even having had sexual feelings at all. Not for her or for her forty-three-year-old creator, Edith Wharton, were what James called the "convulsions and spasms" of physical love. Lily, though a grown and supposedly sophisticated woman, is strangely spellbound, lonely, and unprotected, like a girl in an incestuous house. Some feminist scholars (among them Gloria Erlich, author of *The Sexual Education of Edith Wharton*) are now wondering whether Edith Wharton might not have had some experience of incest as a girl. Perhaps there was some erotic feeling for her father—perhaps an experience in the library. There's something about *The House of Mirth*, something about the way Wharton writes of her father and mother—nothing you can pin down, of course—that suggests she was more than a tourist in the terrain of childhood sexual abuse.

For one thing, there were all the illnesses Edith experiences in girlhood and young womanhood: symptoms of what her Victorian doctors called neurasthenia but which contemporary diagnosis often links to early sexual trauma. Panic attacks, breathing difficulties of all kinds, migraines, debilitating depressions. For the first twelve years of her married life, she suffered from nausea so severe she often had to return to bed; she became incapable of eating. Lily Bart's beauty and powers of seduction turned on her and—in the drawn-out, Kabuki-like *tableau vivant*—led inexorably to suicide. And the young Edith's body would turn on her as if trying to punish her. Just before she published her first book, when the cage door seemed to be opening at last, she suffered a complete nervous breakdown. For four months, she was in

Philadelphia being treated by the famous cure of Dr. S. Weir Mitchell. This involved being isolated from everyone she knew and not being allowed to read or write; undergoing total rest except for electrical muscle treatment and massages; and eating huge amounts of food.

Edith Wharton returned over and over in her fiction to variations on the Oedipal and incestuous theme. This journey to the heart of the psyche must have taken great emotional courage. Sometimes her explorations lead (in this writer capable of such seamless, lapidary polish) to clumsiness of tone and prose. But she brought all her gifts for description and pace to bear to a high degree in what she herself marked as an unpublishable fragment from a never-completed story called "Beatrice Palmato." This fragment was discovered about twenty years ago by scholar Cynthia Griffin Wolff, who was looking through the Wharton archive at Yale. Professor Wolff's astonishment can scarcely be imagined. "Beatrice Palmato" is a piece of elegant pornography; a graphic description (in the firm, no-nonsense, rather manly handwriting) of a father having sex with his recently married daughter. "I have been . . . so perfectly patient," Mr. Palmato whispers to his "little girl" in the hushed and magical room with the deep divan and pink-shaded lamps. She's the Ornamental Woman, naked at last; he's the secret, gloating connoisseur. Wharton's prose camera pans at a snail's pace as (to the young woman's deep satisfaction, after years of mutual foreplay) her father makes a meal of her with eyes and mouth and then penetrates her for the first time.

"PLEASE SEIZE the event, however delicate the problem, to dispel the myth of frigidity," W. Morton Fullerton told Elisina Tyler, a friend and would-be biographer of Edith Wharton, after the author's death. For three years, when Edith was in her late forties, he had been her lover. Her forties were the watershed for her: the decade of the opened cage. First, in 1902, she moved into the Mount, her house in Lenox,

Massachusetts. The Mount was definitely *her* house, named for the residence of a great-grandfather she admired as a go-getter; paid for with her money; built from scratch to the standards of taste and comfort set out in *The Decoration of Houses*, a book that had proved a surprising success. There was a nice big corner bedroom for her and her morning writing, well detached from Teddy's suite. It's a grand enough house, there's no denying it. Its design was based on an English country house by Sir Christopher Wren. There was space for twelve indoor servants who smoothed the path for Edith, Teddy, and the courtiers who began to trickle in regularly from this period on. (There were separate quarters for White, the English butler, and Cook, the chauffeur hired for the brand-new Panhard.) But the house, which is being restored and may be visited by the public, is really quite intimate inside, with rooms proportioned for comfortable talk with chosen friends. French doors lead out to a big wide terrace. Here, in a pleasant breeze under a striped awning, Edith and her companions would sit for hours, looking across the lake to the blue-tinged Berkshire hills.

She wrote *The House of Mirth* at the Mount. It is an extraordinary literary work. And by conjuring up and then killing off decorative child-woman Lily Bart, Edith Wharton took a big step toward her own freedom. The book was a giant hit. One hundred and forty thousand copies were in print within a couple of months of publication in 1905. James called it "an altogether superior thing," although perhaps feeling a twinge of envy. Edith spent some of her profits putting in the Italianate gardens at the Mount. If Edith's literary triumphs—which only increased from now on—caused twinges in Henry James, a universally recognized genius, they had a devastating effect on poor Teddy, an ineffectual gentleman of leisure who had always been financially dependent on his wife. He had always got by with his sporting hobbies and drew some self-esteem from puttering with Edith's trust-fund investments. But they were like the man and woman on a cuckoo clock, these two. As the sun came out to shine on her at last, a cloud began to cover him. By 1902, her mysteriously debilitating symptoms had largely lifted. His illnesses, just as mysterious, were beginning. He had his first nervous breakdown that year, with manic-depressive mood swings.

It was in the autumn of 1907 that James sent his friend W. Morton Fullerton to be a houseguest at the Mount. He was forty-two, and Edith, forty-five. He was slight in build, with a luxuriant Victorian mustache and languid, bedroomy eyes. There was something raffish and dandified about his style in dress, with boutonnieres and bowler hats. Like James and Edith, he was a "wretchedly exotic" hybrid. He was the bisexual son of a Congregational clergyman from a small New England town. He had lived for many years as an expatriate, first in London and then in Paris, as the chief correspondent for the London *Times*. He was a gifted man whose friends included George Santayana, Bernard Berenson, and Oscar Wilde. James called him his "dearest boy" and was more than a little in love with Fullerton himself.

Fullerton had a sexual past that could only be called lurid. Among the highlights were affairs with Oscar Wilde's friend Lord Gower and with Lady Brooke, the Ranee of Sarawak, who was fifteen years his senior. There was also a marriage of about ten minutes to a Frenchwoman who had borne his child. And as he was on his way to the Mount, Fullerton had stopped off at Bryn Mawr to visit his cousin Katherine, who was teaching there, and became engaged. Katherine was fourteen years his junior and had been raised in the clergyman's house believing herself to be Fullerton's sister. Fullerton was a selfish and irresponsible man, you could say. He was incapable of fidelity and always ended his affairs after a few years, at most. Henry James' distinguished biographer, Leon Edel, and Edith Wharton's distinguished biographer, R. W. B. Lewis, use descriptions like "seducer" and "lothario" about Fullerton, if not quite "cad." They are like two white-whiskered family lawyers in old New York, trying (misguidedly, as it turned out) to protect the noble, celibate Edith from herself.

Edith knew what she wanted. And what she wanted, with all the energy of a passionate nature that has been starved and stoppered for a lifetime, was W. Morton Fullerton, warts and all. The year she welcomed him to the Mount, the winter was already setting in. She and Fullerton went out driving in the motor and were forced to stop when snow began to fall, so that Cook could put on the chains. The couple walked a little way into the woods, where they talked and smoked cigarettes. They broke off sprigs of witch hazel. In her and him, something stirred. He must have given off—sitting there on a deep bank in a cold New England wood—that faint and indescribable aura, just short of a scent, that even well-bred, well-bathed, and well-dressed men give off when they are in the habit of frequent and eclectic sex.

She'd heard his footsteps outside her holy of holies, and she had no intention of letting them recede. She began to keep a secret journal, addressing him in passionate terms. The following spring, she was in Paris, and Fullerton was courting her with his well-polished line of flirtation that combined the erotic with the idealistic and the religious. Sometime in the spring of 1908, she consented to unite her soul with his by falling into his experienced arms. "I have drunk of the wine of life at last," she told her journal. "I have known the thing best worth knowing. I have been warmed through and through and will never grow cold again." Fullerton would let it be known to Elisina Tyler that Edith had been an adventurous erotic playmate for him; he compared her to the amatory and literary giant George Sand. Edith couldn't quite believe it: she was in love, she knew "what happy women feel" at last.

At the height of it all, she had no illusions about him. She soon learned about the other imbroglios, about the engagement to Katherine, which was eventually broken off. Swiftly and efficiently, like a wealthy man of the world, Edith arranged to pay off a discarded mistress who was black-mailing Fullerton with some of his letters to Gower and the Ranee. Her adored and shopworn boulevardier took her to levels of experience she might have missed. These included a memorable night in a seedy hotel at the Charing Cross railway station in London. Henry James (the only one of all their friends who was in on the affair) was invited to supper that evening, in their rooms. There was champagne and great hilarity and, after James had gone home, some adventures in the bed "rutted and worn as a high-road," with "sooty chintzes" and "grimey brass." In the morning, she sat up in bed and wrote a long love poem called "Terminus" about the night just passed. Fullerton dressed and, looking back from the doorway, saw her still in bed and engrossed in her work as he went off to catch a train.

Inevitably the affair petered out. No one stayed mad at Fullerton, and he and Edith remained friends. But Edith was busy setting herself up in a new home in the Paris Faubourg and working on *The Custom of the Country* and *Ethan Frome* simultaneously. Teddy was going from bad to worse, with no relief of his symptoms in spite of visits to different spas. His erratic behavior now took the form of embezzling $50,000 from Edith's trust fund as well as supporting a mistress and several chorus girls. In spite of her fear of what she still believed was the social stigma of divorce, she made up her mind and let go of him. And she sold the Mount. Closed the door, got into her motor, and journeyed on.

1993

MY SISTER, MYSELF

*M*Y SISTER has been on this earth for two years and eight months longer than I. At my birth, she could already walk, talk, and make up complicated stories about the fairies who (along with her mother) had served as thoroughly satisfactory companions until I came along. She stared down into my cradle with mingled excitement and contempt; as soon as my eyes could focus, I lay there gazing back. I can't imagine what my life would have been if things hadn't been like this: two pairs of eyes, two female beings taking the measure of each other's lives.

"*I am not my sister,*" writes Patricia Foster in her introduction to *Sister to Sister: Women Write about the Unbreakable Bond*, a collection of essays she edited. "*Who am I if not my sister?*" is the question she asked herself, next. One of the contributors told her that what we think about our sisters is the "big secret." Others said that the prospect of their sisters reading what they had written about them was terrifying. Until fairly recently, like many aspects of women's lives that do not directly involve men, sisterhood has been a largely hidden, untold tale in literature and history. (Goneril, Regan, and Cordelia, King Lear's daughters, revolve, for good or ill, around him.) In drawing female relationships to the forefront, feminist thinking tended, like psychoanalysis, to make a start with the parental bond: relationships between women and their mothers. But now there is a growing interest in siblings' place in each other's psyche, too. What part did the people who shared our earliest memories play in making us who we are? The theme of sisters, in particular, has recently emerged in a steady stream of books, movies, and television shows. Biological sisterhood is examined, too, for the useful clues it offers about "sisterhood" in the world at large—about how women connect to other women, how they support each other or compete.

The subject of sisters from the same family is being approached with varying degrees of emotional courage or sentimentality. Foster's book consists largely of the shadow side of the matter. Her essayists use the first-person feminine voice (full of halts and palpable silence, followed by sudden rushes of confession) to speak of rage and rivalry; of losing sisters to cancer, suicide, or mental illness; of looking on with a child's scant understanding as a troubled teenage sibling degrades herself in promiscuity and then runs away from home. *Sisters*, a best-selling book of photographs by Sharon J. Wohlmuth and interviews by Carol Saline, generally takes the opposite approach. It offers us an unchallenging parade of related feminine faces of various ages, with the same sets of delightfully similar noses or grins. On the book jacket, Christy Turlington, the supermodel, and her two sisters—a kittenish trio, very close in age—pose seated on the stoop of a nice-looking house, their hands and feet affectionately entwined. No Cinderella subtext mars the perfect, glossy surface, according to the interview that accompanies the photograph. Christy's sisters say they are thrilled to be invited into her social set from time to time and to wear her glamorous cast-off clothes. For the most part, the message of the book is

no more complicated than that of the sampler Saline's own
sister gave her—"A sister is a forever friend."

PHOTOGRAPHS OF SISTERS are poignant, to be sure.
Mysteriously compelling, like all family photographs—
hurling us deep down into truth; fixing life on the surface and
telling many lies—they carry the extra weight of female
appearance and the profound effect of this on our lives. My
self began, in a way, not simply when I looked at my sister and
she looked at me but when a camera recorded us both side by
side. Some kernel of she-and-me remains in the moment
when we were very young, in our native England, and we sat
in my grandmother's house being photographed by my
father's brother, Jack. The sofa smelled of Spot and Chip, her
dogs; in the fireplace, coals flared up or made soft *pfft* sounds
from time to time. Grandmother's mother, an old Scots-
woman in her nineties, sat in her snug corner reading a magazine called *The People's Friend*. Our bodies were small and
shaped like pears; our faces were small and shaped like hearts,
back then. My sister's braids were longer than mine by
two years and eight months. For one of these photographic
sessions, we showed off our new Shetland-knit hats and
mufflers; for another we wore matching hair bows, as did the
big, pottery-headed dolls who sat on our knees like a pair of
baby sisters, batting their eyelids at Uncle Jack with unpre-
dictable and tinny clicks. Each time we visited, it took a little
longer for him to take these sisterly portraits because he had
Parkinson's disease, which worsened year by year. He had had
it since youth; his limbs, launching him into perpetual trembling motion, had brought to a halt any life in the world outside his mother's house. (He spent his days fussing with his
cameras or in a shed at the bottom of her garden, painstak-
ingly carving ever more heartfelt wooden gnomes.) My sister
and I sat helplessly, for what seemed an eternity, on the sofa—
our smiles repeatedly springing up and fading away—as we
waited for his hand to stop vibrating too wildly on the button

of his shutter cable and for him to capture us on film. In these twin portraits, my body is often leaning into hers, as if I am yearning to be consoled.

There is something so physical about sisterhood; some body-memory, too deep for words. Throughout history, women have always attended to the flesh-and-blood, nursing sisters through sickness and childbirth, or (like the Brontës) attending each other as they died. I have not lived under the same roof as my sister for over thirty years, but the simple sight of her bare feet reminds me so immediately of my childhood that whenever I see them I get a sort of physical jolt; they seem more familiar than my own. I have all kinds of thoughts and feelings about her, but first and last we are two kindred bodies. We grew at what now seems a short interval in the same womb; even when we are separated by continents, we are moving through time in parallel tracks. In the archeology of our existence, a childhood layer remains: the pair of us lying side by side on the grassy earth in a backyard tent and trying to be brave enough to sleep. Or huddled in the back seat of the family car, singing in girlish voices or mute with the misery of the motion-sick. My sister grew plump as a teenager while I stayed very slim. Her softer silhouette seemed very significant, part of some angry anguish she was feeling: it shut me out. As long as I can remember, she has been more modest than I, more inclined to cover up. We have both lived in America for decades, but she retains a very British reserve—accepting a kiss or a hug from me with kindly, courteous resignation, as if we had just met. My mother is not demonstrative with me, either, although all the photographs of her and her three sisters when they were young show them holding hands or with their arms around each other's waists. I have watched with a kind of envy as my mother throws her arm round the neck of her favorite sister. This old aunt of mine has Alzheimer's—another of those thieving diseases with some stranger's name—and has lived for years in a nursing home. As little girls growing up in the country, she and my mother were confidantes; they had stood together in fast-running streams up to their skinny knees and used their bloomers for fishing nets. "Do you remember me, darling?" my mother will plead, of this once-mirroring sister whose mind was long ago lost. "Do you remember me? Oh, do you know who I am?"

"A SISTER'S LIFE interrogates yours, saying, Why do you live this way? Are you doing what's right?" writes one of the essayists in Foster's book. This interrogation is never more urgent than when sex comes in. Youths fell desperately in love with my teenage sister, precisely because of her rounded figure and the intriguingly hidden, female quality she had developed—her air of gliding through her life behind a veil of privacy, like her own harem screen. She never thought, when it came to me, that I was "doing what was right." On my wedding day, she couldn't keep herself from crying, from the moment she woke up. At the church, she wept so much that my Auntie Margaret had to take her round the back of it and tell her to compose herself. My aunt was formidable, and a farmer; she carried a large, old-fashioned handbag that might serve to stun a bull. My sister's tears obediently dried, but she knew in her bones that my husband would make me unhappy; she was absolutely right.

Another recent addition to the literature of sisterhood—*Sister Stories: Taking the Journey Together*, written by Brenda Peterson—expands the theme beyond the blood relation. Peterson, one of three sisters, discusses her relations with women friends—the consciously chosen female allies, seeking autonomy through work; living in late-twentieth-century ways; occasionally wounding each other, so great is their hunger to be fully seen and heard. In addition, the author paints affectionate pictures of female relations in species other than our own: pointing to sisters, mothers, aunts, and grandmothers among the elephants and dolphins who contribute collectively to rearing the young. Female elephants are so bonded, she says, that after the briefest of separations they will greet each other with ecstatic trumpeting sounds and wildly flapping ears. And it is the ancient, long-barren females who hold in memory the migration routes and watering holes; whose heads are full of the lore the extended family needs in order to survive. Peterson, who has no children of her own, swims with some dolphins, one of her sisters, and her sister's little girls. She honors the way the members of the dolphin "pod" breathe in unison; communicate in their mysterious underwater language of sighs and whistles; and circle each other protectively throughout their lives.

My sister is a mother, and I am not. Three times her body changed and gave birth; each child carried her farther away from me to a place I could never fully comprehend. I have done different things with my life. For one, while she has been busy with the young in our family, I have borne witness to the fading away of the old. Perhaps we made the classic pact between two sisters: out of fear of the horror of competition, we neatly divided up our experience of the world. When my nephews and my sisterless niece were tiny, we would sit around my sister's table after supper sometimes. I would sit there in the candlelight with one of her babies on my knee, and when she looked across at us her eyes would well with tears. "What is it? Oh, tell me what you are feeling, when you see me with your baby on my knee?" I longed to ask. But I never dared. I was reminded of her when I read about the dolphins, warily swimming in circles until they get their heads sideways and fix a sisterly creature with a wise yet inscrutable stare.

1995

A NORMAL MAN

ONSIDERING how obsessively Henri Matisse
depicted both his domestic life and the legions of
female models who streamed through his studio for
half a century, remarkably little is on the public record about
his relations with women. He was rather a private man who
demanded an orderly life. In everything, but especially in the
matter of the opposite sex, we are politely but firmly told to
think of Matisse primarily as an artist and only peripherally
as a man. "I do not create a woman, I make a picture," he
often said. The biography, unlike Picasso's, feels smooth as
silk. Because of his importance, most of the scholars and
experts on Matisse have been men. And there are virtually no
accounts of women stepping out of the pictures Matisse made
of them to get jealous of each other or mad at the Great Man.
In the world of *Luxe, calme, et volupté* he set out to create—
actually using this Baudelairean title for an early work of
nudes like rainbow dinosaurs grazing by the shore—no
women make trouble for Matisse. Apparently, no creature is

tempted to hurl a Matissean flower vase or stamp off to the kitchen and bang pots about. Born into the conservative and puritanical milieu of a small town in northern France, he remained a nineteenth-century bourgeois at heart. The appearance of propriety was vital to him.

His long life spanned two centuries, moved with them from lamplit parochialism to international media blaze. A host of reporters and photographers, making pilgrimage to his final home in Vence on the Côte d'Azur, added to the legend of the serene old magician, sitting up in bed with giant scissors making cut-paper shapes. Formal religion was declining in Western Europe; with his heroic creative struggles and epiphanies, Matisse was perfectly positioned for the new role of secular saint. In his lifetime, he did not entirely discourage the idea of sainthood, which seems to have been nurtured by his family after his death. Women were his main subject, to be sure; but (we may believe) he transcended the flesh through his work. He never abandoned the old practice of working from the live female model, with her clothes or without. He liked to sit extremely close to the women while he worked. One photographer shows him sketching a nude with one hand while resting the other hand on her knee, apparently quite detached. Perhaps he sat so close because, behind his professional wire rims, his eyes were weak; perhaps it was a kind of spiritual celibacy test, along Gandhian lines; or a summoning up of intimacy and sexual energy, which he would use to fuel his work and then leap from at the climactic moment, as from a runaway bus. "Matisse has affirmed that before the most voluptuous models his attitude is no different from what it is before a plant, a vase, or some other object," wrote the poet Louis Aragon, in some awe. He also wondered, bemusedly, whether there wasn't more variety in the armchairs Matisse painted than in the women. But he was thinking of the elderly Matisse, and not the ambitious, fiercely innovative artist of the earlier years ("the madly anxious Matisse," one contemporary called him), when his wife, Amélie, had been his unique and unequalled model.

SOMETIME AROUND 1911, when Matisse was just over forty and he and Amélie had been married for twelve years, he finished the painting called *The Conversation*. In it a standing man and a seated woman—a pair of two-dimensional figures who look vaguely Byzantine or ancient Egyptian, perhaps—face each other unbendingly across a sea of blue. There's no attempt to give the space perspective or to make the figures look round and "real" by the academic standards Matisse had been exposed to at the Ecole des Beaux Arts. "Copy nature stupidly," his teachers used to say. The blue doesn't even seem like an attempt to capture light in the manner of the Impressionists. It feels like emotion, mostly: a membrane stretched between the man and the woman and humming with rage and love. And the figures are on opposite sides of a window that opens in the blueness and frames a vivid, childlike, otherworldly garden view.

It is generally assumed that this encounter is taking place in the bedroom of the comfortable, highly respectable villa Matisse acquired in the Parisian suburb of Issy-les-Moulineaux in 1909. There's a crisis in Matisse's marriage, it seems. One factor may have been an affair he was having around this time with one of his painting students, a young Russian blonde named Olga. More broadly, the standoff may revolve around the world beyond the window: the arena of his art. He asserted the right to reside at will in the sunny, luxuriant pocket jungle—the earthly paradise—while his wife cheered his forays and welcomed his return. The austere, seated figure in the black-and-green dressing gown is Amélie, and she looks fit to be tied. And the monolithic standing figure in the blue-and-white pajamas—frozen, mute, looking and looking at this woman as if looking's the only thing he knows how to do—is Henri. It was a moment, this. The blue place with his Amélie challenging and confining him was too intimate, too real. From now on, he would arrange to live more and more in the contemplative place where he was untroubled by the demands of others: "the private garden where I am alone."

Given his expressed interest in the figure above all other themes, his prodigious production, and his self-centeredness, there are surprisingly few self-portraits by Matisse. And he would never again permit us to see him quite as exposed as he seemed that day in his pajamas. When his image appears in his paintings, later, he'll have a self-protective mask in place; he'll appear as the Artist, sometimes with his back to us, and with a palette in his hand. He'll be seen to be in charge. Madame Matisse was the last of Matisse's models who had the resonance of being the painter's equal, and she ceased to appear in his work around the time of the First World War. Her place was filled for a time by an Italian model we know simply as Laurette, the first of a series of young women of whom he made intense, extended studies. There would be some fifty portraits of her over the course of two years. Matisse had volunteered for service but was turned down as too old: he was forty-four when war began. Many of his friends were killed, gassed, or wounded. His sons, Jean and Pierre, would be drafted before the war was over; his younger brother was sent to prison camp, and his widowed mother was trapped behind enemy lines in the painter's hometown of Bohain-en-Vermandois, in Picardy. Bohain was captured by the Germans three times in the lifetime of its native son: in 1870, 1914, and 1940. Like him, it developed a shuttered obduracy to hide perennial vulnerability. War, like age and pain, was not to be seen in Matisse's work. He said he wanted to convey "the lightness and joyousness of a springtime" and conceal from the spectator all the effort it cost. "You and I were in the trenches, too, in those days," he said to Picasso, a bit pompously, speaking of the war years, when the one was on the ramparts of Cubism and the other was beavering away at his multiple Laurettes.

MATISSE'S REPRESENTATIONS of women and their world are not as cozy as they seem at first glance, but they are fundamentally benevolent. We may thank his mother for this. "My mother loved everything I did," he once said. She gave him confidence and (while he was convalescing from a serious illness at the age of twenty) his first box of paints. She had artistic aspirations, had worked as a milliner, and painted china as a hobby. The father, a grain merchant, seems to have properly played the role of nasty ogre in the fairy-tale journey of the artist-hero, which Matisse so neatly lived out. Matisse *père* insisted Henri become a lawyer and never came round to his art. In a photograph of the youth with his mother, their black clothing—his frock coat, her corseted bombazine—looks sepia brown. They seem like a team—a pair of sturdy little ponies with barrel chests and short legs, made for the fields round Bohain, where Father's seeds grow slowly and surely in cool, gray northern light. Henri sketched his mother on the back of a telegram form, once: freely, from memory, and from the heart. "Exactitude is not Truth," was what he learned; the sketch is lost, but the insight remains in Matissean myth as "the revelation at the post office."

He was a late bloomer. In his life as a family man, as in his career, he made a false start. As an art student—still penniless in his twenties and dependent on a pittance from his father—he lived with a young woman called Caroline Joblaud, who is presumed to be the subject of his painting of 1896 *The Breton Serving Girl*, and who, in 1894, had given birth to his daughter, Marguerite. Only Jack Flam, Matisse's most recent biographer, is straightforward about all this. Nothing is disclosed of what happened to Caroline; she was expunged, in the Victorian way, from the record of his magisterial life, to become one of that generation's many lost women. She gave up her child—that much we know—to Henri.

After Henri and Amélie were married in 1898, they adopted Marguerite. Amélie took on the man and the little girl wholeheartedly. She was the wife of the Great Artist par excellence in the days of early struggle. She had vivacity, stamina, and courage. She gave her all to him while he gave his all to his art. They honeymooned in London so he could look at paintings by Turner. She would pose and pose for him over thousands of hours. In the Spanish shawl; in the Japanese kimono; in the buff in the bedroom, putting up her hair—her figure was central to his tireless, anxious experiments in form and style. She soon produced two sons; he soon produced a slew of representations of his wife. He'd turned his back on conventional painting (with her support) as soon as they married, and housekeeping funds became very short. Marguerite would always stay by her father's side, but Amélie sent her two little boys away—one to each grandmother—to save on food bills and leave her more time to pose. She consoled and encouraged her husband, took him for a walk when the sculpture he was making smashed on the floor, read to him for hours when he couldn't sleep. (He was a lifelong insomniac.) Her mother had been a dressmaker; she set herself up as a milliner to try to bring in extra funds.

It is Amélie, of course, who is the subject of *The Woman with the Hat*. This famous painting, shown in the Salon d'Automne of 1905, established Matisse as a leader of the avant-garde and the so-called Fauves, or "wild beasts." (A wag remarked at the time of the Fauve artists that they all dressed less like wild beasts than like floorwalkers in a department store.) The painting brought notoriety and the beginning of financial success. Amélie's heart-shaped face with its rounded black eyebrows became, in the portrait, green, white, and yellow, and was surrounded by carmine hair. Her head is almost crushed beneath a hat like a galleon, loaded with wildly colored fruits. Color liberated from "stupid copying" and expressive of emotion was the next great revelation for Matisse. In reality, the hat had all been black. Perhaps it was Amélie Matisse who created it.

Matisse's daughter, Marguerite, was also a favorite subject of his. She was painted out of *The Breton Serving Girl*, and exists there as a toddler only in pentimento. But from the time her status was settled, she appeared again and grew from a child to a woman in his work. Like Amélie, whom she increasingly replaced as the years drew on, she was an industrious and intelligent model. "We were a family of artists," she wrote later. "The whole family revolved around the labors of the father." Aragon thought that Marguerite, more than anyone, had been the real love of her father's life. When he was an old man and she a middle-aged woman, he still spoke with an unmatched frisson of tenderness of "his little girl." She is the girlish figure in red on the balcony in a painting made in the first of the emancipatory sojourns Matisse would make in the Mediterranean sunshine in 1905. (A second female form reclines indolently within the painting's room—presumably Amélie. Perhaps she was resting after one of her predawn treks up the hillside to pose for Matisse's painting *Nude in a Wood*.) Marguerite posed nude for a sculpture of a girl when she was twelve; then, in a pinafore dress, as a teenager, with a black cat on her lap; and, in the twenties, she was one of the fashionably dressed young women floating through her father's house in Nice. He also painted her portrait in a variety of hats.

"Matisse cannot get over the fact that he is Matisse," said a friend who had known him since they were students, and watched him become immensely famous and immensely rich. "He can hardly believe his luck." If Matisse had had the misfortune to be born a woman, in his time and place, he is unlikely to have left the world (his "spiritual family," as he called it) his paintings. He might have expressed his creativity only by painting on china, or by making frocks or hats. Indeed one hostile critic sneered that he had "the taste of a milliner." He became fascinated by Islamic art at least partly because, unlike the European tradition, it did not value painting at the expense of the decorative or applied arts. He took a great interest in fashion, fabrics, and textiles all his life, and they were of great importance in his painting. Even when poor, he was elegantly dressed; as his work began to sell and he began to prosper, he encouraged his wife and daughter to wear couture. He would attend fittings with them at the salon of Germaine Bongard, one of Paul Poiret's sisters and a remarkable person in her own right.

WHAT INTERESTED HIM most in painting, he said, was the expression of emotion. A suburban house containing a genius, his wife, his two growing sons, and a daughter by another woman was probably full of emotion. (He was capable of being as hard on his sons as his father had been on him, demanding for some reason that they train for careers in music. Jean became a sculptor and Pierre a dealer in art.) He painted the life of his household at Issy intensely for a while, moving back and forth between the rooms and the prefabricated studio he had built in the garden. Art and life went on in layered combinations like Islamic patterns. A growing collection of objects—fruit stands, china dishes, vases, African figurines, Moroccan pots—filled the house and started to move through the work, to swirl and reproduce with vegetable energy like the Art Nouveau patterns papering the walls. Real female presences were jostled by representations of females, in his sculptures on tables and his canvases all over the room. Objects look strangely human, while humans get blurs instead of faces and are arranged like still lifes. His art was a vortex sucking everything in. "He could think of nothing else," said Marguerite.

"Oh, do tell the American people that I am a normal man," Matisse told Clara MacChesney, who'd been sent to interview him for *The New York Times*. The American critics had called his drawings of women "loathsome and abnormal," so Miss MacChesney was puzzled by this "fresh, healthy, robust, blond gentleman" in his pleasant home. He was, he assured her, piling it on, "a devoted husband and father. I go to the theater, ride horseback . . . have a fine garden, flowers, et cetera, just like any man." Even as he was putting the brush-

strokes to his idyllic picture, he was, in point of fact, already
beginning the process of moving on. He was painting his last
major portrait of Amélie, the *Portrait of Madame Matisse* of
1913. His paintings often revisited earlier paintings of his;
this one shows how far he's come as husband and painter
since *The Woman with the Hat.* (Sometimes, like a man taking
a second wife to a resort or a restaurant where he has been
happy with the first, Matisse would re-create a scene or theme
with a new female model.) Amélie's hat is now a chic,
noseward-tilted black pillbox whose potentially optimistic-
looking feather is abruptly snipped off by the edge of the
canvas at the top. It's a wonderful painting: rich, strange, and
sad. She sat for it for one hundred hours. It became more and
more abstract as he worked at it, and ended with an African
mask of a face, with almond-shaped black holes under the
round black brows. She cried when she saw it. He was saying
goodbye in some way, and she knew it. But in spite of the
abstraction, the portrait as a whole has a quality not often
found in Matisse's images of women: compassion. He releases
her to be a woman, and not a picture, now. Shortly after this
portrait, Amélie sank into depression and a mysterious invalidism that would grip her completely for the next twenty
years.

F O R   M O S T of Matisse's lengthy stay in Morocco in 1912–13,
Amélie had been left behind at Issy. In the venerable tradition
of the nineteenth-century Frenchman, he and his painter
friend Charles Camoin explored their colonial possession and
allowed their imaginations to be stirred by the light, by
authentic life among "primitive" people of a different race.
That life particularly meant the real or imaginary delights of
exotic sex. Henri and Charles set out to tour the brothels of
Tangier. But only, the decorous Henri told his friend, in the
interests of art and in search of women who would model for
them without the veil. "Be careful. We have to go there like

doctors making a house call," Matisse said. On his return to Paris, he would ask Laurette to pose in turban and caftan like Zorah, the prostitute who had modelled for him in Tangier. And in 1917, the normal man, by now approaching fifty, moved without his wife into a hotel room in Nice.

He set up his easel and played his violin a lot (in the bathroom, so as not to disturb the neighboring guests). In time, he would take up rowing and join the Club Nautique. He set himself up for a whole new life. He responded, he said later, as if ecstatically to the climate and the light. "I needed to have a respite, to let myself go," he said, remembering. Still, he felt he had to defend the pictures he would paint in his first Nice period (from 1917 through the first part of the twenties) from charges of hedonism. The hotel room began to fill with female models, inevitably, and it was as if, by denying his paintings' "hedonism" and pointing out their "pictorial tension," Matisse could discourage the spectator from thinking that any hanky-panky was going on. He took a larger room than the first, in the five-star Hôtel de la Méditerranée. There, in the high-ceilinged, rococo room with its shuttered, balconied window overlooking the Promenade des Anglais and the sea, he began to produce paintings of young women at top speed. The curving shapes of their dresses or, if they were nude, the arabesques of hips and arms, worked well with the straight line of the shutter slats, the stripes of the tablecloth, the pattern of red-tile floor. There was an oval mirror, too, that sometimes reflected the young women, or himself watching them. Sometimes it was quite blank and black, reflecting nothing at all.

In 1919, he made another famous series of studies— drawing and painting a model called Antoinette, in a plumed, Cavalier-brimmed hat. He made the hat himself; he was delighted with it. In fact, even when he depicts the lovely woman wearing nothing *but* his hat, you'd swear it was the hat that turns him on. He took Antoinette north when he returned to Issy one summer and painted her lying down in the garden while his wife and daughter took tea some way behind. Marguerite (although not Amélie) came south and posed with Henriette Darricarrère, a young woman who worked closely with him for seven years. Once, he painted Henriette painting at an easel; another time, he had her play the piano while her young brothers played checkers. This was a pictorial revisit of a painting made at Issy when the models had been his children. Most memorably, though, Henriette posed nude for him, as one of the famous odalisques.

After four years in the hotel room—which more and more seemed like an indoor garden where young women with heavy lids and limbs would germinate like flowers— Matisse took an apartment of his own. Here, decoratively speaking, he went to town—with great-looking armchairs and Turkish divans, and screens and patterned textiles he could shift like kaleidoscope chips. He had a whole assortment of props—gauzy wisps of skirt, "slave-girl" belts and bangles, baggy pantaloons—in which he would dress his models, as he or they felt inspired. Henriette would enter into the harem fantasies of the painterly pasha (or doctor, perhaps) with particular zest. In the 1920s, Matisse also began to have girls supplied from a nearby movie-extra agency, the Studios de la Victorine. (This agency kept them coming for thirty years. By 1940, he had the system down pat. "The ones I don't use, I pay off with ten francs. I have them pose in shifts, three hours in the morning, three hours in the afternoon.")

Conservative collectors, seeing these "Oriental" nudes of Matisse at this time, flocked in droves to buy. The French gave him official recognition for the first time by buying the *Odalisque in Red Pantaloons*. (His important early patrons were the Russians Shchukin and Morosov, and the American family of Gertrude, Leo, Michael, and Sarah Stein.) The avant-garde, seeing what Matisse was doing, threw up its hands. But later critics have come to understand that he was really not regressing or standing still. In a way, the odalisques are as mysterious and even subversive as any of his earlier, more radical work. It's probably true (as Matisse's protectors always claim) that they are far more about painting than they are about sex. His combination of a three-dimensional and sculptured nude with a flat, decorative, two-dimensional background leaves the spectator baffled and vaguely anxious about where that spectator stands. These sirens *seem* to be enticing you—you seem to smell their perfume or feel their breath—but then you find you're already sated by something, or you are strangely repelled. It is, as the writer Janet Hobhouse once observed, as though Matisse were playing the roles of procurer and bouncer simultaneously. Matisse himself felt that some kind of sublimation was going on. His, and his model's, sexuality was in there somewhere, but spread all over the painting, he said. It would burn off and into what he called the "decorative synthesis" of the whole effect; or, instead of emanating from the nude woman, eroticism would start spurting from a flower vase or murmuring from the depths of his tobacco jar. "I marry objects," he once said. Aragon observed him later on as he was falling in love with a Venetian armchair. "It's splendid. I'm obsessed with it," the painter wrote in a letter to the poet. "I am going to bounce on it gently when I come back."

BE THIS as it may, there's no getting round the fact that when Amélie Matisse finally moved in with her husband in Nice, his odalisques stopped. Just like that. There's a photograph, taken in 1929, of a sad-looking Amélie—still with the curved black eyebrows but with hair that's now quite white—sitting at the dining table in the Nice apartment. Paintings of naked young women cover most of the wall above her head. She rarely went outside. Her symptoms had become something like spinal paralysis, and she spent most of her time lying down—sometimes, no doubt, on the Turkish divans. In the early thirties, Matisse (who had been working on sculpture and etching, and painting nothing at all for several years) accepted a commission for a giant mural of dancing figures for the Barnes Foundation near Philadelphia. He hired a young Russian blonde called Lydia Delectorskaya to help him with the work and with his sick wife. Lydia moved into the apartment, made herself indispensable to him. In the mid-thirties, he painted and drew her over and over again; she was very lovely, and his obsession was as great as any he had known. In 1934, she posed at length for the painting that became a famous *Pink Nude*, against a blue-and-white grid. As always, he worked and worked at the canvas until it felt right. Her lithe young body became more and more a plastic abstraction, closer and closer to the cut-paper forms that would come to him in his final years. At the end of each working day, Lydia would make a photograph of her image on the canvas and then expunge the parts Matisse didn't want with a turpentined rag.

At last, after all this time, Amélie got mad. Jane Bussy, daughter of Simon Bussy, a friend of Henri's from art-school days, happened to be around at the time and wrote a memoir. "You may be a great artist, but you're a filthy bastard!" Amélie reportedly shouted at him. "She said that to *me!*" said Henri, looking shocked, as if it were a kind of sacrilege. He wanted his wife, he wanted Lydia, he wanted Marguerite. Amélie rose from her bed and rushed about, shrieking and insisting that he choose. There were scenes, there were dramas, there was even (Bussy says) a pistol that was fired. Lydia won out, in the end, and got to look after Matisse until the end of his life. In very great bitterness, Amélie secured a formal separation in 1939 and retired once more to Paris, apparently restored to perfect health. During the war, Matisse suffered a nearly fatal illness, but the girls still kept on coming from the Studios de la Victorine, with Lydia to let them in. Pierre Matisse was in America, but Jean, Amélie, and Marguerite became active in the Resistance during the German occupation. The old prefabricated studio (now used by Jean) filled up with explosives. Amélie was arrested by the Gestapo for typing incriminating documents and sentenced to a six-month prison term. Marguerite was a true heroine:

she was arrested, tortured, and sent off to Ravensbrück but was able to escape. When the war was over, she travelled to Vence, where the old man lived surrounded by flowers and tropical birds. Listening to "his little girl" tell her terrible story was almost too much for his heart to bear. He drew her portrait in charcoal while she talked.

1992

LOVE, LONGING, AND LETTERS

O NE JULY DAY in 1846, an obscure twenty-four-year-old country gentleman named Gustave Flaubert met a famous thirty-five-year-old Parisian woman of letters named Louise Colet. There followed an eccentric and turbulent liaison that would last for eight years on and off. Because she lived in the capital and he lived in his family home at Croisset, a hamlet on the Seine near Rouen, they exchanged many letters. Some two hundred of his and almost none of hers have survived. He used her as a sounding board for many thoughts on art, life, and (in later years) the day-to-day writing of *Madame Bovary*, and their affair proved to be one of the most important in literary history.

Many fellow-writers, including Proust, James, and Gide, have been spellbound by Gustave Flaubert down through the years. His biographers have been legion, often of the very best. Enid Starkie, in England, and the elegant and indefatigable Francis Steegmuller, in America, have brought his personality to life. But up to now we have had to draw on the avowedly misogynist, never-married Flaubert and his coterie of champions for the story of Louise Colet, the woman who came closest to getting past his guard. "She is the only woman who has ever loved me," Flaubert was to say as the relationship with Louise Colet wore on. "Is that a curse sent from heaven?" Francine du Plessix Gray, in her biography, *Rage and Fire: A Life of Louise Colet*, attempts to take the spotlight off Flaubert long enough to put Colet back in the center of her own life.

Louise was a great beauty who knew she was attractive to men. She had blond hair, which she wore in a carefully chosen style of ringlets on either side of her face. She had blue eyes whose color she brought out by wearing sky-blue gowns. She was wearing one to pose for the famous sculptor James Pradier, on the day when she met Flaubert, in 1846. She was also a bluestocking whose energy, ambition, and talent had resulted in the publication of several books of poetry. She had been awarded two important prizes from the French Academy—more than any woman before her. She ran a salon where powerful men gathered, including her official lover, the philosopher and government minister Victor Cousin. She had a weedy musician husband named Hippolyte, who was living apart from her, and a six-year-old daughter, Henriette, whom Cousin believed to be his. She had a talent for self-promotion: her name was constantly in the papers, and she knew "everyone." The sky-blue gowns were famous, part of her look.

Flaubert had come up to town on the newly opened Paris-Rouen railroad with the death mask of his sister Caroline under his arm. He was to commission a memorial bust from Pradier, who was an acquaintance of his parents' and who had been urging him to take a mistress for some time. Flaubert had been fond of his sister, who had died after giving birth to a baby girl. As children, they used to spy on their father, a prosperous surgeon in Rouen, while he worked on dissecting corpses. The tender and the grotesque would always mingle for Gustave. On the night of Caroline's death, he sat up with her body and took the opportunity to reread his love letters from Eulalie Foucault, a hotelkeeper from Marseilles who had introduced him to fellatio.

Nothing in his experience to date had prepared the young man for intimacy with an emancipated woman artist who was his intellectual equal. In Paris, as a student, he'd become an enthusiastic patron of the bordellos (like armies of Frenchmen of his class) and had prided himself on his hard-boiled behavior in them. He often visited brothels with his group of devoted men friends and shared girls. The young men also liked to write letters full of graphically sexual descriptions and cheerful, vaguely homoerotic discussions of each other's private parts. But Flaubert had been celibate for two years prior to meeting Louise, since a shattering attack of what is believed to have been epilepsy. After this, to his great relief, he had abandoned his studies in the law and settled "like a bear in his lair" at Croisset to his vocation of writing novels. He already had a domestic routine that served his fledgling art, and was fiercely protective of it. The idea of a real relationship seems to have frightened him half to death. "A normal . . . regular copulation would take me too much out of myself," he said, just the year before.

At the time of meeting Louise, he was healthy, broad-shouldered, and so handsome that friends from Rouen had compared him to a Viking god. Her friends called her the Muse. "Here is a young man who is going to make a name for himself in literature," Pradier said to the living, breathing beauty in the blue dress. She was a daughter of Romanticism; it was practically a religion with her to be swept away by love. "Perhaps you can be of use to him," Pradier said. He was on target; Gustave was receptive this time. Hadn't his father died that same year, only five weeks before Caroline? He found himself the head of a small, gloomy household where his widowed mother wailed as she cradled her lost daughter's child. Almost worse than these losses was that of his soul mate and brothel-companion, Alfred de Maupassant, who had taken it into his head to get *married*.

Louise would indeed prove useful to the strange bird that was Flaubert. She listened to him and she trusted in his literary genius. But she couldn't persuade him to publish any of his early efforts—*Madame Bovary*, his first published novel, would appear only in 1856, after the couple was estranged—or to curry favor with the literati in Paris. "Laurels gathered there are apt to be spattered with dung," he would say. He was a large-hearted fellow in many ways, but he had a great line in sneering.

LOUISE COLET WAS a professional woman writer, self-supporting apart from a tiny allowance Cousin gave her for the child. She had a knack for entertaining and decorating on a shoestring. At home, an alabaster lamp cast a soft glow on walls that were draped with the same sky blue as her dresses. Flaubert found her there alone on the evening after Pradier's introduction. She'd been working on a poem all day and was tired from the exertion. The gossip columns often noted the breakneck pace at which she worked, and reported the chaotic domesticity of her writing conditions: her boudoir table spread with perfume bottles, manuscripts written in her bold hand, and overdue bills from tradesmen. She was not too tired, that night, to receive her visitor, read out loud from her poems, or talk animatedly about her favorite subjects of literature, progressive politics, feminism, and love. The following evening, he called again and took her and little Henriette for dinner and a moonlit carriage ride in the Bois de Boulogne. The rocking motion of the horse-drawn cab lulled the child to sleep on the cushions and put amorous ideas in the heads of the mother and the man. The next day, he was supposed to meet her at Pradier's but got cold feet. Then he called at her home again and took her on a second cab ride, this time without Henriette. They were driven about in a city lit up by the flashes from a municipal fireworks display. Then Louise went back to his hotel for a wild night of passion. There followed a second night, at her house. He crept away in the dawn with some souvenirs: her bedroom slippers, a handkerchief stained with her blood, and several volumes of her work, including one entitled *Female Saints and Madwomen*. Then, after one more night with her in the hotel, he packed his bag and got back on the train for Croisset.

His mother was waiting for him at the Rouen station—in tears, as Louise had been when he tore himself out of her arms in Paris. Quite correctly, he interpreted these bookends of weepers as a bad omen for the new romance. Madame Flaubert seems to have been a depressed and anxious woman long before her most recent bereavements. Now she clasped the baby and her son with hoops of steel. "I am now the only thing that binds my mother to life," he wrote to his new mistress. He baffled Louise by his submission to his mother's emotional blackmail, but in truth it worked in favor of his vocation. In 1846, Gustave and his mother were already a team. Until her death in 1872, she ran the household and its full staff of servants as a smooth machine to serve his writing. The surgeon's prudent investments had left his survivors comfortably off. Gustave never had to write for money and would infuriate Louise and others of his friends who did by expressing his contempt for writers who "sold copy the way a linen merchant sells handkerchiefs." The house was gracious, with French windows opening onto a terrace and lawns that ran down to the river. He had taken the best room for his study, furnishing it with his huge and scholarly book collection; a nice big round writing table; a bearskin-covered divan; and a favorite armchair of which Louise became positively jealous.

"Be regular and ordinary in your life, like a bourgeois, so that you can be violent and original in your works," his famous maxim for writers, was wasted on Louise, whose life was as histrionic as her love poetry was clichéd. She was hopeless with money. She was too poor to keep anything but a maidservant and too hot-tempered to keep a maidservant for long. The Muse and the Viking were the oddest couple. All they had in common, really, was a love of literature; it was a lot, though. There was sex, of course. "At this very moment yesterday I was holding you in my arms. . . . A kiss quickly—you know the kind. And another . . . and another," he wrote on the night of his return to Croisset, the first of the two hundred letters. He observed dazedly that the grass was still green, the books he had been studying still lay as he'd left them before he'd met her. She knew that he was in love with her, that she'd shaken him to the marrow. He told her that she had stirred the stagnant waters of his solitary pond and— a typical touch—she must expect foul smells to erupt. She discovered that her idea of sex was more straightforward than his, and certainly more exalted. *Grande amoureuse* that she was, she was mystified as to why he wouldn't stay in her bed and why, having left, he pretended that his mother's needs prevented him from returning. She sent him a love poem comparing his sexual prowess to that of an American buffalo, but instead of being flattered, he found her literary style to be a turnoff. Writing came before life, with him. Even his mother, years later, would complain that "the mania for sentences had dried up his heart."

As the days passed, it became clear to an increasingly angry Louise (who knew most of the famous literary men of her era and was well acquainted with their behavior when in love) that she had snared some unclassifiable literary animal who kept wriggling away. He was less interested in hands-on sex than in sitting in his study late at night, contemplating her handkerchief and her slippers, and then pouring out his thoughts to her on the page. Erotic, mystical, philosophical, literary, lyrical, misanthropic, tender, cruel, grotesque; the words streamed out as the famous shifting, fluid Flaubertian prose. With all this in his head, what was the point of "normal . . . regular copulation"? He often referred to his writing as if it were sex. When he came out on top in his lonely struggle for the perfect sentence, he said that something "ultra-voluptuous gushed out of [him]." It was, he said, an "ejaculation of the soul." When Louise begged him to come to her, he fobbed her off saying that people in love can go for ten years without seeing each other and recommended frequent soothing baths. He had no intention of permitting her to visit him, either. The idea of introducing her to his mother—an idea Louise was obsessed with for years—filled him with horror. In the first eighteen months of their relationship, Gustave wrote her at least a hundred letters but saw her only six times. Sometimes he agreed to meet her at Mantes, a picturesque little town on the railroad halfway between Rouen and Paris. Her ravenous sexuality during afternoons there, in the Hôtel du Grand Cerf, found its way into the doomed life story of Emma Bovary, later. And Emma's cab ride with her lover Léon was a famous literary set piece in a book considered so shocking that its author would face prosecution; the scene was a cynical version of Louise's blissful, promising drives with young Gustave through the Bois.

IN HIS LETTERS to his safely distant mistress, Flaubert conjured himself up—the "monk of Croisset," sitting pen in hand in his dressing gown with moths around his late-night lamp. Even at her death in 1876, Louise hadn't completely got over Flaubert. As she had sensed when they met, he was a great artist. He had a personality she once described as both "monstrous" and "magnetic." His enduring power, along with the one-sidedness of the surviving correspondence, must pose a challenge to Louise Colet's biographer. For posterity, he is firmly planted at center stage in his famous study. But the place where she should be is blank, her voice at best a querulous and irritating echo. It is ironic that she should have ensured the survival of her name chiefly by keeping safe the letters her lover addressed to it. She hung on to them even when she was elderly and poor and had chronic lung disease. Apart from sentiment, she may have been guided by literary professionalism; she well knew the value of the archives of great literary figures. Her friend Madame Récamier, a legendary beauty whose admirers included Napoleon and Chateaubriand, entrusted Louise with love letters written by Benjamin Constant, with the understanding that she would oversee their publication after Récamier's death. On Louise's own death, it was her daughter, Henriette—herself now middle-aged and in need of cash—who sold the letters from Flaubert. They were published after his death, in the 1880s.

Many biographers of female subjects have learned that the letters and papers of women are far less likely to survive than those of men. Flaubert was no friend to most women's writing. "Our literature is drowning in tears, breast milk, and menses," he grumbled to one of his men friends. Gray believes it was Gustave himself who destroyed Louise's half of her correspondence with him. One night in October 1879, he hauled out a suitcase full of papers and burned many of them. He lingered over some letters, along with a woman's slipper and a faded rose tied together with ribbon, and then tossed them all into the study fire. The witness, from the armchair opposite, was the writer Guy de Maupassant, nephew to the long-lost Alfred, who had somewhat redeemed himself, not long after his marriage, by dying in Flaubert's arms. (Guy, who was like a son to the novelist, would also die young—of syphilis, and after losing his mind.) Both de Maupassants, like their friend, were known to make virulently woman-hating remarks. Gray, who is very helpful in sketching the social history and ideas that were the background of her subject's life, points out that misogyny was common to many nineteenth-century Frenchmen, partly because they had a collective memory of the uncontrollable and bloodthirsty women of the Revolution. History apart, the thought of Guy and Gustave's bonfire raises Gray's hackles. The aim of her book, she writes with an indignant flourish worthy of Louise herself, is to "resurrect yet another woman whose memory has been erased by the caprices of men."

BY ANY STANDARDS other than artistic merit, Louise Colet had a much bigger life than Gustave Flaubert: nervier,

more packed with people, bolder in the distances she travelled. She grew up on an olive estate near Aix-en-Provence,
where—against all odds for girls of her time—she acquired
some real erudition. She became versed in Latin, Greek,
Italian, and English classics. In addition, like Emma Bovary,
she steeped herself in Romantic novels and poems that gave
her a lifelong addiction to love. Her siblings seem to have
resented her brains, her liberal ideas, her larger-than-life personality. After some years of being treated like Cinderella,
after her mother's death, she was happy to use marriage to
Hippolyte as a way of getting away and to Paris. Gray com-
pares her to a hero out of Balzac, arriving determined to wrest
fame and fortune out of the capital. When she arrived in the
1830s, the new steam presses and the expansion of the middle
class and its consumer culture were causing a proliferation of
magazines and reviews where serious new literature was supported by gossip and squibs about fashion.

In the 1830s, she jumped feetfirst into the city's seething
literary scene. She was a lovely woman who wanted to be
valued as a first-rate poet. She chased after publishers, critics,
and any great men who could help her get prizes, subsidies,
or a blurb. One by one, she collected many of the legendary
names of nineteenth-century French literature as allies,
friends, lovers, or enemies. She was a genius at keeping herself in the public eye. She always appeared in the most flattering and fashionable outfits, even when she couldn't really
afford them. In her first dynamic decade in Paris, fashion was
also on the move, and skirts were evolving from the stat-
uesque, straight-from-the-bosom line of the Directoire (the
sort of thing Madame Récamier wore on her famous chaise)
to the enormous bell-shaped crinolines so often painted by
Winterhalter. The vogue for *orientalisme* translated itself,
Gray reminds us, into women's hats like turbans made of
gold lamé or tulle. An Eastern potentate had given a giraffe
to the Paris zoo: the creature caused a great stir and inspired
such hugely tall hairstyles that women were forced to sit on
the floors of their carriages.

Flaubert was a man, and he had a private income. Both realities helped reinforce his decision to take the literary high road. He worked from the inside out, gambling that if he read, reflected, and struggled in solitude, his work would be published and find fame in his lifetime and after. By temperament and by necessity, Louise represented a newer and more recognizably modern literary world based on self-promotion and celebrity. The difference was one of many the couple sparred over: they were always trying to change each other. "What distorts your life is also distorting your style," Flaubert wrote her, in one of his many jabs of criticism. She was a volcano, a tempest. She was forever acting on impulse—rushing about, bursting in, flouncing out. The publicity she got was often unflattering. Her most notorious moment had occurred some years before she met Flaubert, when she was about to give birth to Henriette. A hack journalist called Alphonse Karr made some snide remarks in his column about her child's paternity. Suspecting that the men in her life were not brave enough (or perhaps foolhardy enough) to defend her honor in a duel, she took things on herself. In her heavily pregnant state, she hid a kitchen knife in her umbrella and set off for Karr's house, where she stabbed him in the back. The wound was mercifully slight. In his next column, he let her off lightly—only noting that she might have done more damage if she hadn't posed with the dagger over her head, like a painting of Marat's assassin, Charlotte Corday. No doubt, Karr said sardonically, Madame Colet had the photo op in mind: "the anticipation of some forthcoming lithograph."

IF IT SEEMS to her biographer that Louise suffered from the "caprices of men," it seemed to Flaubert (and sometimes seems now to readers of her life story) that her chief handicap was her determination to lead the kind of life that makes good copy. Flaubert was always grumbling at her confessional style, her writing that came directly out of life. One of the reasons that trysts in distant hotel bedrooms appealed more to her than to him was that they threw him off the track for weeks, while she started writing about them even before they were over. While retaining his passion for Art all his life, in his maturity he rejected the other forms of Romantic passion to which as a youth he had felt terrifyingly susceptible. In his prose, he aimed at scientific detachment and strove to excise the first tinge of purple. He hated the excesses in Louise's writing, of which he was sometimes supportive but more often not. "You have turned art into an outlet for passion, a kind of chamber pot to catch an overflow," he said reprovingly when she planned a poem of revenge on the poet Alfred de Musset, who had tried to rape her under the influence of absinthe, in another of those Paris cabs.

Whenever she bristled at Flaubert's criticism of her style or got jealous when he showed her his writings about sex with other women, he said he was simply flattering her by treating her like a man. He was always trying to get her to be more "virile" or turn her into a hermaphrodite. She kept trying to get him to observe the sentimental proprieties or send gifts. "To hell with flowers," he growled. He had none of these obstacles with George Sand, a platonic friend in late middle age who became the second of the great correspondents of his life. He addressed her as "chère Maître" and thought of her as a "great man"; she was received most hospitably at Croisset by his mother.

Louise had wanted to be Sand's friend, but Sand kept her at a distance. Women in Louise's life were few and far between. The men in her blue room were heavy hitters, but there were rarely any women at her salons. Gray points out that the women of Colet's generation, however devoutly they professed their feminism, tended to compete with each other. There had been a loving mother in Provence; there was Henriette, the daughter who grew up conservative and Catholic while Louise was liberal and anticlerical. There was Madame Récamier, who was a generation older. But there seem to have been very few peers to help her through her abortions and miscarriages and the times when babies died. Flaubert himself was more often a heartache than a comfort; he was monumentally self-obsessed. He was horrified by the idea that she might be pregnant by him. The onset of her period ("the landing of the redcoats") was of hysterical concern. He was loving to his niece, it seems, but had no desire to bring a child of his own into what he regarded as an appalling world. "May the god of coitus grant that I never again go through such agony," he said, after one of their false alarms.

By the spring of 1847, Flaubert was having an affair with Ludovica Pradier, the sculptor's notoriously promiscuous wife. He had a recurrence of his epilepsy, and Louise suffered paroxysms of jealousy. She began an affair with a Polish émigré called Franc. Her commitment to the cause of the antiroyalist Polish liberals extended from the political to the personal several times. Flaubert was becoming more and more reactionary. He thought democracy was a waste of time, since it merely raised the proletariat to a middle-class level of stupidity. The couple's correspondence sputtered on for a while and then ended in the summer of 1848. They were to have no contact for the next four and a half years. In this time, she nursed Hippolyte and then buried him, as well as the baby boy she had borne to the Pole, who had left her.

Meanwhile, over his mother's objections, Flaubert and his friend Maxime du Camp were making the journey of a lifetime: two full years in the Middle East and Egypt, called the Orient at the time. He paid courtesy calls on consuls and visited the Pyramids by camel; he wore native dress and a tarboosh; he meticulously noted down incidents of bestiality and suppurating wounds; he wrote reassuring letters to his mother. To his friend Louis Bouilhet he wrote more raunchily, describing his researches into exotic sex ranging from dancing girls ("these shaved cunts make a strange effect") to male attendants at the baths. He visited the famous courtesan Kuchuk Hanem and watched her dance the bee dance in her rose-colored bloomers. He described the bedbugs and the smell of her flesh when (after sharing her, fraternally, with Max) he spent the night.

When, in 1851, Louise got wind of his return, she decided to risk what had always been forbidden: visiting him at Croisset. She took the train, hired a boatman, had a note carried in to him at dinner. He sent a servant to tell her to go away; even his mother was shocked at his treating a woman like this. But then he came out in the garden and told her he would meet her later in Rouen. He was fat, bald, and dressed in a flowing shirt and pants. His teeth were blackened by mercury treatments for the syphilis he had contracted, and he had grown a drooping mustache. She barely recognized him. "More like a seal than a Viking," she said in the jottings that served as her journal. It was one of her all-or-nothing actions that paid off. He was beginning *Madame Bovary*, a book about an all-or-nothing woman not unlike Louise; he needed her around. There was Mantes, again, and letters full of worries about the redcoats. He wrote every Saturday night to tell her how his writing had gone; Bouilhet came over every Sunday to help him crush escaping metaphors and purple excess. Like twins, in the cotton shirts Flaubert had brought back from Nubia, the friends sat side by side—"white as phantoms and calm as gods"—editing his masterpiece.

Back in Paris, Louise could never be calm, but it was fruitful for him and for her awhile. She was writing prolifically after a long hiatus; sometimes the kindly Louis helped Gustave edit his mistress. He was hard on her, still, and tetchier than ever. "Nothing one says does you any good," he said. He gave her his travel notes with the description of Kuchuk Hanem. She was especially upset by the bedbugs, which he called enchanting. Once, after being with him, she complained that he had given her a case of boils. She was lucky that boils were all she caught. "Boils are à la mode," he said laconically.

———

D U R I N G   T H E   P E R I O D   when he was writing *Madame Bovary*, she was writing fashion copy in order to make money. Gray seems particularly incensed at seeing a "committed political activist and self-taught scholar" reduced to "grinding out harebrained fashion chronicles." Louise wrote for *La Chronique de la Mode* and *La Gazette des Femmes*; she promoted the gowns and perfumes of Guerlain and was an expert on hats. The milliners rewarded her with free samples of the fruit-laden, feathered bonnets of the day. She wore them around town or sold them out of a special glass-fronted book-case in her apartment. Gray asks us to pity the poor woman writer who must seduce the men who will help her, suffer snide remarks from envious male colleagues who accuse her of casting-couch methods, and stoop to what Louise herself describes as "promoting the inventory of department-store owners." Flaubert despised taste-mongering ("the religion of chic," he called it), but he rather liked women's clothing. He mailed his thoughts on the subject to Louise. He wrote more seductively and descriptively of women's dress, in his fiction, than anyone except Proust.

A woman, reading Louise's life, finds much that is ad-mirable but much that is annoying. There is something alien-ating about her; some approval or identification that we withhold from her femininity. Is this a lingering trace of the ambivalent Flaubert, along with mean-spirited contempo-raries, who defined her for so long? Is this hesitation some-thing in us, in Louise herself, or in her biographer? Louise feels curiously *abandoned*. She is left to fend for herself—give us her own description, even, of her appearance. "I have put on weight; my waist is no longer willowy, but is still elegant," she wrote of herself at thirty-four, presumably after looking in a mirror. "My throat, my shoulders, my arms are excep-tionally lovely." Nowhere do we find a really affectionate description of her like the one Edmond de Goncourt made of Flaubert at Croisset: "with his broad hat and kind face and big bottom in pleated trousers." Even Kuchuk Hanem bee-dancing in her bloomers feels like a human being we can root for and invest with our compassion. There's something pretentious about the ringlets, something exasperating about that lifetime of sky-blue dresses. Poor Louise, bloodied by her Flaubert's scratches. Burning up the road, as she races through her era in a whiff of Guerlain and a cloud of hasty verses. Only crouched, in the end, on the floor of the carriage.

THE AFFAIR broke off again when he could do without it. Flaubert sent a curt, definitive note to the woman who had given him so much, in March of 1855. In middle age, Louise spent most of her time reporting on political causes. She became active in the Italian struggle for reunification, the risorgimento. In Ischia, she nearly got herself lynched; in Rome, she attracted hostile interest from the Vatican secret police. During the bloodbath of the Paris Commune, she was in the thick of the whistling bullets. On the opening of the Suez Canal, she was the only woman reporter invited to join the French delegation. "A rather vulgar fat woman with a virile voice and masculine manners" was the assessment of one of her colleagues. An elderly woman with failing lungs, she had graduated to something like manhood, if not quite to greatness. While in Egypt, she used some of her waning strength to comb the red-light districts in a fruitless search for Kuchuk Hanem.

1994

TRAPS AND DAMASK ROSES

*I*T'S BEEN years since I attended the Paris collections. After those last springtime weeks among the international fashion world, I went directly to England for another final chapter: digging and dreaming my way through a summer in the garden of a cottage I had determined (not without heartache) to put on the market. My life was changing. Sporting a new haircut, I headed north to the cottage—an old stone farmhouse perched on the edge of a grouse-moor in Yorkshire. I settled in. I wound the tall oak clock with its painted face of a sun and a slyly smiling moon. I polished the brass on the bedstead and the fire grate. I staked and weeded the herbaceous border. I walked in the woods, gathering primroses and bluebells to fill a big old tureen where, under a cracked and yellowed glaze, ladies in feathered hats strolled beneath the trees of pleasure-gardens. I called the local real estate agent and gave him my instructions. In New York, my editor was waiting with his habitual patience for an article about my days in Paris.

A wet and gloomy Northern European spring gave way to a string of long, fine days—the first of many in what was to prove an unusually warm summer. Above the dale, the sky was wide and blue. The air was filled with the piping of upland birds, the scent of hawthorn and honeysuckle. Vivid greenness came bursting out of the land and rolling over the hills that stretched into the distance. On the tops, lambs danced round curly-horned sheep that munched blissfully on emerald turf; down in the river meadows, cows stood udder-high in grass, chewing away as if hypnotized. My own particular corner of this verdant world was a sheltered patch of lawn inside the walls of the garden. My raft was an ancient canvas camp bed stencilled with the name of a long-dead friend of my father's called Captain Branton. I spent hours there, ruminating and watching the butterflies on the buddleia. Then I forced myself to go indoors and try to write about Paris.

I'd been tired when I arrived in the city for those spring shows, and when I left I was bruised and depleted. At the entrance to the tents set up for the designers in the Tuileries gardens, fistfights were frequent. Inside, the beauty of the models and the clothes seemed to struggle with imperfect success against a dark and death-driven zeitgeist. I hadn't the heart for any of it: the Roman-circus shouts of the photographers; the Texas matrons with their face-lifts; the female wrestlers, the men in makeup, the witch doctor in full regalia who had appeared on the runways along with the beautiful young women. It rained and rained. Everyone caught colds. Buyers and editors trudged up and down the muddy paths to the tents, forlornly coughing.

I sat at my table in the room whose whitewashed walls took on a tint of the greenness beyond the open door and windows. "If toads or bats had dropped from the bare-branched trees of the Tuileries," I began, miserably. Then I crumpled the page and went out into the garden. Under the clematis-covered wall, I lay down on Captain Branton.

IN EARLIER SOJOURNS in the house, I spent many an hour in the company of my favorite neighbors—an elegant, cultivated couple many years my senior. My house was old, pretty, and a long walk from the village. But their house was older and more isolated still, and spectacularly beautiful. They knew many arcane things about books, art, and music. Ugliness pained them. They owned a pier glass that had once reflected Lord Byron's face, and a chair that had been honored by the Duke of Wellington's bottom. An eighteenth-century silver jug was kept filled, in proper season, with the old-fashioned roses the couple approved of—the *alba* "Maiden's Blush," the damask "York and Lancaster," the Bourbon "Reine Victoria." Hybrid teas seemed hopelessly vulgar to them, along with lobelias, ornamental cherry, and virtually all petunias. One evening, I was sitting in my friends' window seat, watching a hare lollop about their field and half listening as they wrangled about something or other (suicide, perhaps, a frequent topic), when it struck me that these two knew more about aesthetics than they knew about living.

Defiantly, I stuffed the pots on my terrace with nemesias, whose eggy gaudiness would have seemed appallingly déclassé to my old companions, had I invited them to see my garden. But our exchanges of visit were getting rarer. In the endlessly long evenings of a North Country midsummer, I took to pointing my little car down the road that led in the opposite direction from their house. The market town that served the dale had a cobbled square; a medieval castle with massive walls that loomed above a river; and a modest tennis club, with a cedar hut for making teas and a couple of courts surrounded by suburban gardens. I became a member. The regulars were welcoming, their play was courteous and sometimes eccentric. It was the form to apologize to our partners when we lost a point and to our opponents when we won one. We played interminable and giggly mixed doubles, until the hybrid tea roses beyond the fence yielded up the last of the day's scent and a harvest moon rose slowly over the castle.

A BUTCHER; a woman with sensible brogues and teeth like those of her horses; large families in shabby cars, looking chiefly for a field in which to unwrap their picnic. Half the county came to view my house, but the summer wore on and no one bought it. I wasn't sorry. The cantankerous retired major from the manor house down the hill, obliged by an ex-wife to put his home on the market, thought I might like to know his secret for putting the wind up serious buyers. "Tell 'em about the ghost!" he said, in a stage whisper. The hot weather held. I visited the local dressmaker in her slanty-floored little room above the cobbled square and was measured for cotton dresses. I grew tanned and strong and lean; some hurt I had hidden even from myself was healing. Sometimes after tennis, my new friends and I would hurl ourselves into the river and float along on the current under the battlements, while the sun pierced the leaves and danced on the surface around the dragonflies.

I filled and refilled the tureen with the flowers that arrived in succession in garden, fields, and hedgerows: lilac, mock orange, foxgloves, campanula, Queen Anne's lace, and roses. The hills turned purple as the heather bloomed. The Duke who owned the moor arrived with a large house party at his shooting lodge, for the traditional opening of the grouse season. By that time, my own calendar was full. In the mornings, before the mist burned off the heather, I would amble down the fields in my dressing gown to check my mole-traps—lifting out some small, still-warm, and velvety corpse before resetting them. My few acres had moles by the score, and rabbits by the hundreds, and an alarmingly vigorous crop of thistles that I finally mowed, one sunset, with a sickle. Some fellows who knew the local caves took me away from it all, to a secret place inside the limestone mountain. They showed me how to wriggle through tunnels and crevices until we reached a cool and silent chamber where we stood looking with a kind of reverence at the stalactites that sprang to life in the beam of our helmet lamps.

I wrote to my editor in New York, explaining that I would not be writing about Paris. Instead, I described all this to him—the cave, the sunset, sickling the thistles. (I left out the moles, for he was an urban man and very squeamish.) I went to the slanty-floored room to pore over the dressmaker's pattern books again. She got to work on outfits for winter evenings when (I vaguely supposed) my life would be completely different. She made a black velvet dress and one of rainbow silk chiffon. She made a jacket of Chinese silk the color of a kingfisher I once saw flash past when I was in the river. We discovered at the fitting that my waist was inches smaller than it had been at the beginning of that, my last Yorkshire summer.

1994

FRITILLARIES AND HAIRY VIOLETS

*A*PPROACHING the estate of Ashton Wold by night and at the end of a cloudburst, the big car forded milk-blue mist that rose from the road in pools and wisps. Then the headlights were bouncing up a long, rough drive and playing on the creamy saucer shapes of cow parsley (tall, this year, for May) that formed a jostling honor guard along the verge. From my seat beside the chauffeur I had an impression of dark and dripping woods at either hand. Then we were pulling up in a courtyard, and there was a pair of tall stone gateposts with lanterns beaming from their tops. On every side, there was the purposeful, rustling silence of deep rural England, and a sense of plant life laying siege. Underfoot, nettles, grass, and heartsease colonized the frontiers of the gravel paths. Ivies and creepers tackled the upper reaches of an old stone house—scaling and smothering mullions, drainpipes, and chimneys that unfolded like accordions, in the Jacobean style. A horse chestnut stood protectively sheltering the housekeeper's wing and raising a thousand white candle blossoms to where, in a dark-blue sky, a cloud half hid the moon. From a nearby coppice came the drawn-out hooting of an owl.

The mistress of the house—the Honourable Dr. Miriam Rothschild, Commander of the Order of the British Empire, Fellow of the Royal Society, and, in private life, Mrs. Miriam Lane—had retired to bed. (Probably not to sleep, for she prides herself on the stamina and discipline that help her keep long hours: she rises what she calls "relentlessly" at five to speak to her farm manager and head gardener, and reads scientific books until well after midnight in the room where, in 1908, she was born.) I got out of the car and was greeted by Kate Garton, a capable woman in her forties, who was once Dr. Rothschild's personal assistant and is now a full-time conservationist, and had come to Ashton Wold, in Northamptonshire, to help her out with what promised to be a very busy weekend. I followed Kate Garton, who was wearing a flowered dressing gown, as she led me through the house and to my room. Through a back porch with its covey of Wellington boots and its big, squat red flashlight under a sign reading "Mrs. Lane's torch. If used by anyone, please return to same position." Past sculleries and a darkened kitchen, with a blurry gleam of copper pans and bowls up one wall. Down a long corridor (Kate Garton's slippers scuff-scuffing on the parquet) lined to the ceiling with files labelled "Flea News," "Uncle Walter," "Zoological Record," "Trustees Meetings: British Museum." Through the front hall, with its gaggles of walking sticks, deck chairs, tennis racquets, and panama hats. Up a staircase lined with paintings and past a massive billiard table draped with a cloth, to the door of one of the guest rooms. In the passageway outside, someone had mounted—like a case of brilliant lepidoptera of related species set out with pins—a collage of hundreds of family snapshots, a sepia cornucopia of Rothschilds past and present, English and Continental, variously intermarried, more or less prone to eccentricity, and more or less possessed of fabulous fortunes, great intellects, and good looks. Here they were on English lawns or Hungarian tennis courts (Miriam Rothschild's mother, Rozsika, was Hungarian, and was said to be the first of her sex to venture the overhand serve), or cutting figures in lavish baby gowns in the arms of parents or nursemaids, or (later) on magnificent horses or on skis. Here was the house of Ashton Wold in 1900, when it was built, on a baronial scale, by Miriam Rothschild's father, the Honourable Nathaniel Charles. (In 1969, when she returned from Oxford, where she had been living for fifteen years, she took off the whole top story and lowered the roof to turn the house into a more manageable manor.) Here was Tring Park, the kingly estate in Hertfordshire that was home to her grandfather, Nathan Mayer (Natty), the first Lord Rothschild; to her amazing Uncle Walter (seen photographed in top hat and frock coat astride one of his giant Galápagos tortoises and also in his four-in-hand, being pulled by zebras he had broken in); and to Miriam Rothschild, too, for most of each year until 1935. ("We were a very close-knit family," she told me later. "As my father would inherit and my grandmother lived there, one went there for the winter.") And here, displayed among these photographs of the Rothschilds, were various mutations of the compiler herself. For it was Miriam Rothschild who had assembled the memories, the way her Uncle Walter had assembled, for his private museum, a world-famous collection of 2.25 million butterflies and moths, 300,000 bird skins, 200,000 birds' eggs, and 144 giant tortoises, and the way her father had built up his own great collection, of 30,000 specimens of flea. Here was Miriam Rothschild as a little girl of four, milking a cow; as a girl of ten or so, in a straw hat, with pigeons feeding from her hand; and as a striking young woman, in a group of young men including George Lane (also a Hungarian), whom she married during the war and divorced in the 1950s, and her brother Victor, the present Lord.

WAKING the next morning to sunshine at the window and, from outside it, a chorus of cooing pigeons and joyously barking dogs, I found myself in the company of Rothschilds straightaway. A line of caricatures and silhouettes hung on the wall opposite my pillow—an Indian file of shortish, roundish men, marching with supreme self-confidence through nine-teenth- and early-twentieth-century British history: Nathan Mayer (founder of the British branch of the family banking house), Lionel, Anthony, Natty, Leopold, with top hats, bowler hats, spats, canes, waistcoated paunches; financiers of wars against Napoleon and the Boers; first Jews to be elected to Parliament; first to be elevated to the peerage; sweeping the board at the Oaks and Derby with the products of their racing stables; friends and confidants of prime ministers and kings; little black figures on white paper, here at Ashton, facing the English countryside.

I opened the leaded casement and leaned out. Wisteria and clematis lay in waiting, pressing to get in. In the distance unfurled an old, familiar dream: a rolling green ridge hazily shimmering on a May morning, the fields marked by flow-ering hawthorn hedges high as cottages, and a distant frieze of venerable woodland with a church spire peeking out. In the middle distance, a herd of deer like something in a tapestry lifted their heads in unison in a field, then wheeled and scampered away. Closer still lay a garden unlike any garden I had ever seen. The outline of Edwardian lawns and flagstone terraces was there, but floppily uncorseted, left to riotous, rampant seed. Artfully undisciplined lilac and cherry blossoms swayed over unmowed meadow grass that was sprinkled with white cow parsley, yellow cowslips, bluebells, tulips that were blowsy, droopy-petalled, pale pink. The air was full of scent. Butterflies were everywhere, jerkily danc-ing and alighting. Doves spread sun-pierced wing fans and looped with purring drumroll sounds overhead.

Miriam Rothschild came walking through her garden, surrounded by seven dogs. Like an Eskimo and his sled team, the group came forging through the waist-high snow of cow parsley down a winding, mower-wide cleared path. Shelties with fluffy brown-and-white coats came flowing and jostling ahead of her and behind, speeding on paws placed one straight in front of another, woofing, or stopping abruptly to sniff the damp spring earth. Their leader shot out of the flowering tunnel, then craned its pointed nose back over its shoulder to make sure its mistress was there. At her forceful command, it plunged excitedly on. The woman had a handsome head with a widow's peak of white hair under a purple kerchief tied at the nape. Tortoiseshell spectacles, hanging from a chain, bounced on an ample bust. As she, too, emerged from the cow parsley and crossed a part of the lawn that was kept close-cropped and velvety, she was revealed as a square, stout figure in a shapeless dress and matching sleeveless jacket, a style she adopted as her uniform some forty years ago, in order to free her mind for more important things. Today's outfit was in a silky purple-and-turquoise printed stuff. Her arms swung purposefully as she walked; her solidly planted feet left snail-trail marks on the dew-wet lawn with the soles of white Wellington boots. ("These are my summer shoes," she will explain. "And my evening shoes as well! I never wear anything made from animals. In the winter, I wear moon boots, indoors and out.") With a hollow slurping of the rubber Wellingtons, and looking peaceful in her habitat—knowing the hiding places of the fledglings and of the pupae on the leaf—she crunched across the gravel and disappeared from view around a corner of the house.

This morning, my hostess had a great deal on her mind. Today was the seventy-fifth anniversary of the Royal Society for Nature Conservation, which was founded by her father, and Ashton was the movement's spiritual home. Several dozen distinguished British naturalists, conservationists, and entomologists were to gather for elevenses in the drawing room (which at Ashton Wold is called the library), and then other colleagues and friends—some two hundred in all— were to meet under the horse chestnuts on the green of Ashton village (weather permitting) for lunch. There was a butterfly film, to be screened in the squash court; afternoon tea for the two hundred back on the green; and a clay-pigeon shoot organized by Sid Jackson, her farm manager. The house was desperately short-staffed, and there was dinner and Sunday luncheon to be managed, and beds to be sorted out for the several dozen people who were staying in the main house and in other houses and cottages around the village and the estate. There would be a professor of genetics, and one of botany, from Cambridge; Dr. Daphne Osborne, also a botanist, from Oxford; all the members of the Entomological Club (it is the oldest entomological club in the world, limited by statute to eight learned and convivial souls, with Miriam Rothschild its first and still, after two decades, its only woman member); an eccentric poet who had sent her some of his poems and whom she had impulsively invited to join today's festivities; and a man who had recently made the headlines by walking to the South Pole, or was it the North Pole—she couldn't quite remember. And there was the man who had once been a suitor of one of her daughters and, though long ago disappointed, was still around (like an Englishman after the Raj) on occasions like this, as an attentive, self-effacing family friend. And no Rothschild gathering would be complete without some "flea people"—scientists specializing in the study of the insect that has loomed large in her life, what with original research of her own and a recently completed eight-volume, thirty-five-year cataloguing project based on the paternal thirty thousand, now in the British Museum. Among the flea people was Dr. Bernice Williams, a wiry, talkative woman with a Welsh accent and a long ginger-colored braid, who was an expert on cat fleas. She had brought along a friend—Rosemary Mulcahy, a dark-haired young woman with an Irish accent (which, its owner being inclined to silence, was little used), who wore a sweatshirt bearing the legend "British Hedgehog Preservation Society" and was an expert on mites.

Refreshed by chocolate cake and chitchat, the elevenses folk set off in a disorderly crocodile to inspect one of the meadows where Miriam Rothschild grows wildflowers. Over the past decade, and at first virtually single-handed, she has made the British public aware of its wildflower heritage and the threatened loss of that heritage. This is perhaps the most visible and triumphantly successful of a lifetime's public-spirited campaigns: for refugees from Nazi Germany in the 1930s and '40s ("I battled with the British authorities, who behaved excruciatingly badly," she says); for free milk in British schools; for, via her participation in the Wolfenden Committee report, the legalization of homosexual activity between consenting adults ("They were rather frank in Oxford, they called me 'the Buggers' Friend' "); for the use of car seat belts, which she invented; for glass-walled squash courts; for crash helmets for competitive skiers; for help for schizophrenics (she started the Schizophrenia Research Fund and an art gallery, in her village, devoted to paintings by people suffering from the disease); for the better treatment of farm and laboratory animals and against the cruelty of ritual slaughter without anesthesia ("I haven't got much patience with some rabbis on that," she says). At Ashton, a farm of several thousand acres—large by British standards but small compared with the estates of some county neighbors, including the Duke of Gloucester and the Princess of Wales' family, at Althorp—she has filled ninety acres of meadow with the wildflowers of Chaucerian England, in only ten years accomplishing through careful management a task that some said would take a lifetime or more. By producing wildflower seed as a farm crop, she began to disseminate in the nation's private gardens and public places plants that were previously threatened with extinction or discarded as weeds. In a variety of ways, she has sought to balance the discouraging depredation of the British landscape over the past forty years—damage caused by chemical spraying and fertilizing, by the slashing of roadside verges, by the expansion of towns and highways, and by the rooting out of hedges—which has transformed the traditional patchwork of fields into agriculturally profitable but one-dimensional arable acreage, or what Miriam Rothschild calls a "really ghastly mini Kansas corn belt." What's good for wildflowers is good for the nation's ecology. ("Our conservancy trusts would do well to hitch their wagons to the cowslip's star," one of the officials told the gathering in a speech after lunch.) All the flora and fauna—the larks, pipits, and nightingales; the oxlips, primroses, bee orchids, and ragged robins; the fritillaries (both plants and butterflies of that name), the cabbage-white, red-admiral, and skipper butterflies—depend each on the next for shelter, food, survival. Until forty years ago, it was all still in place: the web and texture of Shakespeare's natural world—Milton's, Keats', Matthew Arnold's. (T. S. Eliot's Little Gidding and Rupert Brooke's Grantchester are within a short drive of Ashton Wold.) The loss of each successive species is more than just a void in nature. Even in postindustrial, computerized, Thatcherized Britain, there stirs a sense of damage to the English language itself, of diminution of the national myth.

The group wound its way down the drive (deliberately kept bumpy, it turned out, to discourage speeding); past the Ashton cricket field, with its thatched tea pavilion and its big roller lying timelessly idle, as on an L. P. Hartley afternoon; through woods, with branches trembling with pale-green buds overhead and a carpet of bluebells underfoot; and out into the middle of a field. The men were sensibly dressed in tweedy jackets or thorn-proof Barbour coats; a few of the women had braved summery frocks with cardigans over them. Wellingtons (conventionally colored black or green) were widely worn.

The self-effacing family friend (whom I'll call Michael Fitzpatrick) was one of several gentlemen in tattersall caps. Moving in and out of the dappled shade of the wood, cocking his well-brushed head to listen to the trilling of a bird, pausing to sniff the air or point out a view, he was himself like some modest, sprightly British butterfly. He had a kind of sunniness, in the manner of a Franciscan friar. "Marvellous," he said, coming to a halt after satisfactorily ushering a group of ladies through a five-bar gate. He brought his closed fists in to his heart and flung them outward several times, inhaling and exhaling. "We ought to *bottle* it!" The sky was large, soft, pale, the air buoyant with the fleeting sweetness of an English country spring. A breeze carried mingled hints of the bluebells in the woods and the May blossoms in the cottage-high hedge. "I mean, the only actual moment I actually have is this one, now, isn't it? So why not enjoy it?"

Miriam Rothschild was stalking along with her hands clasped behind her back, leading the group into the center of what looked at first glance to be a perfectly ordinary green field. (It was too early for most of the wildflowers to be in bloom.) In her kerchief and brightly patterned dress among the dun-colored tweeds, she looked as exotic as the kangaroos and emus her Uncle Walter used to keep beyond the ha-ha at Tring Park. She stopped, and the rest stopped with her— little knots of people dwarfed in the expanse of land and sky, breathing deep, buzzing with a furious exchange of observations, bending over and pointing down at the green with excited cries.

"We changed the drill in here to put in oxeye daisies," she was saying. "We graze lightly between harvest and Christmas. Sheep or cattle. Not horses. They're particularly bad."

"Are there masses of meadow browns?" someone asked, referring to a kind of butterfly.

Miriam Rothschild was standing with her hands in the side pockets of her skirt, as if turning over imaginary change. She wore a big black watch on one wrist. "That's a very interesting question," she said, looking pleased. She is an expert on the relations between plants and insects, especially butterflies. Butterflies will feed on a variety of flower nectars during their short adult lives, but are extremely particular about which plants they lay their eggs on; if the right plant goes, the butterflies die out as well. "Interesting" is unquestionably Miriam Rothschild's favorite adjective. "My family has always been very *interested* in everything," she says.

Talk now turned to field plants that are undesirable, at

least to gardeners and to cows: thistle, ragwort, and something that Miriam Rothschild referred to as "that awful brachypodium." "Daphne!" she called in a big, gruff voice across the field to the botanist from Oxford. "What's the germination rate for hay rattle?"

Fitzpatrick has a farm in the Home Counties, and, like a number of landowners, great and small (including the Prince of Wales), he is going in for wildflowers, at Miriam Rothschild's instigation. ("She's got 'em all tearing up their Inigo Jones parks and planting weeds!" someone said, in jesting admiration.) "I had this field, you see," Fitzpatrick said. "So I thought, May as well bung in some wildflowers! My farm manager thinks I've gone mad!"

A man of science had been standing nearby and listening with half an ear. "I don't believe I know what your field is," he said to Fitzpatrick.

"No, no, I *own* a field," Fitzpatrick said, looking flustered. "I've just sown it, you see. With wildflowers."

Some of the conversations were neither scientific nor agricultural.

"I only have to look at a *photograph* of a Victoria sponge," one of the cardiganed ladies was saying as the party trailed into motion again.

"My father, now, he was the sort of chap who never put on an ounce until the day he died," said a second.

"Oh dear, I shouldn't have had all that coffee," a third lady said, looking plaintively in the direction of some shrubbery.

The naturalists were in seventh heaven, comparing notes on lepidoptera.

"It's a very good year for orange tips."

"The blues are magnificent here."

"I've introduced two different burnets and they're doing well."

"I know there used to be a colony of Duke of Burgundies in Rockingham Forest."

A gray-haired man of military bearing, with caterpillar-like brows, said he liked to keep an eye out for skippers while walking the North Downs. "I'm chasing newts at this time of year as well," he said, with a twinkle. "That always makes for fun and games."

"ALL GOOD SCIENCE is in a sense autobiographical," Miriam Rothschild once wrote in an article, quoting (rather freely) from Thoreau. Before the war, she did research on parasitic flukes and fleas. In the 1950s, she branched away from her father's obsession, the flea, to research various kinds of plant-insect relationships. Her book *Fleas, Flukes, and Cuckoos*, published in 1952, pioneered a new kind of writing about natural history for the literate general reader. In the 1960s, she returned to flea studies for long enough to prove how the reproductive cycle of the rabbit flea is dependent on that of the rabbit on which it lives. She spent many sleepless nights watching for fleas to hop from the doe to the newborns at the instant of birth. Subsequently, she made an exact analysis of how a flea jumps. With an acceleration twenty times that of a moon rocket reentering the earth's atmosphere, a flea can reach what would be on a human scale the height of the Empire State Building—and then repeat the feat thirty thousand times without stopping. And she showed how insects already possessed of warning coloration also store plant-derived poisons, to further discourage birds and other predators from gobbling them up. Perhaps in all this her role and perceived responsibilities as one of the wealthy English Rothschilds, her life as a brilliant woman scientist in a world of men, her motherhood (she reared six children, three of them adopted), and the story of her loves and sorrows may be discovered. But her autobiography is found in more than science or natural history.

"She is of inestimable value," a younger friend (one of many whom Miriam Rothschild has encouraged in their careers) once told me. "You won't find her kind of marriage of

the arts and sciences except, perhaps, in the seventeenth century—in someone like Sir Kenelm Digby, a founder of the
Royal Society."

Miriam Rothschild's autobiography has been written, for
one thing, in a long lifetime's prolific correspondence, in a
handwriting that remains sturdy and vital. Like the accou-
trements of her sporting youth—she rode, skied, and played
tennis, cricket, real racquets, and squash, the last to international standards—her handwriting is of uncompromisingly
high quality, a well-maintained and constantly used extension
of herself. "My friends used to say I was like a motorbicycle
roaring through England and throwing out letters at every
hand!" she told me once, with a laugh. "I didn't keep a diary
for that reason." To her beloved cousin the late Alix de Rothschild (of the French banking house), she wrote every day for
thirty-five years—some thirteen thousand letters in all. "We
were like sisters. We'd grown up in the same way. We were
both Rothschilds, we both had difficult marriages. She burned
all my letters, because she thought they were so indiscreet.
But ten years later that doesn't really matter, does it?" In
accordance with the explicit testamentary instructions of her
grandfather, her uncle, and her father, virtually all their correspondence with members of the family was destroyed by
their executors. Miriam Rothschild had cause to regret this
when she came to write *Dear Lord Rothschild*, a biography of
her Uncle Walter, which was published in 1983 and includes
much of her parents' story and something of her own. (Walter
Rothschild, who remained a bachelor, had also been a copious
correspondent, although for a period in his late thirties he was
unable—out of fear of his mother and of a blackmailer—to
bring himself to open any personal post addressed to him,
instead hiding it in enormous laundry baskets in his room on
the nursery floor of Tring Park.)

In spite of the weight of her published books and scientific
papers, Miriam Rothschild's story, like her letters, is something evanescent and written fresh each day. "I'm frightfully

keen on doing my book on haiku," she said to me some days after the anniversary, when she and I were sitting alone.

"Haiku?" I said. I was trying to get things straight. "How many books are you writing at the moment, anyway?"

"Well, there's my book on butterflies and doves in art. Then, there's *Farming for Profit and Conservation*. I've had to sink some capital in research surveys for that—medieval ditching systems, God knows what. Then, I'm doing my book on insects in haiku poetry, with a fantastic man called Kazuo Unno. There I feel I really *have* got something to say."

At this point, the telephone rang. It often does when Miriam Rothschild is in residence at Ashton Wold: allies on the fronts of her various causes; friends in Jerusalem (where she interests herself in wildflower conservation, a crafts center, and the Biblical Zoo), or in Zurich or America; friends to meet in town (this week, after the Chelsea Flower Show), or over luncheon back at home in the country. This particular call was a request, for the second time in two days, that she provide a home for a fox. She has eight foxes, and some of them like to come in and watch animal programs on television with her. People are known to call her Mother Fox.

"Tell me," she instructed the caller, firmly taking charge. "Is it tame? What age is it? Is it *very* nervous?"

She hung up and resumed the conversation about her work. "Oh, yes, I'm writing a book on Proust as a naturalist," she said. "I forgot!"

And day by day her story unreels in pictures as well as words—images constantly dissolving and re-forming with the light, the weather, and the seasons at Ashton Wold.

"The Rothschilds as a whole have high I.Q.s, but we're not really intellectual," she told me. "We are all doers. We don't just dig in the garden, you might say; we think what we're going to plant." If her grandfather pursued constant improvement on his estates—breeding champion shire horses and Jersey cows, and running for his tenant workers what she calls a "mini welfare state"—Miriam Rothschild is also, in the

Rousseauesque surroundings that only on first glance seem carelessly run-down, indefatigably in pursuit of an ideal. The views from the leaded casements of her house were planned and are maintained with care. And she seeks to arrange the garden and the rest of the estate at Ashton (designated by the government a Site of Special Scientific Interest, because of its overall health) as if she were herself a butterfly, seeing it from the air with ultraviolet vision, in search of nectar and a crèche.

LEAVING the naturalists to make their way to the seventy-fifth-anniversary lunch, I wandered down through the path in the cow parsley from which, in the early morning, I had watched Miriam Rothschild and the dogs emerge. I came to a gate in a high, sun-warmed wall and stepped through. Except for the scuffling of a blackbird in some dry leaves somewhere, everything was very still. A pigeon feather lay on a lichened path. There were plenty of nettles, which butterflies love. I pushed through unpruned branches of lilac and buddleia and stood at the rim of a huge, neglected stone-rimmed swimming pool. Curving steps descended into thick brown water, where a handful of cherry petals floated. A solitary water boatman sped about its beetle business at the center of concentric rings. I pushed open a second gate—this one of heavy ornamented wrought iron, somewhat rusty but perfectly balanced and swinging open with ease. I stood in another high-walled garden, larger than the first, and with a thatched dovecote, shaped like a tower and surrounded by an empty moat. On a sloping, bonnet-shaped roof of warm brown reed, pigeons—tan, snow white, or dapple gray— alighted, flew off, turned in circles on their perch, or tucked their heads into their necks and cooed. A second, ornamental pool glinted from a tangle of briar and meadow grass lower down. Loud in the peaceful place, a frog stretched out the hinges of its legs and jumped through the stalks near my feet. From somewhere beyond the far wall came the faint barking of a dog.

SINGLE-MINDED, in giant close-up, the wasp laid its eggs, dooming to a long, slow death the chubby butterfly grub that lay dozing in the cradle of a leaf.

"Ha!" said Miriam Rothschild. She was standing at the back of the darkened, cold squash court, watching the butterfly film over rows of silhouetted heads. She took an absent-minded bite from a piece of bread she was holding, with her eyes still glued to the screen. She has spent countless hours watching how butterflies (among other creatures) court, mate, feed, and die. "I never had much time for dolls," she told me once. "I was rearing caterpillars when I was quite small. I think naturalists are born, not made. Farming, gardening—anything to do with growing things is *grand*."

The party was going splendidly. During luncheon under the horse chestnuts on the village green, buxom women in straw hats and blue pinafores had performed old English clog dances, shaking handbells and lifting their knees. "Nineteenth-century sentimentality," a titled lady at one of the white-draped tables said, with a sniff. She herself had eighteenth-century silver hair, and an eye patch like Lord Nelson's.

"I hope that man who walked to the North Pole wasn't offended," Miriam Rothschild said. "Perhaps we should have made rather more of a fuss over him."

Bernice Williams and Rosemary Mulcahy got into their car and headed back to the house. The Welshwoman rolled down her window and stopped to chaff with a man in another car. "I'll be sending you those fleas, then," she promised, laughing, in her singsong voice.

"Send them by first-class post," he said. "And be sure they don't arrive on a Friday."

"Met him at the International Flea Conference," she said, giving a nod, flinging her braid back over her shoulder, and starting off again. "Nice man."

Then the lengthened tree shadows were reaching out from

the corners of the fields, and it was time to present the prizes at the ending of Sid Jackson's clay-pigeon shoot. Other landowning ladies had no doubt been opening church fêtes and gymkhanas and presenting all sorts of prizes all over England that afternoon. But the Honourable Mrs. Miriam Lane was assuredly the only such lady to have on the seat of her car, as she set off to perform her duty, books entitled *Endopolyploidy and Polyteny in Differentiation and Evolution* and *Genome Multiplication, Growth and Development.* At the top end of a large, sloping field, a group of a dozen or more diehard competitors were standing around in their shooting vests under an oak. Others were leaving the finalists to fight it out and bouncing away over the grass in cars and Land Rovers, headed for their evening meal. The air was echoing with shots as each fellow in his own good time steadied his nerves and—with a loud shout of "Pull!"—signalled another fellow to release from a trap a volley of flying disks. Beyond the semicircle of men, the gun barrel wheeling in an arc, and the disks whizzing and shattering over a field of wheat, the green countryside rolled along.

"The great thing about Northamptonshire is that every-thing here is very *slow*," Miriam Rothschild said indulgently as yet another round began. The men, some with hands in pockets, some with their shotguns resting broken in the crook of an arm, spoke among themselves in low, loamy voices, sounding not too different from the accents of Bottom and Master Quince. Miriam Rothschild is capable of great impatience—with what she deems foolish conversation or staff incompetence as well as with the callousness of some rabbis—but of infinite patience, too. She has an old country person's long memory and sense of unfolding time. "We'll never have a spring like this one, with the cherry and the blackthorn out together—not in a hundred years," she said this year. For all her international travelling and honorary doctorates, she is deeply rooted in her village and her country tales, and now she was recalling the time there was a double murder in Ashton village, and the time Eros, her Jersey bull, was separated from his cows and turned up in the road with the field gate on his horns.

"Was that the bull we put the cat fleas on that time?" asked Bernice Williams, under the oak.

"You couldn't put cat fleas on Eros," Miriam Rothschild said. "He's far too nasty."

The shots and cries of "Pull!" echoed on.

"I was a very good shot with a rifle once, but no good with a shotgun," Miriam Rothschild said. "One of my favorite companions during the war was Clark Gable. A pleasant companion for shooting rooks, but a very conceited man." Six thousand American servicemen were stationed at Ashton during the Second World War. She turned over the big house to the Red Cross for a military hospital. "Over there, that was all covered in Nissen huts," Miriam Rothschild said, with a wave. "The Army, the Air Corps, the Ordnance Corps. The Ordnance Corps were the worst. Every wild animal on the place was killed. They destroyed our fire engine—all the wonderful old things." It was a stick of practice bombs gone astray that had put paid to the moat. "I was very friendly with many of the men, especially a padre who had a chestful of medals but was very much against war." She met Captain Lane, her future husband, while he was recuperating in the hospital. A former Hungarian water-polo champion called Lanyi, he was a handsome man seven years younger than she was. ("I like good-looking people," she says.) Later, he became a prisoner of war in Germany, and after the war ended he was decorated with the Military Cross for his outstanding bravery in a famous do-or-die commando troop. "The war was unmitigated hell," Miriam Rothschild said. She suffered a terrifying attack of amnesia after living through the Bristol blitz. As a scientist, she had been in a reserved category at the outset of the war. "I worked as a dairymaid while they decided what to do with me. Then they sent me into a secret occupation: working side by side with Alan Turing at the decoding center at Bletchley. We worked from four in the afternoon until eight in the morning, with two days off every fortnight. I was comfortably housed at Lord Rosebery's, but I scarcely slept all that time."

The shots and cries had faded and the victor had emerged. Miriam Rothschild shook the hand of the winner. "Very good shooting," she said.

The bystanders took their own well-worn hands from their pockets and clapped, slow and loud. "Well done, lad," said one of the loamy voices, nearby.

Now that silence was creeping over the field at last, a bird began its evening song.

"Fourth prize is Mr. Brightwell," Sid Jackson announced.

"Well done, Steven," the voice said.

"Equal sixth is Mr. T. Wilson and Mr. P. Curtis," Jackson said.

" 'E's gone 'ome," someone said.

Sid Jackson wanted to thank those who had manned the traps, especially a chap who had been up in a tree working the high-board trap. " 'Cause 'e don't like 'ights." Bits of paper were drawn for a raffle. There was some slight confusion. ("That don't count. We'll say Bill Nall won that.")

"No. 28, Mr. Gerald Eastland."

"That's it, Gerald, well done."

Someone stepped up to say he'd like to thank Sid Jackson for running the day so well. The handclaps, like the hooves of shire horses, echoed big and slow across the land.

"Well done, Sid."

THE FOLLOWING MORNING was cold and gray with blustery winds. Michael Fitzpatrick carefully refolded the *Sunday Telegraph* and set off for church. Miriam Rothschild was champing at the bit, eager to show an old airfield to a young nature-conservancy officer, who had stayed in the village overnight. She said she wanted the young man to give up his present job and come to manage the place as a habitat preserve. "Of course, you'd have to move to Ashton," she said, jocular but firm. "I'm sure we can find you a house."

She parked the car in a lonely lay-by where there was a squashed soft-drink can and wrappers from Wimpy, the British fast-food chain. "Britain is frightfully dirty now— paper blowing about everywhere," she said. "The Dutch used to be a very tidy people, but now Holland is awful. Sweden's pretty clean still. But Singapore's the best." The airfield had a melancholy aspect, with squally rain blowing sidewise over crumbling concrete runways—once loud with fighter planes and Flying Fortresses—overgrown with nettle and briar. At a little distance stood ugly farm buildings converted from wartime hangars, and a farmhouse that would have looked abandoned if blackish coal smoke had not been emerging from a chimney and whipping here and there in the wind. Miriam Rothschild stalked off in her Wellingtons, then stopped to gesture with her whole arm.

"See? Look at this! Don't you think it's *good*? We've got *Lotus corniculatus*. Four subspecies of roses, including *Rothschildii*. Saint-John's-wort, and creeping cinquefoil, and a lot of cowslips, over there. It's the only nesting site of the hen harrier in the country. It's *just* the place for the dingy skipper. Oh, don't you think it's a *marvellous* place?" She believes in affirmative action for butterflies—transporting threatened species to hospitable terrain. "You see this area?" she said, pointing blissfully to a particularly unprepossessing corner of turf and scrub. "Not so long ago, we had the grizzled skipper, the dingy skipper, *and* the Mother Shipton."

Bernice Williams and her friend were standing around, their hands and noses turning blue.

"If someone were to send a colony of Lulworth skippers, there's enough of that awful brachypodium they like. And over here would be suitable for the Duke of Burgundy. Do fritillaries like hairy violets? What do you think?"

Kestrels hovered in the grayness overhead. Managers of the Ashton estate had tried to use this disused airfield for growing timber, Miriam Rothschild recalled. "The plantations failed completely," she said, with satisfaction. "There's an old rocket network under these runways, and the rabbits are in the tunnels for keeps. Ate all the baby conifers. In the end, everyone gave up and left the place to me. It makes a wonderful nature reserve." She stomped along, the rain spitting down and marking with teardrop splashes a green kerchief she was wearing that day, with the familiar dress style in a green-and-beige peacock-feather print. "The cinnabar has come, thank goodness, and so has the burnet," she went on. "This was a plowed field in 1940. In another forty years, it will be a wood." Butterflies avoid the shade of dense woods. Once again, she pressed the young man to come. "What bothers me is, when I'm dead there won't be anyone to manage the place."

"Isn't there anyone local?" he said.

"There *isn't* anyone."

Back in the car, she said, "Oh, do look at those two cock pheasants fighting!" She had cheered up again.

"I just want to show you this reed field I've planted. Twenty acres of phragmites. It's going to be a wonderful bird reserve in winter, and we'll get some thatch out of it as well." She pulled up at a brick building, very George Eliot–looking, by a stream. "Excuse my enthusiasm," she said, leading the little band round the side of the building and letting out a delighted laugh. The rain was heavy now—dropping into the dark waters of a millpond and, together with a chub that surfaced briefly, bouncing up and plopping back again. Willows dangled in the water. A fat mallard waddled out of the rushes like a country parson, turning right round in a circle, as if taking a bow.

"We've got kingfishers and great crested grebes, and the otter came back this week," our guide said. To the visible relief of the chillier members of the group, she led everyone indoors, to what turned out to be a little museum. There were relics of the Roman settlement in Ashton ("We organized a dig—it was great fun") and exhibits of fishing techniques, including the use of cormorants, in Japan. "The cormorants, when they perch, all face north—you can steer by them. I was fascinated," she said. There were old tools from the blacksmith's and the thatcher's trades. "My father was very keen on local crafts," she said. "Look, this is phragmites. These are the kneelers the thatchers wear for crawling on the roof. A thatcher is the rarest thing you can catch these days—rarer than a purple emperor. We had one apprentice used to come to Ashton, liked to work naked. Sat up there on the thatch, absolutely starkers. Ha!"

"IT'LL BE rather a scrappy luncheon, I'm afraid," Miriam Rothschild had said to the nature-conservancy officer, inviting him and his wife back to the house. Several dozen of the human species (a motley party of acquaintances entomological and natural-historical, together with some neighbors, members of a younger generation of the genus *Rothschildia*, and the eccentric poet) alighted around two large tables in the dining room to feed on roast lamb with mint sauce and red-currant jelly, roast and mashed potatoes, several other vegetables, and a choice of puddings, the whole washed down with either Rothschild claret or a homemade elder-flower cordial.

"Someone just asked me who all these people are," the hostess said happily. "I said, 'Don't ask me, I haven't the foggiest who half of 'em are!' "

She had seated the young conservancy man next to her in order to talk about what interested her most. "Last year, we introduced those marbled whites," she told him. "I should have let the females out earlier. The fritillaries were a washout."

Like veterans of the war between the Roundheads and the Cavaliers, the pair rehashed battles fought in poetic corners of the English countryside. "We lost the Aston Rowant case," she said. "A really dirty bit of business. But they're reopening the inquiry on the Winchester Bypass—did you hear? Wretched road, going through the best bit of downland. It's a scandal. I couldn't be in conservation all the time—I'd cut my throat."

Michael Fitzpatrick, who had been scrupulously attentive to his partners at table—offering to revisit the sideboard on their behalf, or pass the condiments—was exhibiting some behavior exquisite and rare as the guests lingered on over the cheese board. Sitting upright in his chair, with his napkin never slipping from his knee, and seeming to listen to the conversation—even uttering little humming-and-agreeing sounds from time to time, as if to say "Do please go on"—he contrived to refresh himself with a little nap. At length, the group rose flutteringly and came to rest once more in the drawing room, and almost immediately it was the hour for the housekeeper to arrive with the trays of afternoon tea. The wet gray Sunday damped down the garden beyond the window seats and cocooned the occupants of the room in early dusk. Big logs burned in the fireplace, warming the air until it filled with the scent from great bouquets of roses of old varieties, yellow and blood red. People perched on the arms of square old armchairs or sank into their depths; others lolled on the floor; and one guest sat down on the bench of the grand piano, then leaned forward to peer at the notes of Hungarian dances in a book of music open on the stand. Still others, chatting, holding cups and saucers, snoozing, or reading one of a stack of national newspapers, lined the cushions of big, pale sofas. Creaturely, organic objects, these sofas: hosts to clinging burrs brought in from outdoors; accented by muddy paw prints; and vaguely sagging about the undercarriage, like Jersey cows. One of the heads in the room was bent over a book of ichthyology—one of thousands of books (on insects, Rothschilds, horses, birds and many other things) that covered two of the room's walls from ceiling to floor. "It's a terrible thing to have a room with no books," Miriam Rothschild said. "There are about fifteen thousand books in this house. I can't bear the thought of anyone fiddling with them. They're my friends." A pair of heads—one of them the eccentric poet's—were bent over a chessboard. Other guests played with a rosy baby or with the only one of the dogs to have been admitted, as being the most likely not to bite anyone.

Miriam Rothschild, still wearing the green kerchief, stood

leaning back against the tea table with a piece of cake in one hand. She and Kate Garton were reminiscing about the International Flea Conference that had been held at Ashton Wold ten years before.

"Ninety flea people. With wives who had to be entertained with coach trips—that part was the worst," Miriam Rothschild said.

"Then we had tea for four hundred on the polo ground," Kate Garton said.

"And dinner for three hundred out here," Miriam Rothschild said, waving vaguely out at the mist beyond the window.

"Remember that pop group and your pot plants?"

Miriam Rothschild roared. "I was doing a very serious scientific experiment with some marijuana plants. Those chaps went straight to 'em. Noses like truffle hounds!"

A famous jazz musician—a keen polo player—was a house guest at Ashton Wold at the time of the Flea Conference; he would have performed for the assembly had he not got drunk. (Miriam Rothschild's youngest sister, the Baroness de Koenigswarter, is widely known as a jazz patron, and was a close friend of Thelonious Monk.)

"People were supposed to have breakfast at the pub, but the landlord overslept," Miriam Rothschild recalled. "We had a meal going in the marquee, perpetually. Cooked a whole sheep."

"There was the elevenses party on the green," Kate Garton said, looking dreamy. "Scones. Walnut cake. Shortbread. *Gâteau.* But I shall never forgive myself about that big copper pan that disappeared, as long as I live. I should never have used it to put those strawberries in."

"I had more energy in those days," Miriam Rothschild said, still laughing. "It was quite fun while it lasted."

Later, over a Sunday supper of soup and cold lamb, we were a much depleted group. Miriam Rothschild had doffed her kerchief, revealing white hair swept up in a neat but unpremeditated style. "I'm totally unself-conscious, always," she once said to me. "Even as a young woman, I was like that. When I was about eight, I remember going to my mother and saying, 'Nellie'—she was one of the maids—'says I'm pretty. I don't know what that means.' " This evening, she was hooting with laughter in the light of candles as she regaled Michael Fitzpatrick, Kate Garton, and me with old stories about her former husband, Captain Lane. (She remains on good terms with him, and he often visits her at Ashton Wold.) Recalling his unfortunate habit of knocking men down in night clubs, she was in the midst of a dramatic, blow-by-blow account of a contest between him and a chap at Mirabelle—a former prizefighter, at that—when the telephone rang.

"*Allô! Allô!*" she barked at the instrument. "*Qui est ça? Ah, Jacqueline! C'est toi! Tu as reçu ma lettre?*"

She speaks fluent French, but pronounces it with an uncompromisingly upper-class English accent, like Winston Churchill or the Queen. A table by the window of the drawing room held vases of wildflowers and an array of recently published books on art, science, and poetry, in English and in French. With the departure of most of the weekend's guests, the shelties had been set free from their annex and restored to pride of place. "I like my dogs rather better than my friends," Miriam Rothschild sometimes says. As she settled by the fireside after dinner—head back, legs comfortably apart, forearms stretched along the arms of a big old chair—the pack settled around her feet, looking like brown-and-white fur rugs, and squabbled and snapped at each other in a contest for her lap. In the next armchair, Kate Garton (who had had a very busy weekend) rubbed her eyes with a fist for a time, then curled up like a dormouse in another chair and fell sound asleep. Over on the sofa, Michael Fitzpatrick performed a small charade of interest in his newspaper, then let his lids fall, too, resuming his little humming-and-listening sounds. Some lilacs in a Stanley Spencer painting nodded from the chimney breast.

"I've never been a *collector*," Miriam Rothschild said when

I asked her about the art in her house. "I've just bought things I liked. All the really good things I bought when I was young. You won't buy anything good after you're thirty."

I said I supposed one's tastes became more fixed.

"It isn't taste. It's hormones."

When I asked whether she had commissioned the flea, painted by Graham Sutherland, that was hanging in the downstairs loo, she said she had not. "But did you see the Stanley Spencer nettles in the dining room? I commissioned those. The loaf of bread in there is Avigdor Arikha. The cheese is his as well. His father died in a Nazi death march. My cousin Alix helped Avigdor."

From the direction of the sofa the humming-and-listening could be heard to tilt toward snoring—polite but distinct.

"This new book I'm doing is all about butterflies and doves in art," she said. "The idea is that doves are a symbol of the spirit and butterflies of the soul. I've written a chapter on Nabokov. I'm a great admirer of his. I went to lunch at All Souls and sat next to a man who was a professor of comparative religion. He gave me a reading list. And I plowed through the works of Jung. I'm extremely interested in the concept of the soul. But I don't believe in God. Oh, no. I'm an atheist. I think it's immoral to believe in God."

"Michael!" she bellowed suddenly, abruptly silencing the snoring that had been quite like the cooing of a dove. On her knee, the dog whose flank she had been stroking snapped up its head and twitched its ears. "Wake up, Michael! I'm sure *you* think it's immoral to believe in God!"

He blinked in the lamplight and half pretended to have been listening all along. Then, like the parfit gentil knight, he set off in defense of Faith. "I don't mean an old man with a white beard and plus fours," he said. "Nothing like that, of course."

"Just think of wards stuffed full of babies with AIDS," Miriam Rothschild said indignantly.

A log burned through in the fireplace and fell away from its neighbor with a little crunch. Michael Fitzpatrick did his best to expound the problem of pain, using man-eating sharks as his example. Kate Garton slept obliviously on.

Miriam Rothschild let out a snort. "In a world that was properly managed, sharks *wouldn't* go about eating people. God does a lousy job, that's all I can say. No, within a short time I simply won't know anything. I don't think I have a soul. I don't think we understand natural history, but I don't think it's *divine*. What you can say is I believe implicitly in good will. I think everyone should be willing to help everyone else. Neither of my parents was religious, but no two people ever emanated more good will. My parents and my grandparents were motivated by very high ideals. It wasn't spoken of that way, but, looking back, I can see they had *very* high ideals. I can remember asking my mother 'Is it good to be ambitious?' and her saying 'The only thing worth having ambition about is moral standards.' These things were drummed into me as a child."

Sensing danger past, Michael Fitzpatrick was drifting back into the kingdom of dreams. (Like Kate Garton, he was to leave Ashton at the crack of dawn the next day.) "Poor Michael," Miriam Rothschild said affectionately. "He's had rather a difficult evening—George Lane's misbehavior and the immorality of God!"

She went on, "All my books were written as acts of service. The great thing is a life of contribution—to bring some grist to the mill." She is scrupulous in acknowledging collaborators on scientific projects, whether the collaborator is a Nobel laureate, a gardener, or her son as a boy of eight. But her most recent writing, whatever the ostensible subject, has been transfigured by bursts of the purely personal—remembered voices and visions from a childhood that was like a fairy tale: the palatial houses stuffed with mysteries and treasures; the grandfather who liked to shower gold half-sovereigns from his carriage; the brilliant, dotty uncle with his cassowaries and his white top hat; and the terrible darkening when she was fifteen and her father, who was subject to chronic depressions as a result of encephalitis, took his own life.

"How many times have you read Proust?" I asked her now, beside the embers of the fire.

"I'd hate to tell you!" she said. "My mother loved *A la recherche du temps perdu* as well. I can remember when I was a child seeing her come running down the corridor saying 'I have just finished the most marvellous book!' And I remember a French governess I had—Mademoiselle Bize—reading Proust aloud to me while I was drawing some starfish, during the summer I was seventeen. We read it from cover to cover that year. I must have read it twenty times since then."

BY TEATIME the next day, the cabbage-white butterflies inside the old Edwardian greenhouse were in a dispirited mood: a hundred sets of white wings beat against the green netting of their cage or settled wearily on some orange and purple flowers in a jar. (Earlier, the chauffeur had fetched the colony in a shoebox from the house of a Cambridge professor, leaving in exchange a couple of bottles of Rothschild claret.) Miriam Rothschild folded her notebook and, closing the door carefully behind her, ambled off down the garden path. Long beds radiating from the sundial in the old vegetable gardens now held rows of campion, sweet rocket, forget-me-not, and self-heal. A vixen (infuriating to the gardeners) was raising her cubs within the protection of the gardens' sheltering walls. A greenhouse that once held orchids was now home to an extended family of tame palomino-colored rabbits, which rose on their haunches, woffling ears and whiskers at her as she passed by.

"Pamela?" she said, coming to the last in a row of greenhouses and stopping outside its door. "Where are you, Pamela? Ah, there you are!" From a branch high under a canopy of ivy, a tawny owl blinked down at her with enormous eyes.

"Toowit, toowit, chkk-chkk-chkk," the bird said, opening and closing its curved bill.

"Oh Pammie, Pammie, Pammie dear," Miriam Rothschild said in a low, melodic private chant, lifting a face full of love. "Pammie dear, have you been fed?"

The dogs had killed a wild baby rabbit and had laid its small, warm, bloody body under the table that was set with the tea things, back in the drawing room. Miriam Rothschild lifted a domed silver cover and looked down at the contents of a plate. "I absolutely love burned toast," she said. Wordlessly, her sister Liberty Rothschild came in, sat down and played some passages on the piano with great finesse, then picked up a cup of tea and drifted out. A schizophrenic, she lives in one of the wings of Ashton Wold together with a companion, who is a nun. "She was the most gifted of us all," Miriam Rothschild said. "I think lunatics should be allowed to live at home, as part of your community. She really doesn't bother me at all. Oh, sometimes she'll do frightfully annoying things, like letting my butterflies out. Says they should be free. Once, we were all at a dinner and she was bored with the conversation. She didn't know that's what it was, but she was *bored*. So she got an orchid out of the middle of the table and ate it. Munched her way through it. *Very* slowly. Ha! That stopped us in our tracks!"

Miriam Rothschild had been talking all day, on and off, about the years up to and during the Second World War. "I don't believe in God," she had said that morning, plumping herself down on the sofa and resuming the previous evening's conversation as if no time had intervened. "But I believe very strongly in belonging to the Jewish community. I don't mind who I say I'm Jewish to. During the whole of the thirties, one was totally informed about the Nazi persecution of the Jews, and about thousands of people, some of whom one knew personally, who were being expelled from their country and not allowed into this. Prime Minister Baldwin did one thing for these refugees—he allowed children under eighteen to come, provided they had a sponsor. I formed a committee of my contemporaries—people under thirty—to place them and help them once they were here. I had forty-nine children at

Ashton, and the whole family sponsored many more. I took first come, no discussion. A woman appeared with three children—they were evacuees from the London blitz—and it turned out she was the wife of the best viola player of the day, and the children were musical geniuses. That added greatly to the pleasure of those days. But, no matter what you did, you couldn't get over the tragic circumstances. Among these refugee kids we had three suicides. That'll give you an idea. I learned that my address was being touted in the Frankfurt ghetto as someone who would help. The man in the street in Britain was responsive to the Baldwin scheme, but the Foreign Office and the Home Office behaved extremely badly. The late Sir John Foster, the barrister—a great friend and adviser of mine, I miss him very much—did battle with the authorities when he took up the cause of the Jewish refugees. This was the most stressful time in my life. It permanently injured and scarred me. No one sane could have been close and not been scarred. From the Pope to the gutter press, it was the greatest failure of the human race, the greatest tragedy of our age. Nothing again could matter on that scale."

Her husband's whole family was annihilated; her aunts and uncles on the Continent suffered hideous deprivation or met brutal ends. "My cousin Alix was a refugee, and her mother-in-law took her own life when the Gestapo knocked on the door. But Alix was never as bitter about it all as I was." Miriam Rothschild and Foster initiated a movement, on behalf of the survivors of the extermination camps, to prevent the victorious Allied armies from liberating the "unfortunate remnants" without first giving them time to recover something of their physical strength and their dignity. "We were able to get Churchill on our side," she said. And the pair fought again to cut through the thicket of government red tape that prevented Jews from residing in Britain after the war or taking possession of any property there until they had satisfied the authorities that they had really been "deprived of their personal liberty." She was particularly incensed by the case of a certain count, whose hairdresser had saved him from the Gestapo by hiding him in a cupboard for two years but who was said not to have been deprived of his liberty, because he had hidden voluntarily. "I thought the whole thing was bloody-minded. The late Sir John Foster thought it was a disgrace," she said, heaving a great sigh. "The trouble, the difficulty, the heartbreak of that time, the incredible stresses and strains. Nothing can ever compare."

NOW DUSK came rolling over land and garden at Ashton Wold to curl around the house. Mist pressed damply fragrant at the long mullioned windows and cast the room in shadows of gray-green.

"Sometimes one has to seek out people with power, but I've never been remotely interested in having it," Miriam Rothschild was saying. The day's stack of newspapers had gone untouched. "My mother read four newspapers every day, in different languages. But my mother was a political animal, which I never was. And the late Sir John Foster could get more out of a newspaper than anyone else I've ever known. I can just see him now, sitting reading in that armchair, with the papers all round him on the floor." In the same spirit of time management in which she took up her uniform of kerchief and dress, she gets her news chiefly from the BBC World Service, in the middle of the night. "Professor Ford, one of the cleverest men at Oxford, *never* read the newspapers," she said. She has known a fair proportion of the century's cleverest men—what she calls "the Great Brains." "J. B. S. Haldane was one of those people with a terrific memory, unbelievably brilliant; I *adored* his company when I was young. Isaiah, of course—Sir Isaiah Berlin—is probably the best brain alive." Although she is by now opposed to marriage and is enough of a feminist to have been thrown out of a hotel in Devon for urging its chambermaids to strike, she still calls her children "by far my greatest achievement," and believes that the difference between men and women is that men tend to think big while women tend to think small.

"I'm a good example of thinking small," she said. "My scientific work is all bits and pieces that may or may not add up to something. I've never had a master plan. Proust, for example, was a person who thought big. I only saw the end of the drawing room. For a few minutes." She crossed the drawing room now to open the door to the garden and let out her dogs. From the topmost branch of a cherry tree a song thrush was sounding in the soft green semidark. "During the war, we used to say the thrushes sang the names of Allied battles in North Africa. 'Tobruk, Tobruk . . . Sidi Barrani, Sidi Barrani.' Can you hear?" She stood with her hand on the doorknob, listening and looking out. One of the dogs woof-woofed in the woods some way off.

Not long ago, Miriam Rothschild wrote a memoir of Foster and read it at a testimonial dinner. It touched on his great career, his love of food and laughter, his affection for Americans and women, and his sense, at the end of his life, that he might have failed. "That's the thing about being a Great Brain," she told me. "He wanted to alter the face of the world. He thought you could *force* people to have common sense, but you can't. That's just the difference, you see. He thought big."

1987

STONES OF HIS HOUSE

*E*VEN THE most ordinary life is a mystery if you look close enough. But the life of the English novelist Paul Scott, ordinary enough in many ways, turns out on close inspection to be very mysterious indeed. A superb biography of him by Hilary Spurling answers some of the questions that cling to his solid, serviceable, very English name, while leaving much that is unfathomable. Scott died in 1978, just short of his fifty-eighth birthday, apparently at the height of his creative powers. He was in his mid-forties, and had produced eight mediocre and largely unsuccessful novels, when, having told his publisher that he wanted to write a "really big book," he withdrew from the world for his artistic do-or-die. He disappeared into the back bedroom of his very modest house in Hampstead Garden Suburb and emerged from solitary confinement a decade later aged and broken but having produced a masterpiece, *The Raj Quartet*.

Since his days as a young Army officer in India during and just after the Second World War, Scott's imagination had been fixed on the subcontinent and on the dying days of the British Raj. He once said that for him India was the metaphor that every successful writer needs to find; India was the metaphor that had "chosen" him. He knew intuitively that the turning point of lost empire—the years just prior to Indian independence, in 1947—held some clue to Britain's present and could be for him the way into his own truth. All the earlier years of brooding and mulling and trying to write good books had yielded up their harvest at last: almost a million words, published between 1966 and 1975 in successive volumes, entitled *The Jewel in the Crown*, *The Day of the Scorpion*, *The Towers of Silence*, and *A Division of the Spoils*. For Scott's wife, Penny, to whom he had been faithfully married since 1941 and with whom he had two daughters, the end of the great project came too late. She had lived with him in the modest little house—by the end, not so much sharing it as serving side by side with him in her own solitary confinement, and acting, at his behest, as his jailer and keeping the world at bay. The four novels proved scarcely more successful than any of the eight previous ones, and their author was almost broke. In 1976, Penny left him: taking nothing but her handbag, she shut the front door behind her and walked away.

By 1977, Scott was too ill to receive in person the Booker Prize, for his final, and best-selling, novel, *Staying On*. This was a short book, set in contemporary India, and it formed a sort of minor-key coda to the luminous and magisterial *Quartet*. It is the story of Colonel Tusker Smalley and his wife, Lucy—an elderly English couple living out beleaguered lives in a fast-changing India, which the rest of the Raj has long since left behind. The Smalleys are in a doomed yet plucky skirmish against poverty, loneliness, and death and against the fat, nouveau-riche, rapacious Indian woman who, as their landlord, now holds power over them.

Prizes often alight on a writer's lesser work when the greater work is in the past, but the members of the Booker jury were clearly not the only British readers to prefer the

shorter book. Many English people in the 1970s felt beleaguered themselves. And the tale of Lucy and Tusker, although deeply shadowed, is told with those popular English
literary values irony and charm. In the new, uneasily multira-
cial, postcolonial Britain, it could amuse readers with some
racial types that came close to the head-wagging Indians with
absurd accents caricatured in the fifties by Peter Sellers.
Whatever the reason, it was *Staying On* that gained Scott
recognition before he died. But—strangely, in the case of a
writer who was one of the great literary stylists of his generation—it was television that made Scott's posthumous international name. Granada Television's adaptation of *Staying On*,
with fine performances by the aging team of Celia Johnson
and Trevor Howard, appeared in 1980, and its passionate,
elegant version of *The Raj Quartet*—called *The Jewel in the
Crown*, after the first volume—mesmerized the British for
fourteen weeks in 1984 and American viewers of PBS a year
later.

O N   B O T H   S I D E S of the Atlantic, a discerning few discovered *The Raj Quartet* as its separate volumes were coming
out. (Heinemann published it in England, William Morrow
here. The late John Willey, at Morrow, was particularly loyal,
making sure his author had enough money to keep going.) I
cannot count myself among the pre-television Scott fans, but
I'm certain they read each volume as if spellbound, estab-
lishing an intense relationship with the man who had drawn
them into such an astonishingly convincing world. I'm certain
that's what happened to them because it's what happened to
me when I read all four books, one after another, not long ago.
Even after seeing the television series twice, I read in an undi-
minished hungry daze. The real people and events I encountered during those few weeks seemed to me simply like parts
of Scott's world. And though I read right on the jacket that
Scott was dead, I had an impulse, as I shut the last volume, to
write the man a letter—to reach out to him, get to know him

somehow. He had poured prodigious amounts of imagination, skill, and wisdom into his work, but somehow I wanted him to give me *more*.

I read *The Raj Quartet* at what was for me the perfect time. I had been spending some months in England, during what proved to be the final days of Margaret Thatcher's premiership, which so often felt more like a reign. Everywhere, I had seen the old English culture I grew up in creaking and straining, going through radical change. It was being replaced by something newer, rougher-edged, unformed, or by some touristic, "nostalgic" self-conscious version of its former self. It felt oddly as if England, having lost its empire in one generation, were now its own last colony—a sort of culture-in-exile within its own shores.

When Scott began to write his complex saga of British India—to bring to life Daphne Manners, Hari Kumar, Barbie Batchelor, Ronald Merrick, Lady Chatterjee, and the Layton girls—the Raj was seen in England as vaguely embarrassing, as something of a joke. There was a reluctance, amounting to a taboo, about looking seriously at the events of 1947 or their long-term consequences. Doggedly, Scott drew back the veil and revealed layer upon layer of a whole political and historical moment, a rich social world. He took great pains over the details of life of district commissioners, governors' A.D.C.'s, Englishmen of the Indian Army or the Indian Police, captains and colonels of pukka regiments like the "Pankot Rifles" and the "Muzzy Guides" as they did their jobs of governing a nation and fighting a war. "I tend to write about people in relation to their work, which strikes me as a subject no less important than that of their private lives," Scott once wrote. He himself was a tremendous worker. He was also a formidable psychologist, as he showed by adding, "Because their work is so often affected by their sense of personal deprivation."

Far from being some crusty Tusker Smalley type giving the regimental silver a nostalgic rub, Scott was a lifelong liberal, and as his years of thinking about the British role in

India wore on he had increasing doubts about it. In the end, he came to see something "greasy and evasive" about the way the Raj pulled out unscathed from an India torn by murderous riots, after three centuries of commercial exploitation that was always billed by the British as a God-given duty and a sacred trust. Through the character of Ronald Merrick, the ruthlessly ambitious and sadistic policeman and Army officer, Scott showed the racist underside of the vaunted British system of law and order—a side that surfaces uncomfortably often in Britain today. He showed the British cynically imprisoning distinguished Indian politicians until the order came from "home" to turn the country over to those same men. He showed the shameful breaking of the spirit of Hari Kumar, the hapless hybrid—a man educated at public school in England, then cast out into a no-man's-land of race and class, with his upper-class English accent, which infuriates the originally lower-middle-class Merrick, and his dark-skinned face, which in an Indian crowd makes him invisible even to the Englishman who had once been his best friend.

Silhouetting such brilliantly developed characters against a distant place and a past time helped Scott get at truths about the British which he could never have seen so clearly about the British of his own day. "You write for an age, and this is my age," he once said. The age had not yet come when a man as thoroughly English as Scott could write a truthful novel about racism in an English setting, and the age had probably passed when such a man could write, as he did, in realist style (without rage or ribaldry, like his peers the Angry Young Men), about the whole range of class prejudice at home. Scott was profoundly aware of the subtleties of class, as the British are still. The working-class or lower-middle-class backgrounds of Mrs. Thatcher and her male protégés, as well as of the new Archbishop of Canterbury, were and are of the greatest interest. Indeed, in her expediency, her willingness to do the political dirty work that her "wet" Old Etonian colleagues were too gentlemanly to stomach, Margaret Thatcher had a lot in common with Ronald Merrick.

Mrs. Spurling is splendidly specific about Scott's childhood, between the wars, in the newly developed North London suburbs of Southgate and Palmers Green, with their social pretensions, their streets of semidetached houses with "pocket-sized shrubberies at the front . . . bow windows with decorative stained-glass strips opening on to long, narrow gardens at the back, and . . . tradesmen's doors at the side." They were neighborhoods "full of people moving up from one class to another," and committed to toeing and enforcing the social line. India became an obsession with Scott, the key to his expression, but this childhood world was his heartland—the place where he absorbed the dictionary of snobbery and acquired his knowledge of accent, snub, and cut. For him, the codes of British India—the hierarchy of club, cantonment, and regimental mess—were really just the pecking order of Palmers Green writ large. In a way, as Scott and his English readers well knew, *The Raj Quartet* never leaves home. Its author barely did. Aside from his three years in India (in the unglamorous, administrative branch of the Army, doing the paperwork of supply), he rarely got out of London. In his lifetime's handful of addresses, he never moved more than a few miles from the modest house where, in 1920, in another suburban bedroom, his mother brought him into the world.

SCOTT'S MOTHER, Frances, was a lively, dashing woman who had escaped her background first by rising to a job as cashier in a drapery shop and then by marrying, at the age of thirty, a forty-six-year-old fashion illustrator called Tom Scott. Frances came from a large, poor Victorian family, and opportunities for girls like her were almost nonexistent. Her sister Ruth took the more predictable course of domestic service; after cooking most of her life for a family, and living in a single room in Brixton Hill, she would die (in 1971) alone and penniless in a poky council flat. For Frances, Tom was a catch. In partnership with his unmarried sisters, he maintained a studio in a large Edwardian house called Wyphurst, in South-gate High Street. Even after he had married and was living, with his wife and two small sons (Paul's brother, Peter, was two years older), in a house a half mile off, Tom spent most of his time with his elderly sisters, Florrie and Laura, at Wyp-hurst, which was sacred to his work. Paul was working class on his mother's side, middle class on his father's, and he was sent to a private school to absorb the code of cricket, King, and empire, and become a gentleman. In a very English way, he felt he was a displaced person; Hari Kumar was only one of a line of half-castes and hybrids who haunted Scott's fiction from the start.

Frances had ferocious will and energy, and she focussed it on her gifted younger son. "He bore the full brunt," Mrs. Spurling says, "of her dreams, ambitions, and plans." She could be tyrannical or seductive; she had a habit of storming out on her husband and sons when she was thwarted, and staying away for weeks. "Before her marriage, she used to hide in a cupboard and write novels," Scott wrote of his mother, from whom he was implacably estranged for most of her old age. "On the night before her wedding . . . she destroyed her manuscripts but always remembered the title of her favourite: The Keepsake. I have often wondered whether it was any good; or whether it ever actually existed. She had a vivid imagination." Even as a little boy, he was tuned in to her emotional hunger; he learned early on to shield himself from it by switching off his feelings—shutting down. She called this "sulking," or, later, when he was old enough to smoke, comb his hair like Noël Coward, and write risqué one-act plays, or romantic verse in the style of Rupert Brooke, "listening to his Muse."

Frances was, her son's biographer observes, the forerunner of a "line of lonely, vulnerable, insecure wives" in his novels—"women whose energies have found no outlet and whose talents run slowly to waste." Most of the drama of Paul Scott's life took place within the four walls of his house or inside his head. Mrs. Spurling, who is the author of a biog-

raphy of Ivy Compton-Burnett and is married to a writer, has
a feel for complicated creative people with their slippers on,
at home. She knows that hidden domestic struggles between
men, women, and children can be as lethal for the partici-
pants as great national battles or revolutions. In many ways,
this biography reads like a novel—something in the style of
those stories by Saki in which among the very proper shrubberies and windows open to the lawn something spooky is
going on. It seems right—part of the texture of the Paul Scott
tale—that it should be brought to light by a woman. The million words of the *Quartet*, the nine other novels, the poems
and plays—all this outpouring by Scott is somehow book-
ended by the secret, shadow manuscripts of his mother and
his wife. Penny Scott fared better than her mother-in-law:
she actually published several novels. But she was also
silenced as time and her marriage wore on, and her later
books failed to find a publisher. In the minutely printed footnote listing sources, Mrs. Spurling cites one of these unpublished manuscripts of Penny's—the poignantly entitled "My
Story"—and, together with those novels Frances claimed to
have scribbled, crouching in what was no doubt the only private space in her family's crowded house, it haunts the man's
life story like a stillborn ghost.

In his maturity, Scott's work demonstrates an empathy for
the feminine which is rare in male writers, and especially in
one of his generation. Beside the male characters of the
Quartet—men effecting decisions of state, men fighting wars,
men at work—is an extraordinary range of women characters: young and old, bright and foolish, married and unmarried, rich and poor, beautiful and plain. Many of the
viewpoints between which the narrative shifts with great
virtuosity are the viewpoints of women. The rape victim,
Daphne Manners, tells her own story through her journal;
the elder Layton daughter, Sarah, the insider who is also an
outsider, becomes a more and more visible and perceptive
narrator as the story unfolds. Scott's exploration of female
experience—marriage, maternity, loss of virginity, abortion,

relationships between two sisters, dutiful self-sacrifice to the family—is utterly believable. The large events are often seen through the eyes of the powerless and the marginalized, and Scott gives them their full humanity. Parallel to the great, dark spiritual journey of the villainous (yet in the end not unsympathetic) Merrick is the great, light-filled Calvary of poor Barbie Batchelor, the retired mission-school teacher. No angle of Scott's novelistic prism more clearly shows the breakdown of the Raj than the story of the plain, penurious elderly spinster cast out to die by a society too far gone to take care of even the most vulnerable of its own. The most vulnerable but also the most visionary. To the prattly old Barbie (who, by Scott's account, "ran away with" the third volume), with her Cockney vowels, her little shifts and stratagems, her constant humiliations, and her reckless courage, Scott gives the grandest view—the Augustinian struggle with faith, the prescient dreams, the passage through the scrim of day-to-day life to a deeper than personal truth.

IF YOU LISTEN carefully to Mrs. Spurling's story, you can detect early the fatal sound of a closing down, of a very slowly progressing entombment of Paul Scott the man. "The novelist destroys the house of his life and uses its stones to build the house of his novel," the biographer notes on her title page, quoting Milan Kundera. In Scott's youth, the sound is a faint, Chekhovian *crump*; in his middle age, a string of bangs and slams. When Paul was in his early teens, his father's income dried up, and Tom Scott was obliged to combine his two families under the Wyphurst roof, much to everyone's discomfort. Paul was left with a lifelong horror of rows and emotional exchanges and with a terror, when he was himself a husband and father, of not being able to pay the bills. At fourteen, to his profound shock, he was obliged to leave school and go out to work as a trainee accountant. He worked all day, took courses at night, and began to write. "I grew early into the habit of having no leisure," he said. He became fascinated

by the Wildean theme of the face in the mirror, by the double
self, Jekyll and Hyde. He had a love affair with an older
man—a theatre-and-ballet-going estate agent from Streat-
ham. The budding poet wrote love verses to his mentor; "It
Never Happened," one of them was called.

Along came the war, and Paul was called up. Wyphurst
was lost in the blitz, and Florrie and Laura along with it. The
young man was happy enough with barracks life until a
sadistic superior officer demoted him, threatening to expose
his homosexuality. This crushing experience gave rise twenty-
five years later to the character of Merrick, whose abuse of
power is closely linked to his own secret homosexuality. At
the time, young Paul was beside himself; he might have
broken down completely if he hadn't known to dull his psychic pain with gin. He went on a ten-day bender, from which
he emerged with a determination to take "the normal road,"
as a resolutely heterosexual man. A nursing sister called
Penny Avery crossed his path in Torquay. Right away, he
told her that he intended to marry her. The couple entered
the magic circle on the dance floor and, to the tune of "In the
Mood," fell in step. Penny had been a motherless and unloved
child, and she sensed that Paul was somehow split and damaged. (She seems to have known nothing of his recent trauma
with the officer, or, indeed—until the publication of this
biography—of his homosexuality.) In the old, old female
story, Penny embarked on the old, old course: trying to mend
a wounded man in an attempt to heal the hurt little girl from
her past.

Frances had been complacent about the man from Streat-
ham, but she was livid when, in 1941, after just a few months
of courtship, Penny and Paul were wed. The years in
"metaphorical" India followed, separating Paul and his bride.
(Penny came to feel jealous of India, seeing the separation as
lasting not just for the duration of the war but for the rest of
their lives.) For him, India was a second birth. Wide sky,
huge land, teeming characters; an active, necessary life. Forever, this would be his great moment—the open, unimpris-

oned time. Then he was back home, and the young Mr. and
Mrs. Scott were setting up house in Southgate, calling each
other Honey Boy and Honey Girl. She made her own curtains; he went off down the front-garden path each day with
his briefcase to his job as an accountant in a publishing house.
At home, Penny pushed the big double pram with Carol and
Sally, her two girl babies, born in 1947 and 1948. Although in
"My Story" she was to write of feeling lonely, this was
probably *her* great moment, her open sky.

All through the 1950s, Paul set off every morning like the
rest of the suburban men. By now, he was more substantially
employed, as a literary agent with David Higham. Scott was
conscientious, hardworking, and sociable. His administrative
and financial competence, together with his knack of soothing ruffled egos, made him very good at his job. His clients
adored him and called him a "prince." In his spare time,
he methodically turned out novels and plays. "Mondays,
Wednesdays and Fridays: two hours in the evening; Saturday
mornings, 9.30 to lunchtime. Sundays: either morning or
afternoon; or both if the mood's right." His work habits
impressed his fellow-writers or appalled them. "Bleak and
self-denying," one friend said. His two little girls grew up
rarely seeing Daddy, knowing not to disturb him at work.
They lived for the windows that opened sporadically onto a
loving, playful, giving man: Christmas, the annual fortnight
by the seaside, Guy Fawkes Night.

The kitchen was Penny's domain. It had yellow walls, a
cheerful fire, a tribe of cats, geraniums on the sill. Paul would
walk right through it, passing his wife and girls sewing or
making cakes at the big old table, and mount the stairs to his
chilly, lonely cell. It had a single small window, an austere
schoolboy desk, two bookcases, and a portrait of him as a
handsome young lieutenant, painted by an Army pal. He
needed to know Penny was in the house. She was fiercely
loyal, indignant about his detractors always. He had to write.
"I had a wife, two children, a large mortgage, and a horror of
ivory towers," he said. But that wasn't all. He was trying to

save his life. Each of the books except the first had an actual or attempted suicide in it; the task of writing to relieve his depression grew more Sisyphean with each passing year. He could be a great joker and raconteur, yet from his early youth he was, at heart, in mourning for his unlived life. "All his life, Paul filled his creative bucket at the well of depression," Mrs. Spurling says. An underlying sadness was the price he paid for defensively refusing to feel; for his unacceptable (and, in England at the time, illegal) sexuality and its burial under a false self; even for his magic time in India, where he contracted a chronic intestinal condition called amebiasis, which sapped his vitality until it was finally treated, in 1964. Writing gave him respite from imprisonment in all this. So, he thought, did booze. Drink helped him to live, feel, and write—until it turned on him and started helping him to die.

FRANCES WAS proud of her capacity for gin and taught Paul to drink it at the age of six. As a youth, he had a hollow leg. "Moody devil. Drinks like a fish and never shows it," a fellow-soldier said, trying to warn off Penny, but she was instantly hooked. Through booze, Paul had smothered the homosexual aesthete within him and activated the irresistible ladies' man. It was a Faustian compact, a dangerous "success." In his years as an agent, his clients came in for long, convivial lunches and often joined him for "a spot of Dog-and-Ducking," as he called a visit to his favorite pub. But he was never a social drinker. He drank to try to normalize himself, in an increasingly furtive, increasingly desperate attempt at self-medication. Feelings not useful to his literary obsessions he ruthlessly drowned. He depended on his wife—loved her, no doubt. Yet he seemed to hate her: sneering at her, not speaking for weeks on end, shutting her out. But then he had to jump-start his deadened heart to life again, to provide emotion for his work. "Writing is not observation—it is feeling," he once said.

"Sometimes fear I'll become an alcoholic," he confided in a

letter to a friend—years after his alcoholism had progressed enough to exact from him and his wife and daughters a frightful toll. "The awful thing is that at a certain stage my mind seems to go blank," he said, describing his benders, trying to get a handle on what alcohol was doing to his body and his brain. Something monstrous lay crouched in him, waiting to spring out. He would come home after a night of drinking not knowing what had happened or where he had been. In her yellow kitchen, by the dying fire, an anxious Penny would have waited up. She loosened his clothing, propped him up on pillows in the lamplight, lay for hours at his side, monitoring his breathing, after he passed out. She knew better than to mention any of this the next day. "The silence between them on these matters became unbreakable," Mrs. Spurling says. "Each time it was as if . . . 'It Never Happened.'" One night, he tried to poison himself with carbon monoxide, but the garage doors blew open in a sudden gust of wind. Another night, he crawled on all fours round his study, howling with self-hate; he lunged at his portrait with a dagger, and cut its throat.

People meeting him for the first time were often surprised by his unassuming style of dress—more like an accountant's or a provincial businessman's. "He was *so* gentle and *so* good," a woman who was a client said after his death. "He would have been so easy to look after and make happy." She was not the only one of their friends who tried to lay blame for his withdrawal on Penny, whom we see, in Mrs. Spurling's portrait, fluttering signals from her dark and lonely home that she was in urgent need of help. She began to fall sick, to have accidents in the garden and the house. Using her husband's cast-off typewriter and a pseudonym, she began to write novels herself. When he left Higham's to write full-time, in 1960, her hopes of seeing more of him and regaining her sweet old companion were swiftly dashed. His discipline more self-flagellating than ever, he became even more forbidding with her, more remote. From seven in the morning, he was immured in his room, staring at his inner world and working his way through his daily bottle of Carew's gin. By alchemy, he transmuted every bit of himself into his story— disappearing into each of his characters and lavishing on them a compassion so powerful it makes your hair stand on end.

His early novels, most of which he repudiated later on, turn out to be sodden with booze—filled with chronic, self-pitying alcoholics too sensitive to live in the world. It is more common for this tone to seep into the later works of writers who drink. Yet for almost the whole length of *The Raj Quartet* Scott's mortal obsession with the bottle is unde-tectable. The gin had burned right off his prose in an ether-ized moment that was, for him as a writer, a kind of grace. There was just Barbie, and Merrick, and what Scott called "the mystery of human behaviour," and disquieting spiritual truths. But in the Faustian compact time was running out. By the end of the final volume, something more self-serving, less transcendent, is creeping back. There is some prolixity in the style, something compensatory about the brilliance, as if the author were writing with a hangover, against the odds.

There is a photograph in this biography of Paul Scott in his back garden a year or so before the end. He seems like a dingy zoo animal in his patch of London sunshine that does not warm his bones. He looks bloated in the midriff and puffy in the face—robbed of all his dignity, somehow. His eyes are dead. Penny, by now in her early sixties, had also run out of rope; she had sought help from a center for battered women and was living on Social Security in a rented room in Swiss Cottage.

If I have any reservation about Mrs. Spurling's book, it is that she doesn't seem to understand that the disease of alco-holism did this to the Scotts. Her index lists "amebiasis" in the section on Paul's health, and "drinking habits" under "character and interests." She suggests that after the purge of his amebiasis, in a Paris clinic, he was no longer a sick man. It is true that a miasma seemed to lift for him then; even his prose style changed, opened up. But it was an illusory reprieve, whose effect was largely confined to his art. As an alcoholic who couldn't stop drinking, he was still committing suicide. The disease of alcoholism is as patient as a tiger; it will wait in hiding for its victims for years and years. Like most people of their place and generation, Paul and Penny Scott had no idea what was going wrong. Mrs. Spurling can see the tiger and trace its movements, but she is not willing to take away its power by giving it its name. This baffling disease even charms her sometimes. "Less apprehensive passengers [than his wife] reported Paul a brilliant driver when drunk: at the wheel, as at the typewriter, drink steadied his nerve and sharpened his concentration, enabling him to take risks," she writes, gaily. Strapped for cash at the finish, he ventured all the way to Tulsa to teach creative writing. Alone among acquaintances who, while adoring, were all brand-new, he was hospitalized with advanced cirrhosis and cancer of the colon spreading to the liver. He had no problem "managing without alcohol," Mrs. Spurling says of him in this period, as if the choice were casual and had been available all along. Even to the perceptive narrator of Scott's heartbreaking story, alcoholism presents itself with more disguises than a trickster: as amebiasis, as a lost sexuality, as the human condition, as—a favorite, this—great art. But, mercifully for the families, the artists, the people of our place and generation, we are beginning to see where alcoholism and life divide.

1991

VALENTINA

*T*HE STORY of Valentina, the Russian-born New York designer, is very strange. Even now, five years after her death at ninety in her grand but faded apartment overlooking the East River, she has an aura, somehow. Some essence lingers like a whiff of "My Own," the heady perfume she once launched. In her, the life force was very strong. She was abundantly creative and something of a witch. In her youth, she was beautiful and difficult; in middle age, she was striking and impossible; in old age, she was a hunchbacked holy terror. Many people loved her and hung in with her just the same. She was original in all she did and had enormous charm. She said that people were either flame or water and she was the latter; her moods were mercurial. The list of people she thought "idiots" and of things she found intolerable was long. She was famous for sending back her food in restaurants and tearing up the sheets in luxury hotels.

She was called "legendary" in the 1940s; in the thirties and

the fifties, her name was very well known. Along with Main-
bocher, she is arguably the only real couturier America has
produced—a more substantial artist than Charles James. She
demanded the highest standards from her fabrics, her fitters
and seamstresses, her clients. Once a woman came for a fitting
in a dress whose cuffs Valentina disapproved of; she snatched
up her shears and cut them off, leaving the woman close to
tears. She took a suit jacket of Ingrid Bergman's, turned it,
and tore out all the lining and pads. Her passion was all on the
surface, somehow—wrenching and ripping and tearing,
fighting life to get it right. But behind it was a place that feels
mysterious, harmonious, and calm. There's no mistaking the
serenity in her work. The slightly mad, *Fantasia*-like figure
in a turban, circling the air with giant scissors and shrieking heavily accented pronouncements, was just Valentina's
shadow self, another of her many feints and masks.

She was a true artist who happened to be living with great
astuteness at the heart of a very, very worldly world. "I real-
ized that she believes completely in her talent being god-given
& that it must be kept sacrosanct and not abused," Cecil
Beaton wrote in his diary in 1970, after a visit to her. All his
triumphs were in the past, by now, and so were hers. They
had known each other for decades, but something new was
revealed to him as he watched her expressive fingers packing
a gray chiffon dress—folding and touching the cloth and
arranging the tissue with attentiveness and love. The designer
Geoffrey Beene speaks of Valentina now with similar respect
and even awe. He admires the modernity, intellectualism, and
"monasticism" of her design, what he calls her "stillness at the
heart of the quickening city." You get the feeling that
Valentina could only have become Valentina in one place:
New York.

Her clientele was small. No more than two thousand
women wore her clothes, in all, between 1928 and 1957—the
years her house was in business. But those women were such
bright stars—appearing so often on the Broadway stage, in
the society columns of the newspapers, at El Morocco or the

Colony—that the designer's impact was considerable. The Gish sisters, Katharine Cornell, Lynn Fontanne, and Katharine Hepburn were among the many theatrical ladies who wore her clothes onstage and off. Legions of Astors, Vanderbilts, and Whitneys were her clients. The opera star Gladys Swarthout wore nothing but Valentina for many years of what the singer characterized as "happy simplicity." The designer made everything Mrs. Paul Mellon put on, even clothes she wore for gardening.

It was said that a Valentina dress was one in which a woman could fling her arms round a man's neck without spoiling the effect. Her clothes were always very comfortable. Sleeves and armholes were made for ease of movement; waistlines gave an illusion of slimness but did not bind. It is thought that she studied the bias-cut designs of Vionnet; she mastered the cutting of fabric off the grain, for the greatest grace and give. Her color sense was very refined. She liked beige, greige, gray, off-black, especially, as well as earth tones and occasionally red. "Always a leetle touch of color, angel," she would say in the eccentric Russian-English that served her too well for her to sort out the grammar, however long she lived in New York. She shopped in Europe for the most beautiful fabrics— usually solid-colored wool crêpes, silk jerseys or velvet, handkerchief linens, finely textured dobbies or jacquards. In the way she used fabric she was often compared to a sculptor. Some of her gowns drew inspiration from the Renaissance or classical Greece. They were very simple, or looked that way. She preferred loops of self-fabric to buttons, and avoided extraneous trim. "You want bows? You go Macy's!" she once said to Kitty Carlisle Hart.

She never copied anyone. "Be original, always!" she used to say. She was constantly on her guard against the copyists and spies from the manufacturers on Seventh Avenue. (Her staff once alienated Bobo and Winthrop Rockefeller, who made the mistake of walking into her showroom and asking to see some dresses without announcing themselves.) In truth, the way she cut and placed seams made making and fitting her

clothes a costly process, hard to duplicate. Her clothes, like
J. P. Morgan's proverbial yacht, were not for women who
asked their price; if they did, they couldn't afford them. She
almost never gave two women the same dress. She was
famous for giving her clients not what they had ordered, but
what she thought they should wear. She once made a green
dress for a woman who had ordered a red one. A particularly
voluptuous woman who had requested a sexy-looking dress
was horrified to discover that the designer had covered her
more closely than in a nun's habit. Yet she had such conquests
in the dress that she sent flowers to Valentina the morning
after she wore it. Valentina did not believe in fashion, she said,
but in dressing individual women according to their personalities and their bodies. She never imposed a shape that was
unnatural, and hated linings, paddings, corsets, and bras.
Although she sometimes made beautiful décolleté or backless
gowns, she never exposed the body in any way that looked
vulgar. Paulette Goddard once asked her for an eye-
catchingly bare dress to wear to the premiere of her latest
movie; she was determined to cause a scandal. "A scandal?"
said Valentina, looking thoughtful. "Very well. Let it be a
noble scandal, then."

LIKE CHANEL, who used to boast that she had invented
herself, Valentina was her own best model and a genius at
self-presentation. She understood performers, being one herself, in a way; the star of her own life. "I *am* theatre," she once
said. Few could play a better scene of arriving to take an ocean
liner and going up the gangplank surrounded by porters and
friends. For decades, she summered in Venice, perfecting the
tableau of standing on her balcony at the Gritti, overlooking
the Grand Canal. But from 1923, when she arrived in New
York with her husband, George Schlee, she was most
renowned for the entrances she would make at the opening
nights of the Metropolitan Opera or Broadway plays. Her
gowns may have been simple, but other things stood out. For a

long time, her trademarks were her turbans and the foot-long cigarette holder she used to wave about while talking to friends in the lobby. She would go up and down the aisles greeting acquaintances on either hand, then—just as the curtain was about to go up—take her seat and begin ostentatiously combing her eyelashes with a special platinum comb. In the late forties, when Valentina's fame and success were assured, George would look back with amusement on the early, attention-grabbing nights. "It was terrifying to be with her," he told a reporter. "At the theatre, she would be ahead of me. I would hear people say, 'Look at that crazy woman!' "

In her prime, she was either a beauty or a *belle laide*, depending on your point of view. She had a slender figure that seemed taller than it was, thanks to a beautiful carriage. There was always something dainty about her; she was very light on her feet. Her movements were dancerlike and sinuous. Her hands were in constant motion, her nails worn long and brightly lacquered. Her cheekbones were high and prominent; together with slightly upward-slanting eyes under dramatically arched brows, this gave her features a faintly exotic cast. To the end of her life, her face would twinkle with animation and humor or settle into an inscrutable repose. She was especially vain about her very thick, long, tawny-blond hair. "Green-gold," she said it was, once. She would brush it and brush it with a baby brush and arrange it in a thousand ways. In the twenties, her hair was so long that she would wear it like a muffler round her neck.

George Schlee was a very smart fellow who managed his wife and her business, and did it very well. The couple rose to wealth and social prominence, using her look and skills at commanding attention as the main stepping-stone. They got just the right amount of notices in the press: her name became famous, but she kept the mystique she needed for her psyche and to make her clientele seem like an exclusive club. "Cholly Knickerbocker" would note in his column that the Schlees had been at dinner at the Hearsts; or that Valentina was seen in a hood with a fur topknot; or that there had been one of the couple's famous celebrity-packed Russian Easter parties, with no guest "lower in rank than Cole Porter."

The fashion magazines would carry pages of Valentina wearing her new designs. She was photographed by all the great photographers, but she particularly liked Horst, the German who worked for *Vogue*. Not only was she the model, she controlled every detail of the sitting. Sometimes photographers would be permitted to capture George and Valentina at home alone, with the flowery Utrillos on the green walls and what the *Vogue* reporter called their "scarlet stools like exclamation points." They seemed a stylish couple, living in such luxury and with such zest. They were very much New Yorkers, at the beginning of the 1940s, but they were not, and would never be, exactly American. They look so intensely adult, these two, so bound together by a thousand common interests, as they sit with their cigarette holders, facing each other over the samovar and the backgammon board—a Slavo-European Nick and Nora, but with no sign of the movie couple's terrier, Asta. Nothing twitches or snuffles at the level of the "exclamation points." "I can't imagine Valentina with a dog or a cat or a child," says one woman who knew her well. "Or anything for which you had to be unselfish."

DECEMBER 1941 saw the bombing of Pearl Harbor and the release by MGM of *Two-Faced Woman*, starring the then thirty-six-year-old Greta Garbo. The movie flopped, and although no one knew it, it would be her last. The plot revolved round a bored husband whose frumpy-looking wife tries to rekindle the flame by impersonating her glamorous twin sister. Cardinal Spellman and the National League of Decency weighed in to condemn the film for its "immoral and un-Christian attitude toward marriage." For its December issue, *Harper's Bazaar* dispatched Louise Dahl-Wolfe and a reporter to record Valentina dressed for one of her (admittedly rare) evenings at home alone with George. She wore her

hair down and her face unpowdered, it seemed, and "a mauve
violet shirt, black wool stockings, black kid ballet slippers, and
a little underskirt of handkerchief linen."

All her days, Valentina's inner life was strangely indi-
visible from the outfits she wore. (She is said to have threatened to enter a convent in the years to come; but it is also said
that if Valentina had taken the veil, she would first have
redesigned it.) The underskirt was embroidered with angels'
heads and with a motto written in French. *"Jamais deux sans
toi,"* it read: "Never two without you." Valentina was always
quivering with foreboding and premonitions. She said she
had a vision of the blood of Revolution as an infant. Perhaps
the motto was a sign, or just sentimental, or an urbane accep-
tance of a new arrangement. For whether Valentina knew it
or not, she had embarked on the greatest drama of her life,
which would end only with the death of the last of the
players. She began sharing George with Greta Garbo.

THE GIRL from Kiev who was Valentina Nikolaevna
Sanina could never have become Madame Valentina, the legendary New York couturier, without George Schlee to
oversee each detail of the metamorphosis. The couple met,
according to the story they often told, on the railroad station
platform at Sebastopol, in the Crimea. The Revolution was at
its height, farther north; her brother and her mother had died.
She was a very beautiful young girl, standing all alone, with
the family jewels clutched in her pocket-handkerchief.

"Have you anyone to take care of you?" George asked of
the girl who (according to the legend) was a mere fourteen.
"It's a beautiful story," says Jane Gunther, who with her husband, the writer John Gunther, was close to the Schlees and
often heard them tell it. "I like to think it was true." At the
least, it seems likely that Valentina was not so very young.
Four different passports were found among her papers, and
her birth date is now supposed to have been 1899. Beyond
suggesting that she had escaped by running through the

woods in peasant clothes and that she had studied drama in Kharkov, Valentina never spoke about her life before George. In the new world, other émigrés would gossip about her origins; nobody knew her family or anything about it, and some suggested that she might be Jewish or even Polish. Her history is forever lost behind the smoke and mirrors. As the years wore on, she was more and more inclined to suggest that she had royal blood or that her mother had been a lady-in-waiting to the Czar. Once, she took the actor and play-wright Emlyn Williams by the hand and showed him a portrait of an imposing matron said to be her mother. As so many of her friends would do, Williams indulged Valentina. But he knew he was looking at the fin-de-siècle actress Eleanora Duse.

The columnists enjoyed referring to George as the "dean" and then the "elder statesman" of New York's White Russian set, but like his wife, he was not an aristocrat. Still, he brought with him qualities more useful to her in the new world than titles from a lost one. He had a wily, entrepreneurial mind that was a match for any of the émigrés who had to use their wits and snob appeal to make a living: Prince Serge Obolensky, who married an Astor and worked as a publicist for that family's hotels; Count Vladimir ("Vava") Adleberg, who had been a Grand Marshal to the Czar and now sold jewels for Harry Winston; and H.R.H. the Grand Duchess Marie, who made hats and wrote occasional articles for *Vogue*. George was born in 1896. When he met Valentina, he was an elegant, worldly-wise, charming young man with a sense of style. He'd already got a law degree from St. Petersburg and served as a member of the Duma. His family had long had roots in the Crimea, where his mother, Manya, ran a resort hotel patronized by Chaliapin and Bakst. He is said to have been the youngest general in the White army. He had some knowledge of life. "I was wise young," he would say. "I became silly later."

He was good at meeting people and putting them together, especially if they were famous. He protected people, too. He took responsibility for his widowed mother, sister, and small nephew, Igor Kamlukin, as well as Valentina. The family all left Russia in 1919. George knew that Valentina was a great fascinator when he took her on, and that she was a monumental complainer. Returning to his house, the day of the railroad station encounter, he found the servants in an uproar and Valentina screaming from her bath that the soap was wrong. "Even when she had nothing, she was a perfectionist," he said. As for Valentina, she said she had always levelled with George. "My husband wanted to marry me," she told the writer Hugo Vickers in 1984. "I said 'I can't give you love. I don't know how to love, but if you want friendship, then I'll marry you.' He said 'If you marry me, I'll look after you for the rest of your life.' Which he did, for twenty-two years."

After leaving Russia, the Schlees took the émigré trail in search of the means to earn a living: Constantinople, Athens, Rome, Berlin (where George started an opera company), and Paris, where Valentina is said to have worked as a variety performer in the Chauve Souris and George produced an émigré revue. This show travelled to New York, but proved to be too avant-garde for America. The couple stayed on, and sent for George's relatives. The elderly Valentina would look back happily on the early days in a modest flat in the West Nineties. There were a couple of false starts in the dressmaking business. The couple began to make themselves known around town. In 1926, the beautiful young "Valentina Sanina" sat for her portrait to the successful painter Abram Poole, the husband of the writer Mercedes de Acosta, now remembered largely for her lesbian liaisons with Dietrich and Garbo.

Valentina couldn't sew, but she designed her own clothes and they attracted attention. Where all the flappers were wearing chemises with waists round the bottom and skirts above the knee, she wore high-necked, long-sleeved black velvet gowns with ankle-high skirts that predated the styles of the thirties. (In later years, she would be ahead of the

crowd with such notions as snoods, hoods, boleros, opaque
stockings to match the shoes, pants-pleated skirts, inseam
skirt-pockets, layered clothes, and pillbox and coolie-style
hats.) One day in 1928, according to another of the legends
that attached themselves to Valentina—glitteringly symmet-
rical, like the Maltese crosses she liked to wear—she was discovered weeping over one of the failed ventures by a woman
who offered to introduce her to her husband, Eustace
Seligman, a wealthy lawyer. He was so impressed when
George and Valentina came to his house that evening that he
wrote out a check for $10,000 on the spot. Valentina Gowns,
Inc., started well; enough women wanted to look like the
young Mrs. Schlee for the business to bring in $90,000 in the
first year.

The Schlees made a point of cultivating those whose
wealth had survived the Crash—loading a touring Packard
with a steamer trunk of dresses and following their clients to
Lake Placid or Mount Desert Island, in the season. George
was clever with money, and he and Valentina also had the
knack of living, entertaining, and decorating their homes as
if they were richer than they were. By 1933, they had pros-
pered enough to buy a town house on East Seventy-eighth
Street. George's relations moved into a little upstairs apartment, and he set about creating grand reception rooms that
made rich friends and clients feel at home. The showroom
and workroom moved from Madison Avenue, where the
business started, to space in the Sherry Netherland on Fifth
Avenue. (In 1940, the business made its final move, to the
East Sixty-seventh Street town house recently vacated by the
designer Elizabeth Hawes.)

The business took a great leap forward with Valentina's
first commission for a Broadway leading lady—making costumes for Judith Anderson, in 1933. The then thriving New
York theatre world would nourish Valentina and make her
one of its own. Lynn Fontanne, who with her husband,
Alfred Lunt, became part of the inner circle of the Schlees,
borrowed Valentina's accent, turbans, and eccentricities to

play a White Russian pseudo-countess in *Idiot's Delight*, in 1936; the designer relished it all. The leading theatre critics (who were invited to her parties) would review her work with respect. "Valentina has designed clothes that act before a line is spoken," Brooks Atkinson said. When a female star made an entrance in a change of gown, the women in the audience could sometimes be heard to let out a collective gasp.

She was a prima donna costuming prima donnas, but in the theatre she prided herself on being part of the team: conscientiously reading the script and consulting directors and set designers. Her clothes for the stage were for many years the springboard for her private business. In 1935, after she riveted Metropolitan operagoers with a Carmen dressed as a matador in bolero and formfitting pants, *Vogue* featured the style and it became a fad. In the forties, Judith Anderson had such a memorable final-act curtain—banging on a door, stage back, bemoaning the suicide of her lover—that she started a craze for blood-red aprons over black evening gowns, based on the Valentina costume the actress wore. Clients were requesting versions of the white evening dress Valentina designed for Katharine Hepburn in *The Philadelphia Story* long after the show was on Broadway in 1939. (It was Adrian who did the costumes for the movie the following year.) Valentina and Hepburn hit it off. "At last I have made her look like a woman," the designer said.

THE WORLDS OF THEATRE, fashionable journalism, and society mingled at the Schlees' famous parties. They were a great production: between eighty and a hundred were invited for Russian Easters. There were candles, and flowers, and beautiful women; and amusing, talented men. Everyone came. The great ladies of the stage, with their husbands; the producers John Wilson and Alfred De Liagre, the playwrights Robert Sherwood and Philip Barry, with their wives; the Moss Harts, the Brian Ahernes; the Cushing sisters; Vincent Astor;

Elsa Maxwell and her companion Dorothy ("Dickie") Fellowes-Gordon; the actor Clifton Webb, for whom Valentina made a robe and pajamas for *The Man Who Came to Dinner*; Noël Coward, Cecil Beaton, Marlene Dietrich, when they were in town; and Greta Garbo, always, after she came into the lives of George and Valentina, in 1939. The food and drink were plenteous, with borscht and stroganoff and caviar. Valentina—with her hair loose, sometimes, and always in a beautiful dress—would make a great business of cutting the special almond-and-cream-cheese dessert called *paskha*. She'd wear a little decorative apron, to make believe that she—and not her chef, Petrov—had been in the kitchen all day.

Word of this magic world was spread by guests from the higher echelons of fashionable journalism: Harry Bull and the Baron de Guinzberg from *Town & Country*; Mrs. Snow from *Harper's Bazaar*; Margaret Case, society editor of *Vogue*. In the forties, the Russian-émigré and editorial worlds came together in the persons of Iva Patcevitch, publisher of *Vogue*, and Alexander Liberman, its art director. Liberman and his wife, Tatiana, became great friends of Valentina's.

"She was always playing on her Russianness," Liberman says now. "Crossing herself and making the sign of the cross at others. She had all kinds of superstitions."

At her parties for the Russian New Year, she would melt lead on a spoon and make her friends drop it in water and guess their fortunes from the shapes. Or her guests would have to write their wishes for the New Year on a little scrap of paper and chew it up.

"And did you swallow it?" I asked Liberman not long ago.

"Of course, that was the point!" he said, laughing. "There was always plenty of vodka and champagne to wash it down!"

GRETA GARBO ENTERED the world of George and Valentina completely naked, like Aphrodite from the sea. She had been escorted to the Sherry Netherland showroom by

Gaylord Hauser, the California nutritionist who was Garbo's squire at that time. Hauser led George to the downstairs fitting room, to introduce him to the woman Hauser always referred to simply as "She." (Garbo's friends mostly called her G.G., and she used many pseudonyms, especially "Harriet Brown.") George was stunned to find Greta Garbo in his wife's fitting room wearing nothing at all. The story is told by Eleanor Lambert, who was then Valentina's publicist, and would continue as such until the end of the business, in 1957. Naturally, Lambert has pondered that nakedness in the years since 1939—has wondered whether this total undressing for a fitting might have been a habit from Hollywood, since she once came across Marlene Dietrich preparing for a fitting with the same wholeheartedness. Yet the painter Frances Brennan, for whom Valentina made a wedding dress in 1946, still has the dress as well as an indelible memory of her own trembling and modest young self preparing for a fitting in front of the big Louis-style mirrors on Sixty-seventh Street. "Streep, darrling!" Valentina shrieked. "Streep!"

Although Garbo stopped hearts in the costumes Adrian designed for her movies—Victorian lace for Camille, velvet breeches for Queen Christina—she was notoriously indifferent to fashion, in private life. She favored rather mannish styles in gray or brown and, of course, deep-brimmed cloche hats. Hauser had taken her in hand. He encouraged her to eat lots of liver and Brewer's yeast. (Garbo was rather faddy about her diets all her life, while Valentina cleaned her plate and ate omnivorously, like a peasant.) And he took her to buy clothes at Valentina's as well as to order hats from New York's most fashionable milliner, Lilly Daché. Hauser, a handsome man (and also a client of Lambert's) was a great favorite with the ladies of the international set. A self-styled "doctor of natural science," and millionaire author of the best-selling book *Look Younger, Live Longer*, he had hopes of marrying Garbo, although he had a homosexual partner and "business manager," back home. Dressing "Her" seemed to take up much of his time. Elsa Maxwell wrote in her news-

paper column about Hauser's flurry of visits to the show-
rooms and tried to forestall the thought that this was "hardly
a virile life for a busy scientist. But there is only one Garbo . . .
and she, perhaps, is a vocation in herself."

George, who was shortly to discover this, began to go out
as a foursome with Hauser, Garbo, and Valentina. Garbo was
in the process of shifting her life from California to New
York, although at first she stayed in temporary apartments or
hotels. The city that had made the unknown Valentina
famous was about to make Garbo—the most famous woman
in the world, perhaps—almost anonymous. After Hauser had
gone back to the West Coast, George, Garbo, and Valentina
began to be seen out on the town together all the time. The
sight of the trio was unforgettable—especially when, as happened on several occasions, George would appear with one of
the women on each arm and dressed like identical twins.
Lambert remembers them at dinner at her house in a pair of
the exquisite blouses Valentina was known for: these in deep-
blue organza, with characteristic hand-rolled necks and long
poet's sleeves. With them they wore deep blue, bias-cut skirts.
They often styled their hair in the same way, too. It was often
said, especially in the forties, that they looked alike. Valentina
didn't have Garbo's beautiful big mouth, or the set of her
eyes. "I am the Gothic version of Garbo," she used to say.

At first, Valentina was said to be "ecstatic" to be dress
designer to Greta Garbo. In fact, it is sometimes suggested
that initially the bond between the two women may have
been more passionate than that between Garbo and George.
Even for their closest friends, it would always be hard to tell
what feelings were in play. Garbo and Valentina were very
different, but they were both great actresses, and they had
total control of their emotions in public. Far from discussing
her love affairs, Garbo didn't tell even very close friends
when her mother died. People "could live their hidden lives,
have their exciting secrets," she once told Cecil Beaton, when
they were discussing homosexuality. "But public flaunting of
these things is obnoxious." Valentina may have been rude

and even cruel to George, sometimes even to her clients; but with Garbo, however jealous she felt, she was perfectly civil for years. They had things in common aside from their looks and George: they were powerful, extraordinary creatures, each narcissistic and self-involved. And both of them liked and needed to be given directions by a man.

By the end of the war, it was George who had become the fixer and the impresario in Garbo's life. It was he who accompanied her on her first trip back to Sweden in 1946. When they met him, her Swedish friends said that he reminded them of Mauritz Stiller, the Russian-Jewish movie director who had discovered the young Greta Gustafson and, Svengali-like, created Garbo, the movie star, from scratch. Still, Garbo became involved in a curious affair with Cecil Beaton around this time. Like Hauser, he dreamed of marrying her, although by his own admission he was "really more fond of men." He would leave his lovemaking with Garbo and rush home to his diaries to write it all down. It was the fate of the most private woman of the twentieth century to become involved with some of its greatest gossips.

Valentina Gowns, Inc., was bustling at this time. Valentina was seeing clients every hour, and giving her famous one-woman performances that served as fashion shows. George was always present at these, joking with the clients, whom he called "the girls," to pass time while Valentina changed her outfits. His financial acumen and diplomacy were essential to the business. He was forever soothing the ruffled feathers of the sixty-five employees after one of his wife's fits of temperament. Now (Garbo told Beaton) he was getting fed up with it all. George was possessively in love with Garbo. She waited for him to telephone and tell her what to do. She called him "Schleesky" or "the little man." Beaton, who was jealous of George, called him "the Russian sturgeon" or "the Road Company Rasputin." Valentina formed her own liaison with Jack Barrett, a gentlemanly, literary man who ran the Bollingen Foundation. Valentina would be hard on Barrett as she had been hard on George, her "old friend from

Sebastopol." But Barrett wanted her to marry him and would devote himself to trying to make her happy until the day he died, in 1981.

The idea that Garbo was a recluse was as much of a myth as the idea that she never laughed. In the photographs of the Russian Easter that appeared in *Life* in 1947, Garbo looks melancholy and cross—a noble, caged animal in her absurd lace hair ribbon and Valentina gown. In fact, as Margaret Case would tell a friend, Garbo was in a particularly jolly mood that night. And she was going out so often that some wag described her as a "hermit-about-town." George would go to the Broadway openings one night with Garbo, and the next with Valentina. In 1948, Valentina was horrified to read in a gossip column what George had told her: that he loved Garbo but "I'm quite sure she won't want to get married. And you and I have so much in common."

The façade of George and Valentina's life was never smoother than it was in 1948. They left the town house in the seventies and moved into the luxurious apartment facing the East River, at 450 East Fifty-second Street. (When her friend Alexander Woollcott had lived there, Dorothy Parker christened it "Wit's End.") Their neighbors were appropriately prominent and well heeled. Mr. and Mrs. John Barry Ryan had several floors, as did Mr. and Mrs. Henry Luce. (Valentina made many dresses for Clare Boothe Luce, including the pale-blue, Pietà-like creation she wore when Spellman received her into the Catholic Church.) "The Valentinas," as Beaton called them, occupied the fourteenth floor and took half of the floor below for offices and domestic staff. A huge, L-shaped salon, perfect for the parties, was lined with eighteenth-century panelling and faced east and south over the Pepsi-Cola sign and the Triborough Bridge. The river, Valentina would say, was her own Grand Canal.

The Schlees loved the things of this world, the here and now. "I have no time to get fat or sick," she told a journalist in that same year. "I never theenk of myself. I theenk only of things. I am so happy theenking of things. When I look at a

chair, it weenks at me." George, the former producer, turned
his mind to the dream of masterminding Garbo's return to
the movie screen. "She reminds me of Duse," he once said.
"She had been in retirement eleven years and returned to
greater triumphs than ever." In 1949, George and Garbo
would be in Rome, supposedly to make a movie with the producer Walter Wanger. The plan fell through, amid recrimi-
nations. Wanger blamed Schlee, whom he called Garbo's
"embarrassing constant companion." In point of fact, what
mostly occupied George and Garbo was not her career but
browsing together in search of furnishings for Valentina's
new apartment. They scoured the salesrooms and the antiques shops on Third Avenue, and the place filled with the
trappings of a conservative old European opulence: ormolu
and boulle; Meissen vases and crystal chandeliers; mantel
clocks and overmirrors; Louis XV furniture and Savonnerie
rugs; and many rather decorative paintings, often of flowers.
Bettina Ballard, a fashion editor of *Vogue* at that time,
remembered how Valentina ("the strongest-willed woman I
ever met") used emotional blackmail to get Horst to the new
apartment. "Maybe Valentina's last collection . . . doctors,
nurses, nobody knows."

In fact, it was George who was feeling the strain of these
years; he was hospitalized several times, once for severe
depression. But Horst was commissioned by *Vogue*, and the
spread that emerged was among his finest work and perhaps
the apogee of Valentina's self-presentation. All the "theengs"
are not so much winking at the small, brave figure sitting
quite alone in the palatial rooms as looking balefully on. Perhaps the conviction that she was a deposed czarist princess
really took hold right then. As she moved into the home that
summed up her success—and where she was to go on living for the next forty years—she conjures up the impression
of a whole privileged world where she once had reigned
but which she is being forced to relinquish by giant forces of
history.

George once said that his two closest men friends had married "nobodies" and would be forgotten. "I have married one famous woman and been loved by another, so my reputation is enormous." By the 1950s, the arrangements were well established; George and Garbo would go out with the Gunthers, visit Horst or the Seligmans in the country. In 1953, Garbo bought her own apartment at 450 East Fifty-second Street—on the fifth floor, but with the same layout and the same view from a slightly different angle. It was her first and last real home. She panelled the walls and resumed the trail through the salesrooms and antiques shops with George and also with the Baron Erich Goldschmidt-Rothschild, a wealthy connoisseur and man of leisure to whom he had introduced her. She bought Louis XV commodes and consoles and bergères; she bought ormolu and boulle and Savonnerie carpets; she bought many flower paintings. She was far richer than George; she once bought two Renoirs and a Bonnard in the space of two weeks. When he saw the decor, Cecil Beaton was appalled, especially by the cushions the color of "squashed strawberry" and the brothel-pink lampshades, which he saw as "evidence of Schlee taste."

In 1955, George bought the villa "Le Roc" at Cap d'Ail in the South of France. It was built on a promontory sticking into the Mediterranean. "Hideous but beautifully situated," Noël Coward called it, when he visited Garbo there. Sometimes Valentina would visit, but usually she would give a cocktail party in New York to see George off for his summers at Le Roc with Garbo and then leave herself for Venice with Barrett. Princess Grace would come over to Le Roc for lunch and a swim with Garbo, who was clearly the mistress of the house. Aristotle Onassis would carry the couple off on his yacht; he was crazy about Garbo, and George liked talking to him about investments. In 1957, George and Valentina's dressmaking establishment was wound down. In 1963, George and Garbo were in Paris, staying at the Crillon. They had had dinner with another of Garbo's protectors, Cécile de Rothschild, when George went out to smoke his cigar, col-

lapsed, and died of a heart attack. Garbo hid from the press
in de Rothschild's apartment, while Valentina (who had been
staying with Barrett in Connecticut) flew in to take charge of
the body. On the trip back, she sat with George's topcoat in
her lap, obsessively smoothing the fabric and fretting that
"That Woman" might have come along on the same plane.

There was no longer any need to be civil. Garbo was not
invited to the services in the Russian Orthodox Church,
where all the old faces from the cocktail-party list stood with
dripping candles listening to Pushkin. At one point, the
widow is said to have flung herself on her fur coat on the
floor and moaned dramatically. (No doubt the coat was sable;
she is famous for her remark "Meenk is for football!") She
sent for a priest and had her apartment exorcised. Holy water
was sprinkled even in the elevator shaft and the refrigerator.
"That Woman come up have sandwich!" she said, in expla-
nation. She inherited Le Roc, and had that exorcised,
too, before lending it to friends, including Diana Vreeland.
She soon lost interest in the place and sold it for less than
its worth.

Six weeks or so after George's death, Valentina was riding
with friends when she saw Garbo walking down the street
alone. She told the driver to stop, got out, and embraced her
rival. "That poor woman, I feel sorry for her," she said, as she
got back in. A newspaper reported that they had met in the
little chapel she had built for George and kept filled with
lilies of the valley, on the first anniversary of his death. But
after that, for a quarter of a century, the two aging, childless
women went on living in the same building, looking at the
same light on the same water and never speaking. Garbo did
not hate Valentina, but resentment grew in the ever-obsessive
Valentina, along with the osteoporosis that bent her spine.
She cut the photograph of Garbo in her hair ribbon, and
every other photograph of her, out of her scrapbook. She
never permitted the other's name to be mentioned but called
her "the fifth floor." Generations of elevator men were

trained never to pick up the ladies in the same car. Garbo took her long walks in the daytime, and Valentina went out at dusk.

Valentina loved Venice, and kept going there until she was in her eighties. "Darling, Gritti is only place to stay," she once said. "So easy from my room to pray San Salute—so religious feeling in Venice, very conscious soul." She had her rituals: going at the same time each day by vaporetto to the Lido, wearing her coolie hat, then running every evening to say good night to San Marco. She had always been a demanding traveller, but now each passing year made her more of a trial to the management at the Gritti. She tore up the sheets if she found them rough; she would dine on the terrace and express her dissatisfaction with the food by throwing her plate and her silverware into the Grand Canal. This happened so often that waiters were specially trained to watch her and fish them out. She became so impossible that even her oldest friends began to avoid her. On what turned out to be her last trip to Europe, she was dispatched in the care of a sensible-seeming nun, who sent a desperate ship-to-shore message from mid-Atlantic to say she couldn't take it.

In the czarist salon, the curtains got threadbare and the velvets faded. George's room was left exactly as it had been when he used to return to it from evenings with "the fifth floor." Sometimes Valentina went in there and raised her glass of vodka. He had protected her, after all. The money was there to pay for care from elegant and loving nurses, who tried very hard to make her happy. From time to time, when she was taking the air with one of them, fate would put Garbo on Fifty-second Street as well. "She" was a plain old woman in a plain old coat, now, with something grim about her mouth. She would turn and stand for a long time, staring at the hunchbacked little figure, the "Gothic version" of herself. Valentina's rages were worse than ever, but the nurse could calm her by giving her a box of scraps of silk, which she would sit folding, unfolding, and stroking. It was the doorman who told Garbo that Mrs. Schlee had died; she is said to have cried. She was dead herself within the year. Almost no one went to Valentina's funeral. Her "theengs" were sold at Christie's. She left the lion's share of her $5 million estate to Russian causes, including the Orthodox Church, although she had been a practicing Catholic. Her will stipulated that Henry Lax, her doctor, should be sent a ham at Christmas for the rest of his life.

1995

THE POET OF
EVERYDAY LIFE

*T*HE SEVENTEENTH CENTURY, when Johannes Vermeer was painting his masterpieces, was a marvellous time to be Dutch. The people of the Netherlands Republic were recognizably modern: rather easygoing and democratic, and very good at getting rich. Fleets of mighty sailing ships slipped their moorings, raised the little nation's colors, and ventured forth to every corner of the world. The merchantmen of the famous Dutch East India Company came back low in the water, their holds bursting with silk and tobacco, nutmeg and cloves. Closer to home, the Baltic trade in wood and grain—the "mother trade," as it was called—provided economic stability and kept almost everyone comfortably housed and fed. Unlike their neighbors in Europe, the Dutch had no civil wars or bread riots to distract them from making money and spreading it around. They had a tendency to eat too much, to be sure; they smoked like fiends and drank a lot of beer. But their diet was healthy, and they died of the plague in fewer numbers than the English. The Calvinist preachers who leaned out of their pulpits, fulminating against "Queen Money," had no serious hope of preventing the clever new businessmen from having free rein. There were monopolies, cartels, and a lively, widespread trade in stocks and bonds. (The most famous speculative scandal was the madness surrounding tulip bulbs.) A nation of consumers stood eager to adorn their houses with local factory-made imitations of imported luxuries like Turkey carpets and Ming porcelain. Even the most ordinary tradesman or craftsman could afford to have oil paintings on his walls, if only the popular "genre" scenes of barracks, brothels, and kitchens. (These last were often pictured in disarray, with a sleeping or drunken servant, an unswept floor, a cat that nibbled on the family pie—a spectacle intended to point up the importance of temperance and harmony in a patriotic home.)

Other nations envied and resented the Dutch for their spectacular success. The Dutch got on with being the finest capitalists and the most adventurous travellers of their age (they found Tasmania and New Zealand, they landed in Brazil), but they were comparatively feeble as settlers and imperialists. They almost always headed back to Holland; at heart, they were homebodies to a man. Home was virtually a religion with them, central to their view of themselves as a people singled out by God. This notion was bolstered by their miraculous beginning as a nation that (by grace and their skills in hydraulic engineering) had parted the waters and drained the land. At the end of the sixteenth century, they had gained their independence from the occupying Spanish partly by voluntarily flooding the land again, drowning the foreign army and many idly grazing cows. At least these mooing innocents met their Maker with immaculately clean udders and tails. Not only Dutch cows but also Dutch dogs, streets, doorsteps, linens, and pots were tirelessly washed and scrubbed. Nothing amazed foreign visitors more than this pristine cleanliness of the Dutch; it struck outsiders as eccentric to the point of being weird.

The world of Vermeer is connected to the hustle and bustle of the Dutch golden age, yet forever and mysteriously set apart. It is generally accepted that there are thirty-five paintings by him. He left no drawings or prints. He seems to have worked slowly, producing a couple of paintings a year and perfecting his awesome technique. ("First, you paint like Vermeer," Salvador Dalí once laid down as every artist's goal.) At the outset, there was a mythological Diana and her maidens; a sweet-faced Saint Praxedis, squeezing the blood of a decapitated martyr from a sponge and looking for all the world like a Dutch housemaid nobly washing her stoop. Toward the end of his life, Vermeer painted a fellow studying first Astronomy and then Geography; there were a couple of complex allegories about Art and Faith. There was of course the famous view of Delft, the provincial town where the painter lived from his birth (in 1632) to his death (in 1675). But these paintings were exceptions, and even the young artist's idealized genre scenes—with soldiers and gents and maidens in moral danger being plied with wine—gave way in time. Vermeer is universally loved and considered a great master because of the work of a central, twelve-year period when, in a thoroughly magical way, he painted women alone (or perhaps with another female figure) in a room at home. No one has ever rivalled him in conveying the active, passive, peculiarly feminine inner life.

He is the poet of Waiting, of the interrupted story, the moments between other moments, when nothing in particular (and a whole eternity) is going on. The glance in the mirror while trying on a pearl necklace; the hand on the half-open window or on the polished jug; the reading of a letter; the absentminded tuning of a lute; the downcast gaze. These microscopic gestures are what his paintings spring from; these are their galaxies and continents. The images of Vermeer's world speak to us so directly and forcefully; it is so

felt-slippered, its sound track so muted that the phrase
Malraux used for art—"the Voices of Silence"—applies
supremely well.

AS WE MUST always feel, in the end, when confronted
with the mystery of another person, we feel a kind of awe
before the women of Vermeer. Reasoned art-historical analysis tells us that compositional and perspectival decisions,
glazes, the gray-blue-yellow palette, the blurring of outlines,
or the use of pointillist dots affects us in his work. But what
beams out of the rounded foreheads of the women and illumi-
nates their rooms is an enigma—the light of the soul. The
emotion stirred up in us is akin to what we feel when we look
in a window and see someone lost in the pages of a book;
when we visit a quiet church and see a stranger knelt in
prayer; when a loved one murmurs in his sleep; or when we
contemplate a corpse. We understand and control so little,
after all, we people of a modern age that was already in place
around Vermeer, and that feels as though it is drawing to its
close, around us. Who among us has power over much of real
importance, or even over our breathing in and out? At the
close of our so arrogant twentieth century, Vermeer's work is
a timely reminder that the most interesting things in life are
always far beyond our grasp.

The paintings are full of paradox and ambivalence: limpid
and transparent, yet full of veils. The painter beckons you
into the serene, shallow space where the woman waits in
front of a wall, perhaps with a map on it, or a picture of
Cupid or the sea. (Dutch people of that time, seeing these pictures within pictures, would straightaway know that Vermeer, in his haiku manner, was telling a "story" about love.)
But then he barricades the foreground with a half-pulled curtain, a table covered in an Oriental rug, or one of the Spanish-
style chairs with the lion's-head finials he had in his house. It
is he who is the guardian of the private chamber; he who sees
you starting to step through the looking glass, who puts a

hand on your chest and gently pushes you back out. In this painted place of his, mirrors almost never have reflections in them; windows are blank translucencies containing no vista of garden or street. Many Dutch painters were fascinated by the divide between the public and the private—the swaggering, spitting, rough-and-tumble streets of commerce on that side of the threshold, the starched, swept, scour-bright purity of home on this. Painters were fond of depicting the open door, sometimes with a shadowy male silhouette coming in. With Vermeer, artistic themes and conventions of his day are reduced to their essence, rendered ambivalent and ironic, thoroughly refined. He takes "the tipsy servant" who was part of the vocabulary of genre painting and turns her into an exquisite young woman, perhaps sleeping, or perhaps despairing about a thwarted love, as she sits with disarranged neckerchief, her head drooping and propped on her hand. In other paintings, the familiar narrative of outside-inside traffic and its potential threat to the sanctity of home is delicately suggested by a letter (presumably from a lover) brought in via the maid.

The meditative, tranquil aura of Vermeer's women owes much to the sense that they have lost or never felt the desire to lift the door latch and venture out. But the funny thing is that Dutch women of that time, although certainly expert and industrious housewives, were not known for being secluded at all. The same foreign tourists who were struck by the cleanliness of Holland's streets observed that respectable women, even unmarried girls, were free to walk about in them as they pleased. And outsiders were shocked that many Dutch married couples got on so well that they strolled along in public holding hands and thought nothing of giving each other a smacking kiss. When husbands proved drunken or abusive, the law was on the side of women, permitting them to separate and take a just share of the property along. Widows, especially, were often active in commerce and the stock exchange; they had the important legal right to sign notarized documents. One of Vermeer's grandmothers ran a secondhand-bedding business as well as a lottery—although this seems to have been of slightly dubious legality. (Like much about the painter's life and world, this detail surfaced only recently, through the research of John Michael Montias.)

Johannes Vermeer and his wife, Catharina Bolnes, a Roman Catholic whom he married when he was twenty-one (he grew up a Protestant but converted to her faith), had a very large family indeed. There are thought to have been eleven children at the time of their father's death in his early forties; others had died in infancy. The survivors ranged from a baby up to Maria, his eldest daughter, who was recently wed. His life spanned an increasingly prosperous and self-confident time in his nation's history. A small sign of this, perhaps, is that his wife and his many daughters were almost certainly able to read and write. (A devout nation encouraged literacy in women so they could read the Scriptures for themselves.) Was there ever a painter who better celebrated female letter-writing, who made it look more dignified or more delicious than Vermeer? The letters, like the Cupid and the seascape, would have suggested to contemporaries that erotic love was in the air of these hermetic, dazzling rooms. As with the sparkling wineglasses that appeared in the earlier works, there may have been a moral message, an emblematic warning of sexual danger in this business with the maids and notes. But it is all so beautifully painted, so very seductive, that it is hard to believe that anyone could ever feel outraged by these letters, which were so clearly to and from a suitor rather than the butcher or an aunt. At any rate, we know that this worshipper (or castigator, perhaps) of female letter-writers was himself the son of a woman who couldn't even sign her name; at her marriage, she had to mark the church register with a cross.

With Vermeer, even hanky-panky looks positively saintly. And it is yet another mysterious aspect of his genius that he created his canvases, with their intense visions of absolute tranquillity, in a studio in a house that was bursting at the seams and echoing with the clamor of other lives. Some years after their marriage, Johannes and his wife moved out of his father's house—which was also an inn—and into that of his mother-in-law, Maria Thins, in the Paepenhoek, or "Papists' corner," the Catholic quarter of Delft. (After the representatives and priests of the Spanish King were ousted and the Netherlands became a Protestant republic, a third of the population remained loyal to the Pope; they were not allowed to hold public office and had to worship in "hidden churches," but many were able to rise high in the world, just the same. Vermeer was well respected in his time and served twice as head of the artists' guild in Delft.) Maria was divorced from Catharina's father, a violent man who used to beat up his wife—once when she was heavily pregnant. As a little girl, Catharina witnessed domestic chaos worthy of the most direly hortatory of genre paintings. The family was comfortably off (her father owned a brickworks), but as a child of nine she was dispatched to a neighbor's house for safekeeping, looking, according to an eyewitness, shabbier than "a beggar's child."

Some of the sacred quality of Vermeer's women must spring from the Catholic world he had joined. Where the Protestants believed in meditating on the Word, and were even known on occasion to destroy statues and paintings when they took over the churches, the Catholics revered sacred images and used them to contemplate God. The patient, receptive, grace-filled quality of Vermeer's female figures owes much to historic portrayals of the Virgin Mary. But some of the intensity with which, again and again, he painted peaceful women in their safe place must surely be due to the distinctly unsafe personal history of Maria and Catharina, the women closest to him. The painter supplemented his earnings by dealing in art, as his father had done, but still his ever-growing family probably depended on his mother-in-law for financial support. The sale of two or three of his own paintings a year would never have kept the little

Vermeers in bread or clogs. The household relied on income from properties Maria had salvaged from her marriage along with many paintings, including the brothel scene *The Procuress*. This painting is to be seen hanging on the back wall in several of Vermeer's own works. It is a recurrent motif, along with the Spanish chairs, a jewel box, and a flare-back yellow satin jacket with an ermine trim.

The violence did not stop at one generation. The painter's brother-in-law, Willem, would turn up at the house in the Paepenhoek and make such scenes that a crowd of scandalized neighbors would gather around the door. Once, when Catharina was pregnant, her brother came after her with a stick; the family maidservant came to her rescue. Maria succeeded in getting her son committed to a home for delinquents and the mentally ill, but he didn't stay for long and was a source of constant anxiety to them all until he finally died. Mother-in-law retained two of the four main rooms of the house; when Willem was on a rampage, she locked herself in.

Meanwhile, in his studio, Vermeer was absorbedly painting away. He painted the dewy roundness of an eye or a lip; he painted the ringlets, the ribbons in the hair. He painted an earlobe with its teardrop pearl. (Pearls might have symbolized chaste spirituality to contemporary observers, or perhaps the foolish vanities of this world; but more significantly, the nacreous substance suited Vermeer, the painter, perfectly. It suspended the light as if in an emulsion, yet also beamed it flying and twinkling out.) Like an alchemist making gold, he worked away in that home studio, capturing the light and the shadows and (in the free, silent world of his canvas) moving them about, like his props, to suit himself.

It seems that children were born to Catharina at almost the rate that paintings of restful, untouchable, and child-free women came to her husband. His masterworks gradually filled the walls of the man who is thought to have been his sole patron. The makeshift cots and small beds of children gradually filled the kitchen, the cellar, and the little room off the hall of Maria's house. The household bustled with life. There was the tireless round of work—too much for that courageous family servant—for each of the girls to learn: the right way to dust and burnish, wash and starch. The family flatiron must have been in constant use on linen sheets and Father's shirts; on the snowy collars, coifs, and bonnets that females wore. No doubt, when Mother was busy with the newborn, it fell to the older girls to watch that little Ignatius and Franciscus didn't toddle into the fireplace or fall in the canal. (As a little boy, the painter—the child of middle-aged parents—must have been fussed over by his sister and only sibling, Gertruy, who was twelve when he was born.) Both the early painting of Diana and a *Christ in the House of Martha and Mary* show a central figure being ministered to by female attendants; Vermeer was drawn to the theme. He sometimes called on his womenfolk to serve as models for him. It is thought that the yellow satin jacket belonged to Catharina, and that she or Maria, her eldest daughter, may have worn it in some of the paintings. It was probably Maria who posed for her father while playing a guitar.

There was the murmur of prayer in the house, and the sound of crying babies; on occasion, when Willem was up to his tricks or the midwife had been sent for, there must have been screams. But there was music-making, and love, and surely there was laughter in that home, as well. In my mind, like one of his pictures within pictures, I imagine the paterfamilial genius sitting at his easel (with the extraordinary concentration to which his seductively painted Madonnas attest) while putti-like babies and teenage girls with their heads in curlpapers giggle in rooms and stairs all around.

THE GREAT WORLD of greed and wars and manly things impinged in the end, as it will. Louis XIV of France, the "Sun King," marched at the head of his army into the

Netherlands. His move hastened the end of the Dutch golden age and of the life and career of Johannes Vermeer, the "painter of light." The economic disruptions of the war made it hard to sell paintings and caused the rents from Maria Thins' properties to dry up. Vermeer—whose family had once lived quite comfortably, as the ermine-trimmed yellow satin would indicate—found himself up to his ears in debt. Distraught at the prospect of his brood being destitute, he died very suddenly, perhaps of a heart attack. The city of Delft appointed as his executor a famous scientist and microscopist who happened to have discovered spermatozoa. Catharina held on to the last of her late husband's paintings as long as she possibly could—especially the allegorical *Art of Painting*, which he knew was really good and had never wanted to sell. But she was forced to declare bankruptcy a year after his death and later apply to an orphans' fund for charitable assistance.

Vermeer led a quiet life in a quiet town, and it took a very long time for his reputation to extend beyond a few connoisseurs or even to get beyond Delft. But the popular myth about Vermeer—that he was a kind of hidden, late-flowering tulip bulb, a genius entirely unrecognized until he was "discovered" by the French journalist and critic Thoré-Bürger in the 1860s—is far from the truth. Early collectors were tenaciously loyal, and there were pockets of influential enthusiasm throughout the eighteenth century. Sir Joshua Reynolds admired the painting *The Milkmaid*, and there was a Vermeer in George III's collection, although for a long time it was believed to have been painted by somebody else. Certainly it was Thoré-Bürger—a socialist in political exile, who loved Vermeer for his exaltation of the ordinary as well as for the magic of his light—who tracked down as many of the paintings as was humanly possible, wrote a series of articles, and really put Vermeer on the map. (At the same time as the French Impressionists, it turned out.) Van Gogh admired him greatly, and Proust declared the *View of Delft* "the most beautiful painting in the world." The mogul art collectors of late-nineteenth-century America—with great new fortunes made through cartels of iron and steel and railroads, in stocks and bonds—swept up some of the most enigmatic of Vermeer's Dutch ladies and set them down across the ocean, in the gilded palaces of Boston, Philadelphia, and New York.

1995

MEAT

TWENTY YEARS AGO, when I was fairly new to New York and very new to what turned out an ill-fated marriage to an older man, I lived on Lexington Avenue in the upper Eighties. There was a real French butcher's shop across the street. The proprietor was a lively little old Frenchman in a clean white coat; I was a tall young Englishwoman, afraid of many things but with a deceptively self-confident taste in hats. The bell on the shop's door would go on tinkling for quite a while after I'd stepped in. The butcher would be standing alertly behind his illuminated case of gigots or côtelettes like some kindly old doctor with a row of satisfactorily delivered babies. He would greet me with a twinkling look and a singsong "Bonjour, Madame!" He would coax me into conversing in French with him about my menu, the weather, or my husband, whom I adored. Some days the French words and phrases were in me and some days they were not. I had had a whole French-speaking part of me once, in the years when I had been a mere "mademoiselle" in shops. But the language seemed to have clamped shut in me. Like friendships with my own generation, it was one of the things I quietly put away in order to enter my husband's world.

On the butcher's wall was a chart with a poignantly trusting steer standing quite oblivious to the butcher's cuts that marked off portions of its body. They were French cuts, with French names that gave off an unchallengeable authority. No mere joints of beef, these, but the blueprints of a culture: a system laid down, I felt, by some historic Academy of Meat in Paris and posted in this far-flung mini-France where (beyond the tinkling doorbell) the I.R.T. could be heard to rumble. I was teaching myself to cook from a daily more thumbed-and-food-splattered copy of *Mastering the Art of French Cooking*. Its author, Julia Child, warned most gravely against vagueness when buying beef. It was a sin akin to burning garlic or failing to skim the scum from your veal stock. It could lead to "countless unnecessary disappointments and expenses." I would study the chart surreptitiously while waiting to be served or while the butcher was rummaging about in his cold room. He would disappear into it regularly like the White Rabbit, letting the heavy door shut behind him with a vacuumy *phloomph*ing sound. Then he would emerge looking triumphant, with a brace of squab he might just have returned from hunting through the woods, or a pork roast or soup bone whose presence in his cold room seemed to surprise and delight him. In truth I never really learned the chart. I simply trusted the butcher. He never disappointed. He knew just what was called for in a blanquette or a *bourguignon*, and his *rosbifs* were works of art, wherever they came from. With his special long needles, he larded them with strands of the fine white fat he also used to sheathe them, like silk-wrapped gift bundles in Japanese temples. As a final touch, he corseted the roasts into lozenge-shaped decorum with airy nets of white string webbing.

THE APARTMENT WAS roomy and, like the man I
shared it with, hovered uneasily between charm and gloom.
Although I was working hard at not seeing it, in both home
and his nature the dark was winning out. I put out flowers
and chintzy pillows by the armful, but the pair of us were suffocating in rooms that were starved of sun and crammed a
little more each week with the things he kept acquiring in
household sales. He was a home-loving man, but he had the
paradoxical habit of walking out on homes and wives, of
whom I was by no means the first. So he hit on a method of
instantly acquiring a new nest for a new bride by means of the
neighborhood auction rooms. His flurried and sometimes
capricious bids at Doyle's and PB 84 would set in motion a
regular stream of old stuff. Old-fashioned china and silver, in
numbers large enough for the stately dinners centered on the
Frenchman's beef or paper-frilled crown roasts I was beginning to serve my husband's friends. Ornate mahogany furniture and heavy gilt frames surrounding ugly pictures and
prints. An inky Chinese rug that was cleaned several times
without ceasing to give off reproachful puffs of dust when I
walked on it. It was all a stage set, a piece of sleight of hand,
that home, when I think of it now—a trick for casual visitors,
with him as an eternally faithful householder in a well-
furnished life with all its jagged edges long since beeswax-
polished and rounded off.

In the whole apartment, only the kitchen got the sun. Had
he been a different man, he might have permitted its warmth
to enter his study, but he never raised the blinds. He hugged
the pool of light from his desk lamp as he sat all day smoking
and writing books. Sometimes, as if for a diversion, he picked
up the telephone and shouted angrily at the man who published them. I would be in the kitchen in my apron, humming to myself as I learned to chop a carrot from the diagram
in Mrs. Child. I could hear him cursing far away down the
hall. I supposed this was a way for an American man to show
his affection, since I knew that the publisher was one of my
husband's very few close friends. The shaft of sunshine shone

in on kitchen equipment and a *batterie de cuisine* that had been acquired for me in the usual manner, as end-of-sale-day miscellanies and job lots. Shelves and counters filled with spurious personal history as rapidly as the rest of the house. The utensils could have been my grandmother's or (more likely) his grandmother's. I worked more and more assiduously on my *bavarois* and béchamels, using ancient bowls and rolling pins; blue-glass canning jars and spatterware ladles; gadgets for grinding and whisking and juicing that might have been patented in Victorian Chicago; and old wooden spoons as indelibly and personally molded to some other woman's use as a stranger's lipstick.

THE FRENCH BUTCHER was proud of his veal birds, and I often bought them. Miniature versions of the trussed roasts, they were escalopes rolled round spiced and seasoned forcemeat. He sold them, I bought them; but it was a richer transaction than that. Indeed all the chilly aspects of financial reality were deflected from the little man to his wife. Madame sat at a cash register in a glass booth that was raised like an altar to the tradition of the *petit commerçant*. She counted the money and kept guard over things: watching for my errors in gender or subjunctive, her husband's tenderhearted generosities with his scale. He was the confessor, the artiste, as he proffered his veal birds, his courtly instructions for preparing them. These morsels summed up a culinary culture of witty and Carême-like sophistications combined with peasantlike wholesomeness. They were as delicate as any quail consumed by a fin-de-siècle gourmet under a tent of starched white napkin, yet robust and breezily decent like the ancestral fields and orchards that linger in the collective memory of even thoroughly urban French people.

"*Mes oiseaux de santé,*" the butcher called his veal birds. "Birds of health." They would be sure (he implied) to make my husband happy and well; we would work as a team forever and ever, like the butcher and his madame. It was my husband's birthday, and the publisher and his wife were invited to dine. I went to the Dumas patisserie, a few doors from the butcher, and bought a cake so spectacular and costly that Madame Dumas personally placed it in the box and tied it with string pulled down from the overhead spool with her ruddy, oven-mottled arm. It started to snow. By late afternoon, the publisher, who lived in the suburbs, called to say the roads were blocked. My husband's disappointment was boundless. He threw a tantrum; some of the saleroom china flew about and smashed. I put the veal birds in the freezer that night. Months went by. The publisher had died quite unexpectedly and my husband was half in love with the widow by the time I got out those *oiseaux* and cooked them up.

1993

DEMENTED PILGRIMAGE

*T*O A WOMAN WRITER, exposing family secrets can seem perilously close to going mad. Men
have had the support of the culture as they recognized their own experience and laid claim to it by writing it
down. On the whole, they have been able, without inhibition,
to feed their creative ambitions with the details of other
people's lives. Men had a mandate, after all, to inform the
public about the nature of life. Things have not been—are
not—so simple for a woman. Women have often withheld
their stories, because honesty about emotions and about the
family feels to many women like a sin. It means drawing
aside the curtain, lifting lids. It means renouncing the role of
good girl and ceasing to be ladylike. It may mean expressing
anger and being brave enough to watch loved ones be angry.
Women must set aside the bowl they have used to beg for
approval and praise. George Eliot was not free as an artist
until her respectable family had cast her out. Only a community larger than family, only powers greater than lovers or

husbands, can sustain women writers when they start to ask the big questions: Who am I? Who made me? What is my place in this world?

Germaine Greer, the Australian-born author and academic who became famous in the seventies with her feminist book *The Female Eunuch*, has been asking the big questions of late. She has written a book that seems a very contemporary and very feminine version of the "journey of the hero"— the spiritual quest. *Daddy, We Hardly Knew You* is the title, and its lisping, music-hall charm may seem at odds with the ferocious psychic need and volcanic energy that drive this combined memoir, detective story, and travelogue from first to last. Yet the contradiction seems fitting. The book is a jolting, poetic, broken-winged, exhilarating sort of thing. A brave, gifted fifty-year-old woman discovered her family's secrets and wrote them down. "We children knew next to nothing at all about Daddy and we knew too we had no right to find out," Germaine Greer tells us.

The story begins with the death, back home, of her senile father, Reg Greer, and her resolve to unmask the hazy details of his early life. She will mourn her daddy by demystifying him. Like any detective work, the task calls for patience, stamina, and guile. Countless, often fruitless hours are spent in genealogical-record offices and libraries over several continents—in Britain (where the author has lived since her young womanhood, and where, according to the family myth, Reg's parents came from); in India and on Malta (places where he was stationed as an R.A.F. officer during the Second World War); and in Australia (where, the myth notwithstanding, Reg's people turn out to have lived and died). Through impersonal official records Reg is eerily resurrected as a man in his prime. His trembling daughter, scanning his service medical and psychiatric reports, tunes in to his heartbeat, checks his lungs, his teeth, his hammertoe. She blows off half a century of dust and pores over his recurrent dreams. What kind of unnatural daughter is this, whose obsession drives her to travel across the world and back just to hear her father's old secretary tell how, fifty years before, he used to embarrass her by brushing against her breasts? A daughter desperate enough to risk being honest, it seems, and one still hungry to be loved.

The crime that Reg Greer has committed and for which Germaine tracks him across the world and down the years is not only self-invention and deception. Certainly he stands accused of letting her believe him a war hero, indispensable to the operation of the top-secret "Ultra" code. And she finds him guilty of concealing the facts of his boyhood even from her now widowed mother, then his innocent young bride. By the end, the triumphant detective daughter has found out more about him than her mother ever knew. She knows more than *he* ever knew: the identity of his natural parents. She knows that his name was not really Reg; it wasn't Greer, either. Of her childhood daddy—an advertising-space sales-man for a Melbourne newspaper, with a teasing manner, fancy suits, and a nicotine-stained mustache—all she is left with is "a heap of props, smart clothes, false teeth, and a script full of lying clichés." But the gaps and distortions of his his-tory are only part of a more serious crime: he didn't love her enough. She wonders whether he really loved her at all. She remembers how every time she tried to put her arms around his neck he would unlock them and push her away. "You're big enough and ugly enough to take care of yourself" was a line he used all the time. A Cheshire cat to her Alice, he had a way of vanishing even when he was in the room. The seda-tives on which he depended could not have helped. He would sit hiding behind his newspaper while Germaine's mother walloped her for some insignificant offense. "That my father never once struck or reviled me was reason enough for me to love him," she says, like some Dickensian urchin resigning herself to emotional crumbs. But that restraint was not enough to prove that he loved her. She can't remember his giving her a word of encouragement. To her knowledge, he never read the books she went on to write, or watched her on television.

This is a fast-moving, sometimes wildly emotional book wrapped around a cold, still place. It shows the members of a perfectly ordinary, attractive suburban family shut off from each other by secrets, anger, and inherited shame. It shows how stinginess with love—what E. M. Forster once called "the undeveloped heart"—corrodes both the miser and the one deprived. Ms. Greer is fighting hard to smash out of all this. She is a sort of spiritual work in progress, on the bumpy path of coming to terms. She can no longer be a victim; she writes partly to take responsibility for her life. Reg may have been undemonstrative when she was a child, but later she punished him, by not writing, calling, or going home to see him for seventeen years. "You never loved him. You never loved anyone," her own unhappy face seems to say to her from the bathroom mirror on one of many sleepless nights. She silences the accusatory voice by naming it as her mother, running guerrilla sorties inside her daughter's head. For it appears that Mother as well as Daddy had an undeveloped heart. Some of the most radical scenes in the book show the brilliant, famous middle-aged daughter trying and failing, then trying and failing again, to bully her obscure, elderly widowed mother into giving approval and support. These are honest, disquieting scenes. The daughter portrays the mother as competitive and narcissistic, with a "demonic energy" that Germaine recognizes in herself and fears. She also suggests that her mother is insane, and believes at stressful points in her hunt for the true Reg that she herself may be. The battles over wartime Malta were scarcely more savage than the squaring off of these two angry, loving women over Reg's secrets one day on an Australian beach. They bombard each other with forms of rage that women have so often been reduced to: snide remarks, rapid changes of subject, and silent scorn.

Germaine claims, at least at the time of her book's going to press, that she is not yet ready to forgive her father. Still, there is a thread of compassion for him all along. Whether because he is dead or because he never hit her, she describes with quasi-maternal tenderness his feet so vulnerable to sunburn, the narrowness of his chest; she can see him as a damaged man. In describing her mother Germaine is merciless. As a young woman, Mrs. Greer had been flashy, with her long legs, silly hats, and big, red-lipsticked mouth. At seventy, she is older but no wiser: still working on her lifetime suntan, with her old legs "oozing" out of skimpy shorts "like Brown Windsor Soup sliding down a ladle." She outrages Germaine—who, at least at the time of writing, had no child and no husband, and only her cat for a bedmate—by being on the lookout for a new sexual partner. Germaine Greer, the self-confessed "media superstar" of the feminist movement, looks at the woman who bore her with a kind of revulsion, as if she were an archetypal sinister crone.

The compassion that Germaine feels intermittently for her father and withholds absolutely from her mother—and from herself—overwhelms her when she contemplates the animal world. She is pained to see kangaroos and wallabies massacred by traffic roaring through the outback. "Can't you understand how destructive I am?" she asks a bustard that persists in standing in the middle of the road. At home, in England, she accidentally pierces a hibernating toad with her gardening fork, and she feels crushed. "He flings his arms wide and opens his mouth, spread-eagled. . . . I bury him fast." Nature is full of omens for her. She is in a constant dialogue with the earth, the trees, innocent creatures of all kinds—as long as they know their place in the universe, and are not pretending to be Greers. "Digging to Australia," English children call their excavations in the sand. And unearthing Daddy's story turns up some vivid travel writing, some powerful images. Australia seems big in this book, but only slightly bigger than the implacable, indefatigable Germaine. Her relation to her childhood place is protective and combative; inevitably, she regards it with love and hate. Alien, a solitary pilgrim, she crisscrosses the land, encountering helpful and malevolent strangers, and surviving storm, flood, and raging heat. As she drives in search of yet another remote graveyard packed with irrelevant Greers, the landscape rolls by like a phantasmagoric diorama through the windows of her rented car. The book contains some startling descriptions of botanical and ecological pathology. Mostly, the Australian landscape tells her—shouts to her—about the evils unleashed when things are uprooted from their habitat and transplanted to the other side of the globe. Dainty garden flowers or harmless weeds brought over by settlers from England grow into monstrous, aggressive "opportunists" in the climate of the antipodes; foreign trees shut out the light of the sky.

> In all the cemeteries I visited in this demented pilgrimage I saw the initial invasion re-enacted as the flowers planted on the graves escaped through the railings and took off . . . cypresses have grown to giant proportions, until they have burst the railings, and shattered the headstones. The dead lie crushed under vast gray roots each bigger than a full-grown man. . . . Oleanders twenty feet across feed on the rare organic material furnished by human hair and bone. Scented geraniums, grown hard and odourless, have seeded themselves for miles.

There is a hallucinogenic, mushroom-eating quality to the tale, and it builds as Germaine gets closer to uncovering the big lie. Sometimes things are in stifling close-up (under Reg's chin, the little scar where his beard didn't grow; his taboo-breaking daughter's sweating palms), and then they are viewed from afar, when these "Greers" fall back to take their place with other generations in a wide scan of history, emigration, and world war. The shifts of focus act as a safety valve. Without them, given Ms. Greer's intensity, we might all explode. Reg was, after all, a daddy among other daddies forced to wave goodbye to pretty wives and tiny daughters and be shipped off to war. In 1942, he was but one of many frightened, miserable inhabitants of Malta, the besieged and bombarded "rock fortress" in the sea: not at all the hero that

Germaine, with what she calls her "aggrandising fantasy," had tried to make him but an anxious, claustrophobic man in earphones, crouching hour after hour in an ill-ventilated office deep inside the rock, isolated from his fellow-officers by his colonial background and by the secrets of the ciphers piped into his head. "Did they make of you a 'deception person,' or did they realise you were a deception person already?" his daughter demands of the dead man, with echoes of le Carré. "Once the initial breach has been made in the self . . . it is a simple matter to lead a treble or quadruple life." After chapters on the tides of history, we always zoom back to the real drama: Germaine and Reg. "Liar! Liar! Liar!" she screams, fitting a big piece of the puzzle into place and wondering more seriously than ever if she is going mad. Like the hero of a folktale, her father apparently left his boyhood town with a troupe of travelling vaudevillians when he was sixteen and never returned to his impoverished foster home. From his rite of passage he emerged impervious to humiliations and ready for a lifetime of pretense. With a vaguely public-school manner and accent, and what his daughter calls "a shonky alias," he became a perfect salesman, a cheeky Charlie, a kind of high-class flimflam man.

Whether by oversight or by malice, Reg made no mention of Germaine in his will. Instead of money (he had none anyway) or a keepsake she inherited his bone structure, his claustrophobia, his promotional skills. And, you can't help feeling as you put down the book, she also inherited the breach in the self. To his colleagues, Reg always seemed an easygoing chap, thoroughly at home in the Australian man's world of sporting events and the barrooms of commercial hotels. Yet his young daughter sensed a deeper truth about him: that he was somehow cut off from life. Out of her hours of research and miles of travel, with enough supporting extras for a miniseries—they range from a Hindu goddess to General Montgomery, and there is a giant chorus of librarians—Ms. Greer has made a big, bold book. Her task has called for almost superhuman expenditures of strength and will, and a very large advance from her publisher. (We learn of this through an ill-fated conversation with her mother.) Yet under all the commotion is the voice of a woman who seems to need reassurance that she is not herself a fraud. "I am a bounder's child. The blood of bounders runs in my veins," she moans. Like Reg, like the plants, she is an uneasy alien. In a way that is only partly related to being an expatriate, she doesn't belong.

And in a way that goes beyond being single or recently bereaved of her father she seems alone, even in company. Her drive and her reputation give her access to a wide variety of worlds and inner sanctums. She is as much, or as little, at home among the whispering saris and "spiritual elegance" of a household of serenely religious upper-class women in India as she is when she is roaring with laughter with the master and fellows of an ancient Cambridge college, sharing their ceremonial port and snuff in an old, panelled, firelit room. "These people accept me," she seems to say. On the road, the restless pilgrim is touched by the simple kindness of strangers—a librarian who fetches a heater to warm her, a woman who bakes her a cake. She encounters people who know, unself-consciously, just where they belong—people who have never felt the breach in the self or, having felt it, have been healed. She looks wistfully on the cloistered life of one of the Indian women, who has "purged her discontent like a sin" and is genuinely happy. She observes how humbly the women of present-day Malta nurture each other and still draw strength from the Roman Catholic faith, which was hers, too, as a girl. She has abandoned her childhood beliefs now ("I am not so superstitious as to open a Bible," she says, having already quoted Genesis several times) in favor of a more contemporary amalgam—bits of Eastern religion, weather goddesses, apocalyptic landscapes, a malevolent "primal elder," and magic animals—from which she tries to distance herself with irony, but which seems nonetheless to form a real safety net. And, wherever she journeys on her strange, lonely quest, sooner or later the ghost of Reg comes clanking in. His is the voice that mocks her yearnings: sneering at the piety of the Maltese, the fatalism and general foreignness of the Indians; calling out in his phony voice to the college servant to forget the rare wines and fine cigars, just fetch him a beer and a cork-tip. Germaine Greer is a celebrity. She says in retrospect that before embarking on her voyage she should have visited the shrine of the Eumenides— the fearsome goddesses in charge of avenging crimes within the family. Since she was not in ancient Greece but in twentieth-century Britain, she did what celebrities do to appease the gods: made a ritual appearance on "Wogan," Britain's most popular television talk show. Ten million viewers bore silent witness to the heroine's departure and would be watching the shores for her safe return. Yet for a daughter searching for her daddy's love, even from the other side of death, ten million million of the most benevolent and attentive viewers can never be quite enough.

1990

THERE AT *The New Yorker*:
THE NOVEL I NEVER WROTE
FOR WILLIAM SHAWN

FOR MORE THAN HALF my lifetime, I was a kind of daughter of *The New Yorker*. I was shaped as a writer and a woman by my place in the complex extended family presided over by the magazine's long-standing editor, William Shawn. I arrived in the late sixties, and it was my fate and my privilege to come of age in the crookedy halls and dusty offices of the old premises at 25 West Forty-third Street. Like many members of the staff, I was very young when I joined the fold. It seems absurd to me now—when the man most of us knew as "Mr. Shawn" is gone and all the continuous, familial, and gentle community he once led has been swept away—but back then I vaguely assumed that even when I was old I would still be doing my best to produce articles (as the one-line "contract" I signed each Christmastime mildly suggested) in my office on the eighteenth floor.

"THERE ARE things that you and I have never discussed,"
Mr. Shawn said to me one winter afternoon in the early
eighties. We were working on the proofs of a long reporting
piece I had written about some people who lived for power
and fashion. We were sitting on a sofa in the softly lit, dark-
panelled lobby of the Algonquin Hotel. He was in his mid-
seventies at that time—a short, slight, bald man with an
intelligent, compassionate face. He had a rosy complexion,
which grew rosier when he encountered others (especially
women), and he had very long fingers, whose tips he would
sometimes bunch up and touch to his forehead when he was
concentrating or explaining things. (The long fingers were
useful for stretching over the keyboard when, as was his habit,
he played jazz on his piano at home.) Thinking deeply and
feeling deeply went together with him: they were inseparable,
as he was inseparable from the magazine that had by then represented the week-by-week unfolding of his interests and pas-
sions for more than thirty years.

He had been sitting on the sofa, with his mechanical pencil
in his hand and a clipboard supporting various *New Yorker*
proofs on his knee, for well over an hour. But he was still
dressed in his fleece-collared overcoat with the belt buckled
up. Beside him on the velvet cushion, in a meticulous pile,
were his leather satchel-style briefcase, his umbrella, and his
fedora with the crease well tweaked from tipping his hat
with the old-fashioned good manners for which he was
known. The checkroom woman in the booth near to the Rose
Room (where he lunched on Special K or pound cake most
days) knew about his chivalry and his generous tips. It was
probably Virginia, who was said to have been a dance-band
singer in her youth; she would happily have taken charge of
his things. But he thought we might have to go somewhere
else, if the lamps turned out to be too dim to read by or if we
were disturbed by too much noise. He had already checked
with the concierge to see how easy it would be to find a cab.
What's more, the sofa was in a kind of passageway; perhaps
he had detected a draft. The heavy fabric of the overcoat kept

getting in the line of sight between him and the words he was so focussed on. He would push the folds out of the way again with a weary little gesture, as if the tide of materiality were too much for him to bear.

This decision to wear his coat—like other stratagems of Mr. Shawn's, like many of the procedures at the old *New Yorker*—might have been viewed by outside observers as quaint. But it was simply a solution to a practical problem. He was terrified of catching cold, because that might keep him from working. It might slow what always looked in him like the semisacred task of getting out the magazine each week in a form as close to perfect as he could make it. He was also phobic about self-service elevators, especially if they were full of strangers, people with emotional demands, or people with colds. I've never known anyone to match him in the imagination he brought to getting around some problem—to thinking things out. Working on his proofs at the Algonquin was simply the solution to that day's dilemma: how to do his work, when he had to leave the office early because the fellow who operated the manual elevator was going off duty at three in the afternoon. (This elevator was the only one Shawn could ride serenely, and it had been expressly retained by the building's management after the other elevators were automated.)

Now, I can think of a thousand things that Mr. Shawn and I never discussed. But what we had never discussed back then, it turned out—he looked jolted to realize it—was one of the basic principles of *New Yorker* reporting, that of avoiding "indirection." This was of the utmost importance to Harold Ross, who founded the magazine in 1925. Shawn, who began as a "Talk of the Town" reporter, in 1932, had learned much from Ross, becoming his managing editor in his early thirties and succeeding to the editorship after the founder died in 1951. Indirection, Shawn said, meant that you couldn't talk about a man taking off his hat unless you had earlier established that he was wearing one.

"Did you *plant* that earlier in the piece?" he asked me, of some item of information. On his lips, the horticultural metaphor was striking. He preferred reading about nature to being in it. The months he spent in the well-groomed suburb of Bronxville—where he repaired each summer with his wife, Cecille, and sons, Wallace and Allen, before they left home—always brought him a measure of disquiet, as well as pleasure. He startled me one day by comparing all the Irish, English, and American fiction he had read in the previous fifty years to a "field of wheat," and portraying himself as a kind of husbandman, digging in the soil and plucking short stories up by their roots to see if they had taken.

Ross, a man from the American West who had been in the army, might have resented being caught by some previously "unplanted" fact in a kind of ambush; Shawn might simply have thought it rude to run the risk of confusing someone else. Sometimes, with his courteous pole vault into the mind of a fellow human being—his flier at what might conceivably ruffle someone else's feelings, because it would certainly ruffle his—Shawn reminded me of Proust, who once intercepted room service at the threshold of a friend's suite in a resort hotel and served the meal himself, because *he* would have been embarrassed to have a waiter see him dressed, as the friend was dressed, in his bicycling trousers. Himself a man with many secrets—his own and those of hundreds of others—Shawn liked to learn as much as he possibly could about people and the world. And he assumed that you, too, would not want to be confused or left in the dark. This made him a brilliant and patient explainer—at least of the things he was willing to have you know. Although he and I often spoke about writing fiction, it was only after his death that I learned of his tenacious dream of doing so himself. It turned out he had even tried to give up his editing job at the magazine to be a full-time writer when he was still young, but couldn't do it. And he really committed himself to producing a novel of his own only after his career at *The New Yorker* was at an end and he was well into his eighties.

The afternoon wore on. The lobby was filling up. It

occurred to Mr. Shawn to ask whether I would like something to drink. He tapped the brass bell secured to the low
table in front of him. He seemed to take a childlike delight in
the resounding ping.

"It never does any good," he said, cheerfully. "The waiter
never comes."

We had got to a scene in my piece where the people who
lived for power and fashion were at a party in an elegant
restaurant. He made the deftest of editorial fixes with the
mechanical pencil. On the page, a woman was sitting on some
man's knee and calling out to another friend in greeting.

"At least these people seem to be having fun. More fun
than I am," Mr. Shawn said, with a chuckle and a little shake
of the head. For several years, he had been embattled over his
choice of his successor as editor of *The New Yorker*. Across
the street, within the tribe, a painful, fatal struggle was
undermining the foundations of our ever more Chekhovian-
seeming house. The old ties, truces, and civilities that had
bound us for generations were breaking down. Within a few
years, the way would be clear for a new owner with only a
passing interest in Mr. Shawn and his careful explanations of
the traditions and principles without which, in his mind, *The
New Yorker* would not be worth publishing because it would
not be *The New Yorker* at all. For now, though, Mr. Shawn
was still here on the sofa, doing the work that made him
happy. I watched him pencil a note in the margin of the proof
in his infinitesimal handwriting. After several hours of close
work, he looked fresher than when he had started out. His
face was glowing.

"No, Mr. Shawn," I said. "You're having more fun than
they are. I'm sure of it."

IN RECENT YEARS, I have found myself wondering
what my life would have been like if I had not learned the
fundamentals of the literary craft at *The New Yorker*, and that
largely under the watchful eye of more or less elderly men.

After a provincial English girlhood and a spell at university (where I spent hours dreamily punting on the river in romantic hats), I landed on a Manhattan that was quite distinct: a literary landscape largely conjured up by the men of *The New Yorker*, whether dead or alive. The geography extended north, as if as a courtesy, to E. B. White's Maine and Cheever's Ossining, and east (at the right time of year) to the Fire Island dunes of Wolcott Gibbs. It stretched raffishly uptown and down to take in the prize-rings and saloons of A. J. Liebling; it encircled the waterfronts of Joseph Mitchell. But mostly the terrain was within easy walking distance of the office: encompassing Times Square and the West Forties, where Ross had lived with his first wife, Jane Grant, while he was launching the infant magazine and testing his publisher's faith by running up gigantic losses at poker; the Century and the Coffee House clubs, where many of the *New Yorker* men were members (but not the women, of course); the once-favored gin mills and watering holes like Bleeck's or Costello's, over on Third Avenue; eating places like the Blue Ribbon or the Lobster, where I vaguely imagined our writers and artists working their way through steaks and chops, shad roe and soft-shelled crabs, according to the changing seasons. As a young female person from England, I had an instant toehold in the New York of Mayors Walker and La Guardia; my nostrils had a whiff of stale ale in them, and my ear was cocked for the long-silent rumble of the "El."

It took me many years as a staff writer before I had the courage to try my hand at "real" *New Yorker* reporting. In part this was because my life was linked, for quite a while, to that of H., a rather distinguished *New Yorker* reporter who, though certainly not elderly, was much older than I. He had started his career in the checking department; and he discouraged me from writing about serious facts, on the grounds that when I told a story, I never got it right. But even before H., and long before "indirection" came up on the sofa, I felt the silent presence of *New Yorker* men, stretching back to the twenties and thirties, donning and doffing their hypothetical hats.

After Shawn's *New Yorker* came to an end and the magazine's history ceased to be organic, I lost my context, for a time; my imaginary New York, centered on the office and on Forty-third Street, came crumbling down in clouds of dust. And it began to feel imperative for me to write as a woman— to write specifically about women and their lives. I don't know whether this would have been the case had Shawn still been around. For my first twenty years as a writer, he had been the only reader whose opinion mattered to me at all. In practice, Mr. Shawn was a patient developer and staunch supporter of women writers—who, he observed, sometimes came into their own only in their forties—and his magazine regularly published the work of M. F. K. Fisher, Mollie Panter-Downes, Sylvia Townsend Warner, Janet Flanner, and Emily Hahn (among others) when they were well into their seventies or even their eighties. This was the most encouraging signal a young woman just setting out could possibly receive. But he would have balked at describing people as "women writers." In his mind, they were simply individual *writers*, to be cherished even (especially) when silent and discouraged, but capable of giving him, now or sometime in the future, what he honored with the term "Good Writing."

I T   W A S   Mr. Shawn himself who showed me, on my first day on the eighteenth floor, the eight-by-twelve-foot room that was to be my "office." With a gesture, he invited me to sit at the battered old wooden desk, which seemed so much like something from the city room of some defunct newspaper— the *World-Telegram*, perhaps, or the *Herald Tribune*—with drawers just right for a bourbon supply and with what looked like cigar burns on the top. He stood in the doorway smiling and picturing the Good Writing I might conceivably produce on the old Underwood with its chipped round keys. (Neither he nor I knew whether I could really write.) I expect he also imagined the companionable chats I would have with colleagues, as yet unmet, who would be dropping in to sit in the room's second chair. There was a battered old black telephone (the number of the editorial offices was OXford 5-1414); a pile of shiny-jacketed new books, each of which I was supposed to review in a few anonymous words under the rubric "Briefly Noted"; and a stack of white typing paper, which Shawn, reaching out with a murmured "May I?" aligned with his long fingers and moved across the desktop an inch or so to the right. Realizing that something was missing, he went off down the hall to the messengers' room—still known as the "boys' room," in those days—and returned with a sheaf of freshly sharpened pencils in his hand. For the first of many times, outside my office (or one whose occupant I was visiting) I heard his light, quick step on the linoleum as he approached—the skaterly glide of the soles of his shiny black shoes as he covered the last few feet before knocking tentatively on the door and sidling in.

That little office, in a line of similar rooms, each with their desks and sturdy old round-backed wooden chairs, wasn't really an office, of course; it was a room of my own. I sat there in silence, reading my review books, for a year or so. Very few people spoke to me, and I was too shy to speak to people I didn't know. For lunch, I would send downstairs to the luncheonette for sandwiches that, like everything about America in general and New York City in particular, privately astonished me. (I remember, when I visited the luncheonette in person, being vaguely shocked by the sight of Mr. Shawn's ladylike, Southern-born secretary opening wide her jaws to bite into a giant, thoroughly un-European-sized hamburger.) From behind one wall of my silent room, I heard a froglike chorus of clicking sounds, from the switchboard where Anne, our motherly telephonist, plugged and unplugged the board, personally connecting the tribe to each other and to the outside world. From behind the other wall, I heard the

less predictable sounds of Freddie Packard. He had been one
of the platoon of possible right-hand men Ross had hired and
then reassigned in the early days before settling permanently
on Shawn. Packard had been head of the checking department, too. (Indeed, at first he *was* the checking department.)
Now, as far as I could tell from glimpses through the half-
open door of his room (for although we were neighbors for
some years, I do not remember us having a conversation), he
devoted his time to producing some of the magazine's small
pen-and-ink drawings, known as "spots." Sometimes I would
freeze in my reading or my chewing as I heard him roar in
frustration and hurl his pen or his inkpot at the wall. Or from
his unimaginably crammed and untidy lair I would hear the
thunder of what he called a "slide," as some teetering, ceiling-
high pile of proofs and newspapers cascaded from desk to
floor.

The New Yorker occupied several floors of the building,
and in many ways resembled a rambling old country man-
sion, with attics haunted by shadowy and eccentric aunts and
uncles and with basements and strange closets stuffed with
memos and drawings everyone had forgotten about. The sole
occupants of some of the rooms might not have visited them
for months or even years; it seemed entirely possible that they
might have died. Snatched peeks into rather small rooms
housing people with rather large obsessions revealed yet
more teetering piles of papers and books. On the branches of
wooden hatstands there hung primordial fedoras and
broken-spoked umbrellas like wounded bats. Cracked and
dusty galoshes waited humbly in corners as decades passed.
The single cleaner, overwhelmed by the accretions of history
and forbidden by many writers to touch the surface of desks,
contented herself with emptying the big, army-green, rib-
sided metal wastebaskets. I remember with affection the
repeated sound of her working her way along the hall,
gonging the wastebaskets back onto the linoleum at the end
of winter afternoons. Someone's typewriter would be clack-
ing round the bend in the corridor, and the lights beginning

to go off, one by one, in the office buildings across the street. A burst of conversation and laughter would reach me through an open door. Mr. Shawn, who seemed to remember every piece that every writer had ever written, once observed that for him no *New Yorker* writer ever died; that he could still quite clearly hear their laughter and their voices in the halls.

I HAD NOT the remotest idea, when I started out at *The New Yorker*, about writing or the life of writers. This gave my apprentice reviews a mercilessness that makes me shiver, in hindsight. But I spent many hours happily listening to William Shawn explain that you could learn to write only by trying different things, and that you had to be willing to keep going until something he called the "tone" was right. Then there was the polishing. "The self-criticism of the writer isn't always very sound," I remember him saying. "Sometimes he may change or throw out the best of his own writing."

People confided in Shawn. Decades of picking up the pieces in the personal lives of writers had led him to some conclusions. He told me that he thought it was better if writers didn't marry other writers, and that they should exercise caution about acquiring real estate. (In vain, for I was to go ahead and marry H., and we would even buy a house.) "The magazine never lends money to writers to buy houses," he once announced, quivering over the seriousness of a "policy" laid down, as so many had been laid down, after some moment of managerial weakness involving idiosyncratic contributors who were probably long gone. He told stories about writers—of how Jean Stafford had married A. J. Liebling, of how St. Clair McKelway—another of Ross's managing editors—was subject to periods of madness which he put to good use by writing about them dazzlingly when he was sane again. But I don't remember Shawn saying an unkind thing about a *New Yorker* writer, even those with modest talents, flaky lives, or the urge to hurt or betray him.

The writers and artists I could see walking the halls or
stopping at the watercooler outside my door seemed to me to
be miraculous and sometimes fragile beings. I knew from
what they published that they had grown-up lives and a fully
developed craft with which to express experience. In 1968,
my first summer at *The New Yorker*, Shawn told *Women's
Wear Daily*, a paper for which he felt a capricious affection,
that there were "at least five generations" of writers still at the
magazine, beginning with "the original group" from the
1920s, including White, Flanner (still publishing the crys-
talline prose of her "Letter from Paris," which had originated
in the letters she wrote to her friend Jane Grant in 1925), and
our nattily dressed racetrack correspondent, George F. T.
Ryall, who since 1926 had written pseudonymously as
"Audax Minor." I had no idea that Shawn's willingness to
grant this interview was extraordinary. Mr. Shawn never
made public appearances, and as a rule he didn't believe in
speaking for the record about the magazine; he thought this
locked things in and killed its spirit. He was very sophisticated about publicity and promotion and generally wanted
no part of either. He thought it natural, if not desirable, that
some of the writers and artists he revered most were known
largely to other writers and artists. He explained to the
awestruck reporter from *Women's Wear* that he was simply
pursuing the philosophy he'd inherited from Mr. Ross, for
whom "disregarding what was popular, fashionable, or com-
mercially successful" was a point of pride.

From my desk, through the half-open door ("Open or
closed?" Shawn would ask as he put his hand on the doorknob to make his exit from each writer's office; he knew that
such fine-tuning of solitude and collegiality mattered) I
would catch sight of stray representatives of the five generations. And then I would stand gazing at an assortment of
books by those same people, behind a glass-fronted bookcase
down the hall. Together with identical bookcases filled with
a faintly ludicrous miscellany of new editions of worthy
books that no one had wanted to review, this comprised what

was grandly called the "writers' library." It was kept locked, but its key kept getting lost, and anyway no writer ever seemed to use it. The modest room that housed the magazine's official library had a more systematic collection of thousands of books (Nabokov, S. J. Perelman, Peter De Vries, V. S. Pritchett, Muriel Spark, Penelope Gilliatt) whose copyright page read, "The contents of this book originally appeared in *The New Yorker*." Other shelves were lined with battered black binders whose spines were marked in wobbly white handwriting with years and the names of writers. In the shadow of these tomes, and in the fumes of rubber cement, young women spent their days in the unending, Dickensian task of cutting each week's issue into columns and pasting these into new or old black binders.

While staying alone in a midtown hotel—the Algonquin, perhaps—E. B. White once wrote an essay about New York City. He said that it was a tightly packed place where you could still be agreeably solitary; that it blended "the gift of privacy with the excitement of participation." He might just as well have been writing about the premises at 25 West Forty-third Street. The architecture around the place was famously amateurish and improvisational; walls and doors had been thrown up as the need for private space arose. Archipelagoes of hall, too narrow for two pairs of shoulders to pass each other in comfort, were lined with the rooms of writers and artists. Further doors, like those of a shabby motel giving onto a pool too small to be useful, faced the closest thing we had to a collective space—a wider hallway with the watercooler and the glass-fronted bookcases; a dime-store wall clock with its electric cord laconically drooping below it; a couple of love seats covered in a dingy brown synthetic tweed; and a table lamp that looked (as so much of the furniture around the place looked) as if it had been picked up in the closing moments of a garage sale.

The presence of the five generations of people at all stages of lives and careers the magazine seemed committed, willy-nilly, to sustaining; of Joe Mitchell, who came into the office every day (wearing a Panama hat in the summer) and who was cherished as a writer of genius but who happened to have published nothing at all for ages and ages—all this made up the archeology and the ecology of the place where I found a home in America.

M Y   E D I T O R   for my apprentice years was Rogers E. M. Whitaker, who was known as "Popsie." His office was on one of the corners of the nineteenth floor of *The New Yorker* and, in a hot contest, it was by far the most densely packed. Piles of proofs, newspapers, books on football, and yellowing railway timetables reached ceiling height from desk, floor, and bookshelves as well as typing tables shoehorned in as reinforcements. (In addition to his editing work, he was also a loyal Princeton man who wrote a column on college football over the initials "J.W.L." and a traveller who as "E. M. Frimbo, the world's greatest railroad buff," often appeared in "Talk of the Town" stories written by Tony Hiss.) With my hair flying, in my boots and velvet hot pants, I would run up the stairs and down the hallway to his office.

"It's me, Mr. Whitaker," I would say, putting my head round his slightly open door. He gave a sound between a growl and a snarl; sometimes Hiss wrote of him as "the Old Curmudgeon."

"I didn't think it was Bella Abzug," he said once, referring to the congresswoman, who was famous for wearing hats, but not hot pants. He would be sitting at his desk by the window, with the proofs spread out in a space he had cleared with an impatient sweep of the side of his hand across its jumbled surface. He was a heavyset fellow, close to seventy. He was said to have come over to Ross's magazine, with the encouragement of the writer Lois Long, from Frank Crowninshield's *Vanity Fair* in 1926. In profile, everything about Popsie seemed weighted down: large head; pendulous lower lip; a paunch draped in a waistcoat with food-stained lapels and emitting terrifying rumbles after he had eaten a hearty lunch. How formal it seems, now, that relationship between the elderly man and the young woman. The only remotely personal thing I remember him telling me was when I asked how some vacation had been and he waxed lyrical about a trip he had made by train through Abyssinia, and about the sparks shooting into the African night when "darkies" fired the engine with wonderfully sweet-smelling sandalwood. Apart from working, riding the rails, or cheering on the Tigers, his hours were said to be spent in New York night clubs, drinking Brandy Alexanders and cultivating enduring friendships with famous jazz musicians. He was said not to discourage the idea of a past involving Ziegfeld girls and even with a number of *wives* in it, but I found it hard to give this credence. He was very much a bachelor—a man of the Jazz Age, but with chalk-striped, custom-made suits and black homburgs (did he have a watch chain?) that made him seem more of an Edwardian. He was known for making wittily cutting remarks, especially to other men, that could tilt in the direction of cruelty. (On account of one such remark, Popsie and Freddie Packard were locked in a feud that made them pass in the hallway without greeting each other for more than thirty years.) I pair Whitaker in my mind with the far sunnier character of Hobart G. ("Hobey") Weekes, another tailored Edwardian clubman, Princeton man, and light litterateur who had been very useful to Ross. Hobey had a nervous habit of sticking out his tongue like a cat—a sudden, disconcerting gesture that was somehow part of his charm. He is still remembered with great affection in his gentlemanly haunts; he endowed the Coffee House with the funds to throw a cocktail party in his memory.

Whitaker and I sat side by side at the desk. Past his bulky silhouette and through the window I could see an unusable terrace, which ran round much of the building at this level. I remember sitting for what felt like hours staring at the balustrade of crumbling cement urns shaped like Indian clubs and at the glinty-windowed granite cliffs of the old midtown skyscrapers. We would sit there shoulder to shoulder thinking up the perfect word; through him I learned that truth, clarity, and making readers see things mattered very much. He *was* an old curmudgeon. But something about the purposefulness with which he would push himself out of his chair and stand with his big head bent over Webster's dictionary, or the solemnity with which he unscrewed the cap of his huge black fountain pen and marked our changes on the proof, made me feel that what he and I were doing was somehow grand: a moral act.

The giant digits of the clock on the wall of the *Newsweek* building visible from our window, the clock in the eighteenth-floor hall, and the street clock outside the Morgan Guaranty on Forty-fourth and Fifth (where many of us did our banking) were all I needed, back then, to tell the time. I didn't wear a watch; I lived *New Yorker* hours. Even when a piece was going to press, there seemed to be no rush. The magazine rolled smoothly into existence each week in an old-fashioned mood of industry without bustle. After I had begun to write the "Feminine Fashions" column, I would sit with Popsie Whitaker until the dusk drew in and the Indian clubs grew dim—until at last my words could bring some periwinkle peplum or some organdy sleeves just as clearly to his mind's eye as those Abyssinian sparks.

W H I T A K E R   H A D also edited Lois Long, who had written the "Feminine Fashions" column for the "On and Off the Avenue" department for some forty years before I succeeded her. I was twenty-two when Shawn invited me to write for the magazine on fashion, a subject about which I knew nothing apart from what I had absorbed from reading Baudelaire and from being part of the generation in England that first adopted the miniskirt. Shawn seemed to consider my ignorance of my subject and even of the magazine an advantage, on the whole; he was faintly depressed by young people who had grown up reading *The New Yorker* and who tried to copy people who had written for it in the past. He had a great affection for the pretty trappings of femininity, an empathy for the iconoclasm of the young in the 1960s, and an unprecedented freedom from advertisers who might get the foolish idea of expecting quid pro quos or exerting pressure on editorial content. All this, combined with his daily reading of *Women's Wear*, seemed to give him complete confidence that under his guidance, I could produce the kind of fashion column he wanted.

First, we had to bypass Lois and all the old ways of reporting about fashion. As I was preparing to write my first column, Shawn invited me to have dinner with her at the Algonquin. He paved the way for the meeting by telling me about all the brilliant writing she had done for the magazine since her arrival in the 1920s, when she had written a column about night clubs called "Tables for Two," under the pseudonym "Lipstick." She had been a sort of Zelda Fitzgerald figure, only married not to a famous writer but to the famous cartoonist Peter Arno. She was beautiful and witty and he was handsome and worldly. They had been, Shawn said, the most glamorous couple in New York. "First marriages are *such* fun!" she was to tell her young assistant, Elizabeth Guyer, when she said she was getting married. (I'm certain that Shawn didn't tell me what I learned later: that Arno used to knock Lois about.) Lois liked to suggest that many of the witticisms attributed to Dorothy Parker—who was still alive, but invisible to me and moving toward a lonely and alcoholic end at the Hotel Volney, at this time—had really come from her. Lois used to sit in her office in her Lilly Daché hats, with a cigarette dangling from her mouth, laughing at her own jokes as she banged them out for her column.

A woman who came to *The New Yorker* in the same year and at the same age as I did told me recently that she immediately started to pretend she was far older and wiser than she was, and that this kept her immature for decades. I understood her exactly. (I also reflected that somehow the world we had each entered and whose myths we took on as protective camouflage made it strangely difficult for two young women to ally themselves in a simple friendship.) One of my earliest signed reviews was entitled "Life Begins, and Ends, at Sixes and Sevens." But it was Whitaker who had come up with the phrase, as well as the commas, and they hung on me just as if I had borrowed his waistcoat or his homburg. Like any young writer, I had experience for which I had no words and words for which I had no experience. That evening when I arrived at the Algonquin to be introduced to Lois, I could observe that Mr. Shawn was sitting in the lobby with his folded coat and his hat on his knee, looking awkward; and that she was not glamorous at all anymore, but only an old woman with pebble-thick glasses and an absurdly large wig. She was facing him as I approached from behind her and, seeing me, he got to his feet to greet me. She reminded me of a tortoise, stretching her neck and swiveling her head round the wing of her chair to take in the girl who was displacing her. Only in hindsight can I see and name what Lois was, at that, our only meeting—with William Shawn and almost half a century between us. First, Lois was frightened, then she was tipsy. At that time, I could have told you only that she was rambling on and on and that I found it hard to concentrate. I kept catching the eye of H., who was wearing a bow tie and sitting at a nearby table with the vivacious young woman who was then his wife. (She also worked for *The New Yorker*, and went on to give Mr. Shawn a lot of Good Writing.) H. was making her laugh, and something about the sight of the trio of Shawn, Lois, and me made the couple laugh harder than ever. Lois talked a lot about writing her memoirs, a book she wanted to write about the 1920s—the era when she was not a plain old woman who kept repeating herself, but the glamorous "Lipstick," brief of witty phrase and hemline. Shawn was encouraging. But even I somehow knew that she would never write that book.

Something about the encounter must have troubled Mr. Shawn. Late that night, he telephoned.

"Is this a convenient time?" he said, in the quavery voice that retained the twang of his native Chicago.

He wanted to assure me that, like so many *New Yorker* writers, I would write on many different subjects in the course of my career, "trying all kinds of things." He felt sure that I could do reporting of various kinds and that I would be able to write fiction. After all, I wouldn't be writing my column for the rest of my life. He spoke with sadness about our evening with Lois.

"I don't want you to think that all *The New Yorker*'s fashion critics end up like that," he said.

Whitaker, who was very loyal to Lois, must have known how hurt she was that I never sought her help, but he never suggested that I should. And Mr. Shawn, who had led Lois to believe that she would be consulted by me, told me to find my own way as best I could and on no account to ask the older woman for guidance.

T W O   B O O K S by women whose lives had been changed by *The New Yorker* appeared in my first year there, and I looked to Mr. Shawn for clues as to how I should respond to them. The first was by Jane Grant, and it was boldly entitled *Ross, The New Yorker, and Me*. Grant, who was a friend of Lois Long's as well as Flanner's, belonged, like Lois, to the Lucy Stone League, whose members were committed to keeping their maiden names after marriage. She was clearly a woman of courage and accomplishment: the first woman to report on stories of general interest for *The New York Times*, she had met Ross in Paris during the First World War, when they were both working. She contributed money and imaginative energy to the birth of the magazine, and presided over the lively, Bohemian household in the West Forties where the newly married couple lived, along with the writer Alexander Woollcott. From the evidence, Ross was not the best material for a husband; after Grant he was to try marriage twice again, with only mixed success. She went on to a long second marriage, putting down roots with a man with whom she founded the famous White Flower Farm nursery, in northwestern Connecticut. It seems natural that she should have written a memoir of her experiences with Ross and *The New Yorker.* Although she was long divorced from the first and had had a long-smoldering dispute with the second over money, the tone of her book (forty years on) is rather cheery and detached. The publication of *Ross, The New Yorker, and Me* seemed painful to Mr. Shawn. It violated Ross's privacy and Shawn's own principle against speaking publicly about *The New Yorker.* I remember Shawn being pressed to give an opinion of the book, and the chilling finality of his judgment. "It was a mistake," he said, tersely.

The second book was by the Irish-born writer Maeve Brennan. It was a collection of the remarkable vignettes she had first published as letters from "The Long-Winded Lady" in "The Talk of the Town." In a way, this book was the obverse of the other. Grant had written about *The New Yorker* from the standpoint of one who was, at this stage, an outsider to its close-knit tribal ways, an escapee looking back over fieldstone walls and daylilies to expose some family secrets. Brennan had the use of an office, because of her "Talk" stories and her own contributions to "Briefly Noted," which were brilliantly deft. (She also published enough short stories to fill a couple of books, but people who only wrote fiction were not given offices.) She had made her intramural marriage—becoming St. Clair McKelway's fourth wife in a union that fulfilled the forebodings of the couple's friends by proving brief and disastrous. She was, in the private-yet-participatory *New Yorker* way, an insider looking outward at the world—at least, reporting back on as much of the world as could be seen by a respectable and creative woman walking midtown streets alone, or drinking a martini and reading Balzac at a table-for-one within a stone's throw of 25 West Forty-third Street.

I read Maeve Brennan's book, and the stories that continued to appear at lengthening intervals with her name scrawled on the "Talk" proofs that were pinned up on the eighteenth-floor bulletin board, next to the men's room and the fire escape. And I wanted so much to write like the Long-Winded Lady. She was an expatriate like me, but she seemed at home in Manhattan, which she called a "half-capsized city," with its "inhabitants hanging on, most of them still able to laugh as they cling to the island that is their life's predicament." She was a female *flâneur* in the modern city. In the fifties and the early sixties—the period covered by the essays—she progressed in age from her thirties to her fifties. In Times Square and the West Forties, the brownstones were being replaced by office towers; and the theatre, radio, and newspaper businesses that had once thrived were giving way to less legitimate forms of enterprise. She seemed to move house a lot, and be familiar with the neighborhood's residential hotels, which had once been elegant but where elevators were likely to break down and old women "cut off from real life" complained in vain to desk clerks dozing over television game shows.

The Lady had pluck. There was a tremendous charm of surface detail in Maeve's little sketches—a Gypsy-like and feminine humanity of florists and newsstands, ailanthus trees and pigeons, of straphanging on the subway while reading the evening paper, of visiting Monsieur Paul, the hairdresser on the second floor of the Royalton. She could listen in on the conversation of a couple in a nearby booth in the Adano or the Steak de Paris (her two favorite restaurants) or watch a woman reading a letter in a window across the street and make up a whole little tragicomedy around it. She could make you see and feel things. Before I had lived a round of Manhattan seasons, I learned from her book how Sixth Avenue looked in a blizzard, or how the city's sidewalks smell after rain, or what a real heat wave was, when "there was nothing to breathe but heavy displeasure."

In reportorial lineage, "The Long-Winded Lady" was like a modest, nameless female gleaner, coming along after the tradition of brilliant *New Yorker* men but in a way that was

far more precarious. Liebling died prematurely, no doubt because of his gargantuan taste for food and booze; Mitchell fell silent for what seemed like half a lifetime; McKelway (along with a couple of other distinguished *New Yorker* writers, of equally delicate mental health) took to writing meaningless words on the walls of the eighteenth floor. My first little apartment had a rented piano, a chair from the Salvation Army, and a transparent plastic sofa that you blew up like a beach balloon. Once, in the middle of a night during my early days at the magazine, Mac turned up at this modest home along with half a dozen New York City cops who started battering down my front door. I came out in my nightgown and urged them to stop. He was by now a rumpled-looking man in his sixties living, like his ex-wife, among the people "cut off from life" in the shabby midtown hotels. But his powers of persuasion and air of authority were still so great that—in a manic phase when he had built me into a fantasy of assassination—he had convinced the N.Y.P.D. that I had been murdered. (Mr. Shawn told me not to discuss this episode with anyone but him, and to stay away from the eighteenth floor for a time.) The fragility of *New Yorker* writers was distributed evenly between the sexes. But, although the men delighted in writing about characters on the outer fringes of polite society, I never felt, as I read their work in the big black binders, that they saw *themselves* as being marginal.

With Maeve Brennan, on the other hand, I can see—rereading her now, when I am old enough to have known what it means to feel shipwrecked—that her position is precarious and she knows it. I don't suppose anyone stays the course in New York if they lack a tolerance for drama; a thirst for it may even be an asset at the outset. But the reports from the Lady, which begin with an affection for parades and brass bands, progress through bangs, howls, and crashes that echo in the streets to a positive zest for four-alarm fires. The style is ever more elegant and witty, but events are ever more disturbing: a woman drops dead of a heart attack right on the

sidewalk just as the writer is having dinner at a table in the window; a mysterious little man takes it into his head to smash the plate-glass window of the Schrafft's at Sixth Avenue and Forty-ninth Street as she is sitting at the counter. Most troubling of all are the small defeats that overtake the observer directly: she finds it hard to get out of bed or get ready to go to a party, so ends up late and tumbling down the stairs in the hallway of some sublet, dirtying her clean white gloves, and weeping.

No one knows why it is that the little man, who is wearing a black suit and carrying a bunch of red roses, has broken the window. As luck would have it, the Lady was sitting on a stool at the far end of the counter, out of the range of flying glass. I am sure that Mr. Shawn was relieved at this: the idea of his writers being in pain or in danger caused him anguish. (Paradoxically, he inspired and published some remarkable reporting from various wars.) The book of the Long-Winded Lady amounts to a kind of non-fiction novel in the epistolary form. Just as Flanner had written letters first to Ross and then to Shawn from Paris, and they had published them, Maeve was reporting familiarly back to Shawn about New York, the city that suited him so perfectly. She told him stories about the neighborhood where he had spent the majority of his hours, and about people, events, and places (except for the hotels with untrustworthy elevators, to be sure) he might experience himself. The Lady and her shy and phobic editor shared what Virginia Woolf once called "trespass vision"— seeing as much as you possibly could of life and human nature through a kind of keyhole, and reflecting deeply on a restricted world.

I can feel Mr. Shawn behind the writing of the veiled "Lady," of "The Talk of the Town." The "W.S." to whom the book is dedicated, with a discretion that must have given him particular satisfaction, is a rosily attentive second presence—half-concealed, but throughout the pages just the same. The precision with which the miscreant of Schrafft's is described as he stands meekly in custody on the sidewalk—"a

very small man, about five feet one"—is a sure sign that Shawn, who was five foot three, has marked his proof with the mechanical pencil and requested clarification. (He was equally scrupulous on the subject of baldness.)

Especially, I imagine the pair of them marooned in the quiet city in midsummer—the solitary woman writer and the editor who dignified her life with his attention, with space for her "talk" in his own quite singular "Town." You feel that she was in New York, creeping along to the oasis of air-conditioning in her office or the Adano, because other possibilities (marriage, a house in the country) had not worked out. You feel that he was there—scooting into his banquette in the Rose Room; slip-sliding into the revolving door of the Morgan bank; reading and reading away in the office that also had its balustrade of crumbling urns—because possibilities (being the editor of *The New Yorker*, in particular) had really worked out very satisfactorily indeed.

I wanted so much, back then, to write stories for *The New Yorker* and for this pinkish, shortish, baldish man who travelled in every day from Bronxville and then sat at his desk in his shirt-sleeves—with a fan turned on if the heat was overwhelming, but never ever the air-conditioning. I wanted to write enough stories to fill a book and have him hold it, wearing the look of tender pride I saw as he placed Maeve Brennan's collection on the arched bookshelf in the living room of his Fifth Avenue apartment, where he kept the hundreds of volumes he particularly cherished. Even though the Long-Winded Lady made no secret of the thin ice she stood on, I was drawn to the way she lived as a writer: with "W.S." there to stand sentry—like the bartender who stood silently polishing his beer glasses in the Steak de Paris, and gazing out with her at the passing world.

WHEN NEWS got out that H. had left his vivacious wife and was going to marry me, Edith Oliver, the magazine's wisecracking off-Broadway theatre critic, remarked that she hadn't been as shocked since she heard that McKelway was planning to marry Maeve. I am embarrassed to admit it, but I was profoundly gratified by this remark, which augured so badly for my own union. I had arrived in the *New Yorker* tribe; I fitted some sort of mold. H. tried to persuade me not to tell anyone I was getting married—not even Mr. Shawn. Earlier, H. had had his own telephone installed in the kitchen of my little apartment; he revealed the number only to his estranged wife (who was probably encouraged to think that he was merely having a nervous breakdown) and to Mr. Shawn. That telephone would ring as I was cooking supper, but I was not allowed to answer it. Shawn had tremendous power in the lives of almost everyone I was close to. For many years, I was accustomed to feeling the whole chemistry of a gathering changed by a telephone call from him. We might be laughing, quarrelling, or sobbing, but everything stopped at the sound of his voice on the phone. Our voices cracked, went strangely loud or quiet, as we tried to act naturally, sound casual as we said, "Oh, hullo, Mr. Shawn," and then waited with bated breath for him to say that he had read and liked some piece of work we had turned in to him only hours earlier. If he didn't like it, the phone didn't ring.

For a time, it was H. who seemed to protect and encourage me in my writing. He taught me all about the inverted comma. He tried with mixed success to get me to write prose as plain, honest, and American as the chairs and hatstands at the office. Now it was I who was laughing at his jokes at the Algonquin, and enjoying the feeling of security when he called for the check—pulling his squat American wallet from the hip of his too short American pants. There had been a couple of wives, even before the vivacious one. Perhaps my furniture reminded him of his domestic life: flimsy, insubstantial, and in danger of exploding. At his insistence, I deflated my transparent sofa; the air rushed out of it, like a sigh.

It must have been around the same time that I took a stab

at what I hoped would be one of the "different kinds of writing" Shawn had encouraged me to try. My hair was so long that I could have a foot-and-a-half length cut off and still leave enough to bind into the chignon that I thought made me look mature enough to be seen around town with H. I took this chopped-off tail to be made into a hairpiece by Alfred Barris, a nonagenarian wigmaker from England who was still, amazingly enough, in business somewhere in the theatre district. I wrote a story about visiting first the hairdresser—letting down my hair and having it cut—and then the ancient Barris, who had faded photographs of various Barrymores on the walls and who hadn't been back to his native land since coming to New York at the time of the First World War.

I showed my effort to H. He studied the story—the typing was amateurish, the letters jumped friskily about, like girls in hot pants—and annotated it in the margin. His handwritten letter *E* was Greek in shape, perhaps taught by some encouraging schoolmarm in his native Midwest or by the college where he studied the Hundred Great Books; those graphic vowels of his strike me as touchingly American in their idealism, now. I cannot deny that my story had a description of a street in the West Forties, where I noted the melancholy hoofbeats of a policeman's horse. H. told me firmly that the street and the sound would not do: he said they were "Joe Mitchell's kind of thing." But that remark alone would not have been enough to discourage me, to make me hide the story away in the back of a drawer, as I did. It was the injunction my teacher/lover had written in the margin in pencil, but with the *gravitas* of some text in classical stone: "Describe. Color. Texture. Feeling," I read, next to what I had typed about unpinning my hair. And then a sly parenthesis— "(Never did this in public before)"—shifted the balance of my story, plunging Barris, his wigs, and the horse into darkness and highlighting what now felt like an erotic secret between H. and me. It was unthinkable after that to show the story to Shawn. I had let down my hair like Rapunzel, but by admitting this critical prince to my tower, I had blocked my exit and locked us in.

H. hated "The Long-Winded Lady." But then, there were many things he thought he hated at any given time. He was always full of conflicts: about *The New Yorker* and its editor; about his friends; especially about his wives. He once told Mr. Shawn, in my presence, that he loathed the English. This was shortly after he had married me and we had bought a house in England. He had even found an English tailor, from whom he commissioned beautiful trousers that broke, like a proper Englishman's, on the tops of his shoes. Shawn was getting a little deaf, by then; he gave in and wore a hearing aid later on.

"Yes, yes, the English are wonderful," he said, beaming.

"No, Mr. Shawn, I said I *loathed* them," H. said.

MR. SHAWN TRIED to help me write a novel, once. Traditionally, the writing generations crossed freely back and forth between fiction and non-fiction, signed and unsigned pieces, all kinds of forms; McKelway, who had started out as a newspaperman, wrote a famous short story called "First Marriage," about a time in his life before the madness or the experiment with Maeve, his final one. It was only after the end of my own marriage that I felt brave enough to try some reporting myself. I practiced within the cozy anonymous confines, the reassuring collective We, of "The Talk of the Town." Then I tried longer articles, in that *New Yorker* reporting style that drew so much on fictional techniques. I liked telling stories about people; I delighted in describing things.

"Why couldn't I do this before?" I asked Shawn plaintively, one day. I knew I had lost a lot of time. "Why couldn't I have written like this five years ago?"

"You just couldn't," he said. "That's all."

FOR SEVERAL YEARS after my husband and I had parted, his name went on appearing on the personnel sheet that was circulated for the use of the editorial staff, but the space for his address and telephone would be an inscrutable blank. Beside the name of Maeve Brennan, the space was equally bare. No letters from the Lady had appeared on the bulletin board for many years. I heard that their author wasn't doing too well: that she had been in Payne Whitney; that she had been found in a sorry state on the sidewalk outside the office; or that she had taken to sleeping in the ladies' room on the nineteenth floor. Then the name of my former husband and that of Maeve Brennan vanished entirely from the list. He had found some excuse to sever his connection with the tribe. (He didn't "resign," exactly, because like most of the writers and artists, he had no salary, obligatory assignments, or anything resembling a conventional job.) It was rumored that he was trying to write a book about *The New Yorker*. I felt afraid for him when I heard this, as if he had taken to writing gibberish, with his Greek letters, on the eighteenth-floor walls. (Indeed his feelings about his former world were so complex that the project tormented him and would be left unfinished when, some years later, he took his own life.)

I had shown Mr. Shawn some extracts from the journals I had been keeping for years. Some parts were about the days I spent in Manhattan; some were about my days in the country, in the English house. Naturally, there were some pages I kept secret from him. As he came into my office one afternoon, he had the pages in a folder and was clutching them to his chest. He was brimming with thoughts and feelings, with the desire to help me produce Good Writing—he thought perhaps a novel—from the notes. I sat looking up at him; he stood on the other side of the cigar-scarred desk. I had plenty of clutter of my own, after many years at *The New Yorker*, as well as a precarious heap of hopes and doubts. Seeing this, he looked particularly intense. He was beginning to look physically frail, and I noticed that his dark-blue suit seemed to hang on his small frame. He stood leaning the tips of his splayed fingers on the desk as if a high wind were blowing through the halls of 25 West Forty-third Street and he was going to need all his strength to steady himself. He stared over my head and out the window in the direction of the Century club.

Once, years before, I told him I had no imagination. I can't remember why.

"Could one, in England, leave someone a house?" he began.

"You mean when they die? What do you mean?" My words tripped over themselves.

"Just answer the question," he said.

"Yes, of course they could."

"How about a woman character in England who inherits a house from her father. . . ."

He looked flushed and almost fierce. His fingers stretched wide on the desk, as they did on the keyboard when he was playing his beloved Gershwin.

"She is married to an American. A character not *at all* like H.," he said, firmly. "And they have love affairs and so on." He gave a wry smile. "And she has a job—*not* as a writer— perhaps in the fashion world, which you know so well."

"I'm not sure I do."

"Well, something."

He sat down, suddenly, on the very edge of the Salvation Army chair, which had by now stood in my office for many years. The stuffing was escaping, and a strange ochre-colored sand of desiccated foam trickled out, as if from an hourglass, from the corner of the seat. I was terrified that this would make a mess of his dark suit, but I didn't want to say anything that might make him break off the conversation. He talked some more about what I knew and what he knew: about what worked in fiction nowadays. How in order to function, fiction writers seemed to have to get far away from the interesting things that were happening right under their noses. He stood up; there were so many things I longed to ask. What should I do next? How should I proceed?

"These are literary problems to be solved," he said, hurrying out. "For me to say any more would be inappropriate."

THAT EVENING, he telephoned me at home.

"I have thought of an elementary suggestion," he said, without preamble. "Write a scene, with two or three characters. It need not go in the beginning of your novel. Write about a man and a woman, talking to each other in a room."

My heart sank. Back then I couldn't hear myself speaking. I was still waiting for the men in my life to give me my cue. I couldn't foresee that I would have to listen with such attention to other women's life stories before I could move ahead with my own.

"Oh, Mr. Shawn," I said sadly, to the man I owed so much, "That's just the problem. I'm not sure I *can* imagine a man and a woman talking to each other in a room."

1995